"William Simmons certainly has his finger on the pulse of global Christianity and the phenomenal growth of the Pentecostal and charismatic movement, as well as the concomitant need for sound and lively theology for this church. He has written a helpful New Testament theology of the Spirit that honors the third person of the Trinity and opens the door for a drawing together of the incarnational and the pneumatic—that is the person and work of the Son and the Spirit—in Christian life and thought. This book may be a further contribution to the movement called 'Third Article Theology,' in which theology is viewed from the lens of the third article of the Nicene Creed. This attempt to overcome dualisms and bring together what is not separated in organic theology—that is exegesis and devotion, theology and praxis, the Christian mind and Christian spirituality and ethics—by the power of the Spirit, by means of a focus on the Spirit in each book of the New Testament, is indeed commendable."

Ross Hastings, Sangwoo Youtong Chee Professor of Theology at Regent College

"Pentecostals and charismatics read the Bible as the Word of God for us today, insisting that the Spirit actively speaks through the text. That same Spirit, of course, indwells and empowers us as he did the first followers of Jesus. William Simmons builds on these emphases in *The Holy Spirit in the New Testament* while incorporating thoughtful and practical (another typical Pentecostal value) exegesis of New Testament texts. As a Pentecostal myself, I am grateful for a kindred spirit like Simmons who is also living in that sometimes awkward but also hopeful space between the church and the academy. May his book remind us all that the Spirit is present there as well."

Holly Beers, associate professor of religious studies at Westmont College

"A book like this is long overdue, and Dr. Bill Simmons is the one to address this topic. His years of research, training, and teaching of the New Testament in a Pentecostal setting imminently qualifies him to author *The Holy Spirit in the New Testament*. It speaks not only to the mind but also to the heart."

Tim Hill, general overseer, Church of God (Cleveland, Tennessee)

"The Holy Spirit speaks holistically, addressing our mind, our heart, our emotions, and our conduct. *The Holy Spirit in the New Testament: A Pentecostal Guide* demonstrates the integrated work of the Spirit on every page. This scholarly work is tailored for the ministry of the local church and is an excellent source for small groups as well."

Mark L. Williams, lead pastor, North Cleveland Church of God

T0346503

WILLIAM A. SIMMONS

The

HOLY
SPIRIT

in the

NEW
TESTAMENT

A PENTECOSTAL GUIDE

ivp
Academic
An imprint of InterVarsity Press
Downers Grove, Illinois

InterVarsity Press
P.O. Box 1400, Downers Grove, IL 60515-1426
ivpress.com
email@ivpress.com

InterVarsity Press® is the book-publishing division of InterVarsity Christian Fellowship/USA®, a
movement of students and faculty active on campus at hundreds of universities, colleges, and schools
of nursing in the United States of America, and a member movement of the International Fellowship
of Evangelical Students. For information about local and regional activities, visit intervarsity.org.

All Scripture quotations, unless otherwise indicated, are the author's translation.

The publisher cannot verify the accuracy or functionality of website URLs used in this book
beyond the date of publication.

Cover design and image composite: David Fassett
Interior design: Daniel van Loon
Image: dove stained glass © Fred de Noyelle / Stone / Getty Images

ISBN 978-0-8308-5274-1 (print)
ISBN 978-0-8308-4378-7 (digital)

Printed in the United States of America ♾

InterVarsity Press is committed to ecological stewardship and to the conservation of natural resources
in all our operations. This book was printed using sustainably sourced paper.

Library of Congress Cataloging-in-Publication Data
Names: Simmons, William A., 1954- author.
Title: The Holy Spirit in the New Testament : a Pentecostal guide / William
   A. Simmons.
Description: Downers Grove, IL : IVP Academic, [2021] | Includes
   bibliographical references and index.
Identifiers: LCCN 2021013504 (print) | LCCN 2021013505 (ebook) | ISBN
   9780830852741 (paperback) | ISBN 9780830843787 (ebook)
Subjects: LCSH: Bible. New Testament—Criticism, interpretation, etc. |
   Holy Spirit—Biblical teaching. | Pentecostalism.
Classification: LCC BS2545.H62 S56 2021 (print) | LCC BS2545.H62 (ebook)
   | DDC 231/.3—dc23
LC record available at https://lccn.loc.gov/2021013504
LC ebook record available at https://lccn.loc.gov/2021013505

| P | 25 | 24 | 23 | 22 | 21 | 20 | 19 | 18 | 17 | 16 | 15 | 14 | 13 | 12 | 11 | 10 | 9 | 8 | 7 | 6 | 5 | 4 | 3 | 2 | 1 |
| Y | 37 | 36 | 35 | 34 | 33 | 32 | 31 | 30 | 29 | 28 | 27 | 26 | 25 | 24 | 23 | 22 | 21 |

To my lovely daughter,

LAURA

Truly a gift from God

CONTENTS

PREFACE

THE INTENT OF THIS WORK IS TWOFOLD: to select those themes in the New Testament that are of interest to Pentecostals and charismatics and relate these themes to the church. Although the Holy Spirit is the focus of each chapter, the approach will emphasize what the Spirit *does* rather than on who the Spirit *is*.

Regarding method, *The Holy Spirit in the New Testament* emphasizes *praxis* over *theory*. The reader is not only to be biblically informed but also spiritually transformed. The goal is not only to master the content of the Bible but also to hear the voice of the Spirit in the Bible. Thus an overt emphasis on discipleship and spiritual formation will be part of each chapter.

Some might feel uncomfortable with comingling serious biblical study with pointed devotional lessons. This sense of unease demonstrates how alienated the academy has become from the church and vice versa. It also shows the need for a more integrated approach of the kind found in *The Holy Spirit in the New Testament*.

These kinds of goals necessarily affect format and writing style. For example, each chapter will open with a key verse that typifies the core message the Spirit plays in this section and creates the spiritual tone for the entire chapter. What follows is a biblically informed treatment of themes that are of particular interest to Pentecostals and charismatics. A brief summary will round out the chapter, which is then followed by the "What does it mean for me?" portion. It is here that the spiritual claims of the text are brought to bear upon the reader. The effectiveness of this section depends on the readiness of the reader to hear what the Spirit is saying through the text.

All of this affects the writing style of *The Holy Spirit in the New Testament*. The text is intended to be read comfortably and devotionally. Apart from introductory matters, the use of secondary sources and footnoting are kept to a minimum. The primary source for the work is the Greek text of the New Testament.

The Scriptures serve as the touchstone for the entire work. It is crucial for the reader to look up each citation as he or she studies along. For the sake of continuity, it might be best to read straight through the chapter and then go back and read the supporting texts.

It is my sincere hope that *The Holy Spirit in the New Testament* will not only be a source of biblical knowledge but also a means for personal growth in the Holy Spirit.

A word of gratitude is in store for those Pentecostal scholars who have set such a high standard of excellence. Notables like Gordon Fee, and more recently Craig Keener, come to mind. Such scholars have held together their masterful exegesis of the Word with their heartfelt communion with the Spirit. A special thanks goes out to Paul Conn, president of Lee University. His commitment to academic excellence and to continued faculty development has made this project possible. My stay at Tyndale House in Cambridge, and the constant encouragement of my colleagues there, was of great help to me. Finally, my students are a constant inspiration. They are the church of the future and by all measure, the future is in good hands.

Why
a PENTECOSTAL GUIDE
to the HOLY SPIRIT?

CONSIDERING THE WIDE ARRAY of sources on the Pentecostal and charismatic movements, do we really need another book on the Spirit? The gulf between the scholar's chair and the church pew has never been wider. This book seeks to bridge the gap between serious study of the Bible and the need for practical discipleship in the church. In addition, current demographics demonstrate a need for a book like this. The number of believers who identify as Pentecostal or charismatic is growing at an astounding rate. This rapidly expanding sector of the church needs informed biblical study that addresses the role of the Holy Spirit in everyday life. This current work seeks to meet that need.

A CLARIFICATION OF TERMS:
PENTECOSTAL . . . LABEL OR LENS?

Labels are helpful when they serve to clarify, define, and describe. However, the limited value of a label becomes apparent as soon as it is applied. Every label has the tendency to fixate, restrict, and exclude. As such, no single label can fully capture all the aspects and values of a thing. Life simply has a way of escaping the confines of any label. This is especially true with religious labels. *Reformed . . . evangelical . . .*

Pentecostal . . . The very mention of these terms births such varied interpretations that, in short order, the label becomes meaningless. How then are we to label the living and dynamic presence of the Holy Spirit in the church? In other words, can the charismatic grace of the Spirit in the life of an increasingly diverse and global church be labeled?

In response, the term *Pentecostal* in this present study is not used as a *label* that defines but as a *lens* to look through. *Pentecostal* in this work does not refer to a specific denomination or even a particular historical religious phenomenon. Nor does it mean ascribing a cluster of Scriptures with an importance that goes beyond the rest of Holy Writ. Rather *Pentecostal*, in this present context, refers to a special kind of interpretive grid. *Pentecostal* is being used here as a hermeneutical lens that informs all of reality—God, humanity, creation—and frames that reality as a seamless interplay of all that is true.[1] The truth-bearing theme that colors this lens is the living presence of the Spirit of God.

Even so, what lies at the heart of *Pentecostal* so described? In brief, *Pentecostal* means the collapse of the transcendent. A *Pentecostal* lens is framed by this one central premise: God has become immanent among his people by way of the vibrant presence of the Holy Spirit (Rev 21:3). The power, the presence, and the praxis of the Spirit has invaded this world and established God's people as a beachhead for the reclamation of all creation (Jas 1:18). In this sense there is a decidedly incarnational aspect to a *Pentecostal* interpretive grid. The Spirit inhabits the redeemed, and by way of the preeminent sacraments flowing from Jesus and the Scriptures, the Spirit empowers believers to see things as they really are (1 Cor 2:11-12). Paradoxically, the collapse of the transcendent births another kind of transcendence whereby those immersed in the Spirit are no longer defined by, or better, confined to this present world (Phil 3:20). As the faithful "walk in the Spirit" (Gal 5:16),

---

[1]The challenge here is one of nomenclature. It is difficult to find an expression that captures the tremendous diversity found in a spiritual phenomenon that is occurring on a global scale. Although *Pentecostal* and *charismatic* are used as umbrella terms throughout the work, they are at best an upside-down umbrella. They catch a lot, but not everything. Perhaps expressions like *Spirit-centered* or *Spirit-focused* better account for the dynamic and ever-expanding work of the Holy Spirit in the world today.

the presence of the kingdom is brought forward and, in measure, realized in their lives.

All of this means that the task of interpretation (hermeneutics), the clear teaching of the Bible (exegesis), and the present state of the church (ecclesiology) call for a particularly Pentecostal guide on the Holy Spirit in the New Testament.

A PENTECOSTAL LENS FOR INTERPRETATION: BOTH HOLISTIC AND INTEGRATED

One can readily see that Spirit-centered interpretation has huge implications for experiencing God and understanding his Word. This way of engaging the Scriptures is both holistic and integrated. It is holistic in that it involves the human mind, heart, and spirit. The venue of the Spirit's revelation is not confined to human thought but includes human emotion and worship as well (Lk 10:27). A Pentecostal approach is integrated because it knits together the shared experience of the Spirit across time. The generative Spirit at the dawn of creation (Gen 1:2) is the same Spirit that inspired and performed miracles through the prophets (Num 11:29). This is the same Spirit that not only conceived Jesus in the Virgin Mary (Lk 1:34-35), but also charismatically empowered Jesus throughout his life (Lk 4:18) and raised him from the dead (Rom 1:4). The charismatic Christ baptizes the church in the selfsame Spirit (Mt 3:11) and empowers the first believers to preach the gospel to the uttermost parts of the earth (Acts 1:8). This gospel is not only shared in word, but also in the miraculous power and demonstration of the Spirit (1 Cor 2:4).

In sum, a Pentecostal lens sees the primordial person and work of the Spirit to be the same person and work of the Spirit that has operated in the lives of the faithful throughout the ages, including our own. Regarding the ancients, their story of God is our story of God and their experience in the Spirit is our experience in the Spirit. In other words, there is an unencumbered merging of spiritual landscapes, the biblical world of the Spirit, and our present communion in the Spirit. In this way the contemporary believer participates in the life of the Spirit that has always been, now is, and will continue to be.

All of this tends to dismantle the "wall of separation" so evident in many modernist, Western modes of interpretation. By this I mean that artificial barrier constructed to distance academic study from spiritual formation. Yet *Pentecostal* does not mean the displacement of sound biblical scholarship by an unreflective devotional experience. For what lies at the heart of being Pentecostal is a profound sense of revelation. This means that the proto-revelation of the Spirit, that is, the Scriptures, is the authoritative touchstone for any Pentecostal study. Also, the Spirit does not reveal only in word, but also in the world (Luke 3:1-3). God speaks in history, so historical context itself is revelatory for the Pentecostal (Gal 4:4). Language . . . grammar . . . history . . . are all imbued with the Spirit and are part and parcel with God's revelation. Yet this pluriform revelation is intended *for* us, to be active *in* us and expressed *through* us (Rom 10:8).

A Spirit-centered interpretation deconstructs that contrived partition that alienates reason from spirit, thought from heart, and mind from emotion. A Pentecostal rubric celebrates that divine sympathy with the Holy Trinity whereby the joy of the kingdom (Rom 14:17) and the heartfelt fruit of the Spirit (Gal 5:22-23) are an ever-present reality. At times, this divine-human dialogue exceeds the strictures of human speech. It is then that discourse is so directed by the Spirit as to express devotion in a language framed more by the grammar of heaven than of earth (Acts 2:4; 19:6; 1 Cor 14:39). All of this means that a Pentecostal lens replaces an anthropocentric understanding of "God" with the living communion of the resurrected Lord as mediated by the indwelling Spirit. Modern existentialism gives way to being "in Christ" (2 Cor 5:17) as transformed through the Spirit (2 Cor 3:18). There is no cessation of the gifts of God (Jas 1:17) but a continuation of divine benevolence granted for the common good (1 Cor 12:5-7).

Pentecostal interpretation does not objectify Scripture as an ancient artifact to be dissected and analyzed. Rather the Word is alive and exacts a more powerful interpretive effect on us than we on the

Word (Heb 4:12). This means that the Scriptures are to be studied devotionally (2 Tim 3:16-17). They were not given just to be mastered by human reason but to be obeyed by godly servants (Jas 1:22; 2:17). The revelation was not given to be domesticated so that it might accommodate modernity. Rather, the revelation itself becomes the archetype by which the children of God must conform and be changed (Rom 12:1-2). In other words, the original intent of the authors of Scripture has become paradigmatic for us and the Spirit expects us to respond accordingly (Rom 15:4).

A PENTECOSTAL LENS FOR INTERPRETATION: BOTH COMPREHENSIVE AND COSMIC

If all of this sounds like a dramatic and definitive mandate from on high . . . it is. The Pentecostal lens of interpretation provides a wide-screen view that is both comprehensive and cosmic. It takes in everything, from beginning to end, and informs everything in between. This means that a Pentecostal lens of interpretation is necessarily an eschatological lens. The promised outpouring of the Holy Spirit on the first believers (Acts 2:1-21) marked the last days' fulfillment of Joel's prophecy (Joel 2:28). This end-time work of the Spirit not only empowers God's select people but will also restore all creation (Rom 8:19-23). The coming of the Spirit is a momentous, end-time work of God on the order of the incarnation and ascension. The invasion of the Spirit at Pentecost was a paradigm-shaping event that altered the fabric of the cosmos for good (Acts 2:19-20). This end-time reclamation of the Spirit started with those who are created in God's image and so enshrined the saints that their physical bodies became the sole dwelling place of the Spirit on earth (1 Cor 6:19). The Spirit started with us, but it won't end with us, for the Spirit himself is a kind of "first fruit" (Rom 8:23) or "down payment" (2 Cor 1:22) of the cosmic redemption of God yet to come (Eph 1:13-14).

It's clear that for the Pentecostal, *eschatological* or *end time* does not mean "totally future." For the Pentecostal, the outpouring of the Spirit represents a kind of prolepsis, or an advance consummation of all things in the here and now. To be sure, even as we presently "walk in the Spirit" (Rom 8:4), we "wait in the Spirit" (Gal 5:5) for our complete redemption. It is this anticipatory presence of the Spirit that "groans in our spirit" and eagerly looks forward to the redemption of our bodies (Rom 8:23). All of this means that for the Pentecostal, the distance between the "already" of God's kingdom and the "not yet" of our present state has been narrowed. Indeed, a Pentecostal interpretation realizes that the separation of "this age" from the "age to come" is not an impenetrable separation but divinely permeable (Lk 11:20). By way of the Holy Spirit, the presence and powers of the kingdom of God are streaming into the life of the church even now (1 Cor 12:8-10).

SOUND BIBLICAL EXEGESIS CALLS FOR A
PENTECOSTAL STUDY OF THE NEW TESTAMENT

When God established his covenant with the Hebrews of old, he was already announcing the coming of a qualitatively *new* covenant, one that was thoroughly infused by the Spirit (Jer 31:31-33). Ezekiel prophesies that God will put his Spirit into our hearts and cause us to walk in his statutes and observe his laws (Ezek 36:26-27). Following on, Jesus speaks of an organic connection between the new covenant in his blood (Lk 22:20) and the outpouring of the Holy Spirit on his disciples (Acts 1:4-5). The moment this promise is fulfilled in the church, a direct link is made with Joel's prophecy concerning the last days outpouring of the Spirit (Acts 2:16-21). Luke consistently portrays the church as a charismatically empowered community that brings the redemptive power of the kingdom to bear by the power of the Spirit (Acts 8:13; 19:11-12). The same holds for the apostle Paul. By alluding to the prophecies of Jeremiah and Ezekiel, the apostle understands that a new covenant has been enacted by way of the Holy Spirit (2 Cor 3:2-3). For him, Spirit-filled Gentiles are the fulfillment of God's covenant with Abraham (Gal 3:1-9). It is the "Spirit of adoption" (Rom 8:15) through whom they cry out, "Abba! Father!" (Gal 4:6). The writer of Revelation says that he "was in the Spirit on the Lord's day" (Rev 1:10).

This rapid overview of the Scriptures yields an undeniable conclusion. The writers of the New Testament, from beginning to end, understand that the Christocentric plan of God was being realized by way
of the Holy Spirit. This clear and consistent teaching of the Bible is of
special interest to Pentecostals and charismatics and requires a special
study of its own.

THE GLOBAL CHURCH CALLS FOR A PENTECOSTAL STUDY OF THE NEW TESTAMENT

The reported death of the church has been greatly exaggerated. The
church is not dying; it has simply changed address. While there are
signs of decline in the West, there is tremendous growth in the Global
South, Africa, and China.[2] A huge portion of this astonishing growth
comprises those who self-identify as "Pentecostal" or "charismatic." The
findings of mega-studies such as *World Christian Encyclopedia* (2nd ed.)
and the *Pew Research Center for Religion and Public Life* are astounding.
The fact that these mega censuses devote entire sections to Pentecostals
and charismatics is telling. For example, in 1900 the World Christian
Database numbered Pentecostals and charismatics at less than a million.
Today it is estimated that there are more than 670 million Pentecostals
and charismatics worldwide.[3] Presently over 25 percent of Christendom
is Pentecostal or charismatic. This same census projects that by 2050 the
total number of Pentecostals and charismatics will be over a billion with
one in three Christians claiming to be Pentecostal or charismatic.[4]

It becomes clear that any attempt to number Pentecostals and charismatics is like sampling a river. The very moment a cupful is taken, the
subject matter has moved on. Any global census of the movement becomes outdated as soon as it is made. It is for this reason that thumbnail

---

[2]Wes Granberg-Michaelson, "Think Christianity Is Dying? No, Christianity Is Shifting Dramatically," *The Washington Post*, May 5, 2015, www.washingtonpost.com/news/acts-of-faith
/wp/2015/05/20/think-christianity-is-dying-no-christianity-is-shifting-dramatically. See also
Philip Jenkins, *The Next Christendom: The Coming of Global Christendom* (Oxford: University
Press, 2007), 17.

[3]Todd M. Johnson and Gina A. Zurlo, eds., World Christian Database, worldchristiandatabase
.org, accessed October 25, 2018.

[4]Philip Jenkins, *The Next Christendom*, 9.

estimates range wildly. One estimate speaks of 40,000 Pentecostals and charismatics being added to the church daily, while another claims that the number is closer to 70,000! Thus, George Weigel asserts that Pentecostals and charismatics compose the fastest growing religious phenomenon in world religious history.[5]

The data from the Pew Forum is no less impressive. Of the Protestants surveyed in nearly twenty nations in Central and South America, every nation but one reported being over 50 percent Pentecostal.[6] Protestants in three of these countries (Brazil, Panama, and Nicaragua) were determined to be at least 80 percent Pentecostal. Additionally, nearly 60 percent of Catholics in Brazil, the most populous Catholic country in South America, self-identify as charismatic. Similarly, charismatic Catholics in Panama number over 70 percent.

And then there is Africa. Beginning with the 1970s, the Christian population in Africa has increased fivefold. The largest portion of that growth has occurred among the Pentecostals and charismatics. While studying in Cambridge in the summer of 2018, I received two unsolicited comments from church leaders in Africa. Independently they both simply said, "Africa is Pentecostal." Admittedly anecdotal and clearly an overstatement, their comments were telling. Closer to the truth is the Pew Forum's claim that Pentecostals in all African nations, from top to bottom, number anywhere from 10 to 20 percent *of the entire national population.*[7]

Due to a number of factors, not the least of which is what Fenggang Yang calls the "control apparatus," the Christian population in China cannot be determined.[8] Yet, Christianity is the fastest growing religion in China. Yang estimates that by 2025 the Christian population in China will be over 160 million, making China the most populous

[5]George Weigel, "World Christianity by the Numbers," *First Things*, February 25, 2015, www .firstthings.com/web-exclusives/2015/02/world-christianity-by-the-numbers.

[6]"Religion in Latin America: Chapter 4: Pentecostalism," Pew Research Center: Religion and Public Life, November 14, 2014, www.pewforum.org/2014/11/13/chapter-4-pentecostalism. The exception here was Bolivia, which numbered 49 percent Pentecostal.

[7]"Overview: Pentecostalism in Africa," Pew Research Center: Religion and Public Life, October 5, 2006, www.pewforum.org/2006/10/05/overview-pentecostalism-in-africa.

[8]Fenggang Yang, *Religion in China: Survival & Revival Under Communist Rule* (Oxford: University Press, 2012), 154.

Christian nation in the world.[9] If the presence of global Pentecostals and charismatics is replicated in China, and by all indications this is the case, the numbers are staggering.[10]

Nevertheless, the number of Pentecostals and charismatics is only part of the story. Their overall impact on global Christianity is noteworthy. More than twenty years ago Ralph Martin commented, "My research has led me to make a bold statement: In all of human history, no other non-political, non-militaristic, voluntary human movement has grown as rapidly as the Pentecostal-charismatic movement in the last 25 years."[11] Luis Lugo, the director of the Pew Forum project, went so far as to say that the faith is well on its way to becoming "Pentecostalized."[12] John Allan speaks of the "relentless advance of Pentecostalism" that shows no sign of slowing down. He goes so far as to say that Pentecostalism may be the very thing that saves Christianity from oblivion.[13]

Some reasons for this incredible growth were expressed by Harvey Cox over a quarter of a century ago. He says that the Pentecostals have tapped into "primal spirituality," expressed in "primal speech," lived out in "primal piety," that births "primal hope."[14] Even though the reasons for the incredible growth of the Pentecostal and charismatic movements is beyond the scope of this work, the self-reported reason is practically universal: the living presence of the Holy Spirit.[15] Moreover,

---

[9]Tom Phillips, "China on Course to Become 'World's Most Christian Nation' Within 15 Years," *The Telegraph*, April 19, 2014, www.telegraph.co.uk/news/worldnews/asia/china/10776023 /China-on-course-to-become-worlds-most-Christian-nation-within-15-years.html.

[10]Ambrosia Viramontes-Brody, "The Global Impact of Pentecostalism," *USC US-China Institute*, July 28, 2011, https://china.usc.edu/global-impact-pentecostalism.

[11]Ralph Martin, *The Catholic Church at the End of an Age: What Is the Spirit Saying?* (San Francisco: Ignatius Press, 1994), 87.

[12]Mathias D. Thelen, "The Explosive Growth of Pentecostal-Charismatic Christianity in the Global South, and Its Implications for Catholic Evangelization," *Homiletic & Pastoral Review*, June 28, 2017, www.hprweb.com/2017/06/the-explosive-growth-of-pentecostal-charismatic -christianity-in-the-global-south-and-its-implications-for-catholic-evangelization.

[13]Allen Anderson, *An Introduction to Pentecostalism* (Cambridge: University Press, 2004), 180, 285-86.

[14]Harvey Cox, *Fire from Heaven: The Rise of Pentecostal Spirituality and the Reshaping of Religion in the Twenty-first Century* (Cambridge: De Capo Press, 1995), 81-82.

[15]Although there is great diversity among Pentecostal fellowships worldwide, there is amazing continuity with regard to experiencing the Holy Spirit. See Anderson, *An Introduction to Pentecostalism*, 380-81.

even if the reasons for growth are debated, the effect of the movement is not. It is nothing short of a new Reformation, the consequences of which are even greater than the first Reformation.[16]

SUMMARY THOUGHTS

The church of the first century would not have even used the terms *Pentecostal* or *charismatic*. The miraculous presence and power of the Holy Spirit was a given and required no special labels. The unceasing benevolence of the Spirit as manifested in miraculous gifts was both normal and normative. It was just the way things worked among God's people. For these reasons, the writers of Scripture simply address the saints as "the church."

Spiritually, the present status of the church is different from that of the first century, but we are getting closer by the moment. An ever-increasing portion of the global church self-identifies as Pentecostal or charismatic. So in answer to the question, "Why a *Pentecostal* guide to the Holy Spirit in the New Testament?" the simplest answer is, "Because the church requires it."

Yet there is one final reason why this kind of study is so critical for our times. This reason encompasses all other justifications for a Spirit-centered approach to the Scriptures and constitutes the unique contribution of this book. In the minds of many, the worlds of academia and the church have been alienated for far too long. What is desperately needed is what Alister McGrath calls an "organic theology."[17] What is required is a more dynamic interchange between the respective gifts of the scholar and the charisms of the saints; a more fluid dialogue between the academy and the church.[18] This kind of interdependence

---

[16]As Eugene Botha states, "In one short century the movement has certainly changed the face of Christianity fundamentally and irrevocably." Eugene Botha, "The New Reformation: The Amazing Rise of the Pentecostal-Charismatic Movement in the 20th Century," *Studia Historiae Ecclesiasticae* 33, no. 1 (May 2007): 295-96.

[17]Alister McGrath, *The Future of Christianity* (Oxford: Blackwell Publishers, 2002), 150-52.

[18]Thus Craig Bartholomew rightly emphasizes the praxis of biblical interpretation. That is, an authentic interpretation of the Bible has not taken place until the reader has been addressed by God. Craig Bartholomew, *Introducing Biblical Hermeneutics: A Comprehensive Framework for Hearing God in Scripture* (Grand Rapids, MI: Baker Academic, 2015), 3, 11.

must necessarily transfer the intent and expectations of the Spirit to those who study the Scriptures. Reciprocally, those who have given their lives to the study of Scripture must be heard by those who are filled with the Spirit. This means that the devotional intent of the New Testament must be part of a Spirit-centered study of the Bible. Yet historic and linguistic elements are part of the Spirit's work as well. Furthermore, an approach that appropriates the selfsame Spirit that inspired the New Testament in the first place is an approach that expects the text to be believed and obeyed. Therefore, what Craig Keener calls an "epistemic commitment" to the claims of Scripture and to the living voice of the Spirit must be *a priori* assumptions for any Spirit-filled hermeneutic.[19] It is this very assumption that guides and shapes every chapter of this book.

---

[19]Craig Keener, *Spirit Hermeneutics: Reading Scripture in Light of Pentecost* (Grand Rapids, MI: Eerdmans, 2016), 162-63.

The HOLY SPIRIT *in* MATTHEW

HALLMARK OF THE KINGDOM

I baptize you with water for repentance. But after me comes one who is more powerful than I, whose sandals I am not worthy to carry. He will baptize you with the Holy Spirit and fire.

MATTHEW 3:11 NIV

THE SPIRIT IS MENTIONED only a dozen times in Matthew. However, this low number belies its importance. The Spirit literally brackets Matthew's Gospel from beginning to end. Starting with the generative work of the Spirit in the virgin birth and continuing until the very last words of Jesus in the Great Commission, the Holy Spirit sets the agenda for Matthew's Gospel. For Matthew, there is no messianic era apart from the Spirit. Sickness, demonic oppression, and crushing poverty are no match for the in-breaking of the kingdom. This kingdom is exclusively brought to bear by the Anointed One, Jesus of Nazareth, who operates in the power of the Spirit of God.

Herein lies the hope-filled message for us as believers. Matthew's portrayal of the Spirit assures us that the heavens are not closed but open. The Spirit speaks to his people by way of revelation, dreams, prophecy, and miracles. The incarnational presence of the Spirit in Jesus creates an open interchange between Creator and creation. In this way, God's anointed Messiah brings about a Spirit-infused solidarity between heaven and earth. Even more wonderful, John the

Baptist promises that Jesus will baptize us in the Holy Spirit and fire. This means that believers are immersed in the selfsame Spirit who inaugurated, sustained, and even now carries forward God's end-time plan for the ages. For Matthew, the Spirit is not over this world or against this world, but in this world and for this world. The Spirit works in Mary's womb in the virgin birth and works in Joseph's mind to cope with that extraordinary birth. The Spirit is with Jesus at his baptism and in the wilderness of temptation. And he suggests something that at the time was unthinkable. God's Messiah really cares about unclean Gentiles. After all, in a story unique to Matthew, the Magi from the East were Gentiles. They were some of the first visitors to the newborn king (Mt 2:1-16). Finally, the Holy Spirit does not recoil from our diseases, defects, and demons. For Matthew, the Spirit does not reject the world because of sin. The Spirit reclaims the world because of God.

Yet Matthew does not want his readers to be naive concerning the things of the Spirit. An unreflective receptivity without mature discernment can do more harm than good. Even though Matthew emphasizes the fulfillment of prophecy, he repeatedly warns against false prophets, false messiahs, and lying wonders.

PAUSE FOR PRAYER

For those who celebrate the power of the Spirit, Matthew's caution merits special attention. We must not only worship in Spirit but also in truth. Indeed, the gift of *discernment* must be brought to bear on all aspects of the church so that we might judge what is of God. This kind of spiritual accountability is itself a prophetic ministry that is desperately needed in the church today (2 Pet 2:1; 1 John 4:1). Pray that God will grant you that special gift to discern what is true from what is false, what is from God from what is not.

THE PRESENCE OF THE HOLY SPIRIT IN MATTHEW

The Holy Spirit "births" the messianic era (Mt 1:18-25). Matthew is careful to note that prior to Joseph and Mary coming together as husband and wife, Mary became pregnant through the Holy Spirit. The virgin birth came about through the direct agency of the Holy Spirit and was a fulfillment of prophecy (Is 7:14).[1]

Matthew's account links the presence of the Holy Spirit and new birth. From the first day of creation to the virgin birth and even extending to the regeneration of all who believe in Christ, the Holy Spirit births new life (Gen 1:1-2). For Matthew, the incarnation wrought by the Spirit represents the new humanity of God, which in turn is the first installment of the restoration of all things (Rom 8:29; Jas 1:18). And unlike Adam, who failed God and humanity, Jesus is led by the Spirit into the wilderness to triumph for God and his people (1 Cor 15:45; Rom 5:12-21). In sum, the "in-fleshing" of Christ by the Spirit conveys the intimate and immediate connection between the Spirit and all of creation. The Spirit longs to indwell God's people and transform their physical bodies into the temple of God (1 Cor 3:16-17; 6:19-20).

Matthew informs us that the work of the Spirit can be awkward.[2] The Spirit enters Mary's life while she is unmarried and brings about a pregnancy that, in the eyes of all others, is illegitimate and shameful. As a conservative Jew, her fiancé, Joseph, has a real-world solution to an embarrassing problem: divorce Mary privately. God was fully aware of the social and religious factors facing this young couple. He engages them in the midst of these earthbound issues and directs Joseph via another divine gift: a special dream. Joseph takes action and, in spite of the enduring shame, takes Mary to be his wife.

The Holy Spirit actualizes the kingdom of God (Mt 3:13-17). If the Spirit-conceived Christ marks the beachhead of the kingdom in the

---

[1]In quoting Is 7:14, Matthew does not quote the Masoretic Text (Hebrew Bible), but rather accesses the LXX (Septuagint; the Greek translation of the Hebrew text). The former simply has *almah* ("young woman"), but the latter has *parthenos* ("a virgin"). Matthew wants his readers to understand that the virgin birth is a miracle wrought by the Holy Spirit that fulfills a critical messianic prophecy.

[2]The leading of the Holy Spirit can be counterintuitive. The public outing of Ananias and Sapphira for lying to the Spirit must have been difficult (Acts 5:1-11). The directing of yet another Ananias to pray for a Pharisee who had tortured and killed Christians was distressing (Acts 9:10-17). Peter's visit to the home of a Gentile centurion was awkward to say the least (Acts 10:1-43). The inherent tension in this passage is resolved when the Holy Spirit "falls" and is "poured out" upon uncircumcised Gentiles and they begin to speak in tongues (Acts 10:44-46).

world, then the Spirit-anointed Christ is an all-out assault against evil. From the moment Jesus receives the Spirit at baptism, he begins a relentless campaign to roll back the curse. He does so by way of healings, exorcisms, and raising the dead. Indeed, some form of the word *heal* or *healed* appears twenty-one times in Matthew. Jesus explicitly says that when he drives out demons by the Spirit of God, then the kingdom of God has come among them. The very clothes of Jesus have semi-sacramental significance to effect healing (Mt 9:21; 14:36). Frequently Matthew states that Jesus healed *all* who were brought to him (see Mt 4:24; 8:16; 12:15; 14:14; 15:30; 19:2; 21:14). This kind of charismatic deliverance ministry brackets Jesus' calling of the twelve apostles and is the hallmark of the Spirit-empowered church (Mt 10:1, 8; 2 Cor 12:12).

The Spirit, prophecy and dream revelation. For Matthew, the Holy Spirit is the Spirit of prophecy and revelation. Even King David prophecies "in the Spirit" about the coming of the Messiah (Mt 22:41-45).[3] In Matthew prophecy is the primary witness that Jesus is the Messiah. Some form of the word *fulfill* is used fifteen times in Matthew. All these instances are in conjunction with major messianic prophecies. For example, from the virgin birth (Mt 1:22-23) to the betrayal by Judas and subsequent arrest of Jesus (Mt 26:54-56; 27:9), fulfilled prophecy is proof positive that Jesus is the Messiah.

Matthew also emphasizes that the Spirit speaks through dreams. From the beginning of his Gospel to the end, Matthew uses the phrase "in a dream" no fewer than six times. Most of these dream revelations come to Joseph, the husband of Mary. Joseph is told in a dream not to hesitate to take Mary for his wife, for the child has been conceived by the Holy Spirit (Mt 1:20). Some dream revelations come to persons who are outside the pale of Judaism, such as the Magi from the East (Mt 2:12) and also to Pilate's wife (Mt 27:19).

---

[3]Peter's explanation and application of Pentecost (Acts 2:1-13) also quotes Psalm 110 (Acts 2:34-35). Moreover, once Peter has joined the Joel prophecy to the events of Pentecost (compare Acts 2:16-21 with Joel 2:28-31), he launches into a litany of quotations from the Psalms (Ps 16:8-10, 132:11, 16:10). Thus important aspects of Christology and pneumatology find their home in Pentecost and are hermeneutically explained by way of psalms.

This feature in Matthew taps into the ancient Jewish belief that God reveals himself through dreams. From Genesis to Joel, the word *dream* or *dreams* appears over one hundred times in the Old Testament, with the greatest concentrations occurring in Genesis (30×) and Daniel (25×).

Once again, the prophecy of Joel comes into play. Joel states that the Spirit will be poured out on all flesh and that one of the charismatic consequences of this outpouring is that "your old men will dream dreams." On the Day of Pentecost, Peter links this prophecy to the outpouring of the Holy Spirit on the church and is careful to include the part about dreaming dreams (Acts 2:17; Joel 2:28). Indeed, Paul had a dream of a man from Macedonia asking for help, and this led him and his missionary team to take the gospel westward into Europe (Acts 16:9). This decision would dramatically affect the church and by extension all of Western civilization. Although Paul's experience is often translated as "vision," Luke uses the same word as Matthew for "dream." These world-changing revelations all came by a Spirit-inspired dream.

All of this constitutes a kind of "divine circularity" for Matthew. The Spirit that first inspired the prophecy is the same Spirit that reveals when the prophecy is fulfilled. Yet prophecy for Matthew is not just "foretelling" by the Spirit but also consists of "forth telling" through the Spirit.[4] When describing the last days' persecution of the saints, Jesus tells his disciples that they should not worry about what they will say to their oppressors, for the Holy Spirit will give them the words to speak (Mt 10:19-20).

The Holy Spirit: God's final and effective work of salvation. One of the most important Scriptures in Matthew is found in 12:18-21. Once again Matthew is quoting a key messianic prophecy found in Isaiah 42:1-4 (see also Mt 11:5 and Lk 4:18-19). These passages join the person and work of the Holy Spirit with the end-time deliverance ministry of the Messiah. The operative words here are *nations* and *justice*. The word *nations* can also be translated "Gentiles." The Holy Spirit is realizing the expansive ministry of Jesus that will eventually transcend the ethnocentricity of

---

[4]The noun "prophecy" (*prophēteia*) and verb "prophesy" (*prophēteuō*) are both formed on the same Greek root which can either mean to tell in advance (to foretell) or to proclaim (to speak forth).

first-century Judaism (see Is 49:6). All of this feeds into the Great Commission (Mt 28:18-20). Here the Holy Spirit works as a full partner with the Father and the Son in bringing salvation to the world.

Justice (mentioned twice in Mt 12:18-21) speaks to the defining equity of the Lord, which the Holy Spirit brings about through Jesus. As part of the messianic era, all injustice and oppression will ultimately be exposed, judged, and swept away. In this way, the impeccable fairness of God is seen in his love for non-Jews and his care for the poor (Mt 22:1-13). By extension, crosscultural mission and benevolence are essential to the Spirit's work in the church.

Sign seekers and the blasphemy of the Holy Spirit (Mt 12:24–32). Wherever there is power and influence, people will seek to exploit these qualities to their own advantage. The same holds true for the power of the Holy Spirit. Since the Spirit was so central to Jesus and his mission, Jesus has some harsh words for those who would abuse the Spirit. Matthew repeatedly warns of false prophets whose goal is to exploit the people of God and take advantage of their sincere faith. They peddle magic in the name of God and are savage in their abuse of the saints. They attempt to keep their ruse alive until the very end and yet are soundly rebuked by the Lord and experience eternal judgment (Mt 7:15-23).

Similarly, the enemies of Jesus taunt him to misuse his power. Whether it be the devil (Mt 4:1-11), corrupt religious leaders (Mt 12:38-42) or Roman officials (Lk 23:8), they all demand miraculous signs of the Lord. They have no intension of becoming genuine disciples of Jesus. They want him to compromise his relationship with the Father, grant some cheap trick to satisfy their cynicism, or succumb to an ungodly abuse of power. Such persons are evil and adulterous in the manner of Israel's unfaithfulness to Yahweh (Ezek 6:9; 16:32; Hos 1:2). Jesus does grant them a sign, but it is the sign of Jonah. Matthew's point is that only the miracle of the resurrection fully authenticates Jesus as the Son of God, the promised Messiah (Mt 12:39; 16:4; Lk 11:29-30).[5]

---

[5]What's interesting is that the sign of Jonah was given to the Ninevites, a people beyond the covenant and sworn enemies of Israel. What might this say about the Sadducees and the Pharisees?

When addressing those who would misuse the Spirit, an even more heinous sin is revealed. After Jesus' extraordinary season of healings and exorcisms, the Pharisees charge Jesus with casting out demons by Beelzebul, the prince of demons. They maliciously want to distort and displace the power of the Spirit with the power of the evil one. Their intent is to discredit Jesus and dissuade people from following him.

In response, Jesus levels his most severe indictment against these opponents. He points out that their charge is illogical and contradictory. He casts out demons, not by the power of Satan, but by the Spirit of God. This is a sign that the kingdom of God has come among them. He concludes by stating that every manner of sin will be forgiven, even speaking evil against the Son of Man, but blasphemy against the Holy Spirit will not be forgiven in this life or in the life to come.

Why is Jesus' judgment so harsh? Why does this sin, among all others, lay beyond the scope of repentance and forgiveness? In seeking an answer, one thing is clear. God's best and final offer of salvation, the Spirit's work through his Son, is labeled as coming from Satan. This deliberate and evil distortion strikes at the very root of God's work in the world. There is no higher court of appeal. There are no other options. Those who frame the redemptive work of the Spirit as demonic have sealed their fate.

SUMMARY THOUGHTS

In writing his Gospel, Matthew has a single goal in sight: Jesus of Nazareth is God's Spirit-empowered Messiah. Jesus has been conceived of the Holy Spirit and by way of the Spirit, he fulfills all the ancient prophecies of Israel. Through Jesus and his miraculous demonstration of the Spirit, the kingdom of God is sweeping into this world and pushing back the darkness. Jesus shares this end-time ministry with those who love him and commissions them to teach and make disciples until his return.

WHAT DOES IT MEAN FOR ME?

Matthew's message is encapsulated in three words: power, promise, and problems. The God of all creation has sent his Son in the power of the Holy Spirit. The universe is not closed but open, and God is in our midst establishing the kingdom even now. This wonder-filled reality grants great promise to all who believe. The dark forces that often bedevil our lives have been served notice in the Spirit. Yet problems remain. People will seek to commandeer the power of the Spirit and turn it to their own advantage. They will exploit sincere faith and even put God to the test. These charlatans appeal to God, but only on their own terms. Their interest in the Spirit is directed by their own selfish desires.

The Gospel leads in a totally different direction. In Matthew, the miracle-working power of the Spirit brings glory to God, affirms the supremacy of Christ and relieves the suffering of others. Matthew's portrait of the Spirit is like a mosaic. From a distance we can take in the whole picture, but as we draw nearer, we are challenged by the parts. The critical question is, How do we fit into Matthew's picture of Christ and the Spirit?

This is certainly something to pray about as we seek to follow Jesus and grow in grace (2 Pet 3:18).

+ To what extent am I really open to the leading of the Spirit? Healings and deliverance are welcome, but what if, as was the case with Mary and Joseph, the work of the Spirit becomes awkward? How receptive would I be if, as was the case with Jesus, the Spirit leads into a wilderness of trial? When we say that we want all that the Spirit has for us, do we really mean *all*?

+ Am I open to dream revelation from the Spirit? As noted, throughout the history of Israel and the early church, God revealed his mysteries by way of dreams. Sigmund Freud has been reported to have quipped, "Sometimes a cigar is just a cigar." Similarly, sometimes a dream is just a dream and nothing more. Yet according to Scripture, sometimes a dream is a message from God. That's something to pray about.

✦ When seeking the good things of the Spirit, what are my true intentions? Am I seeking miracles to bolster a failing faith? Am I a "sign seeker" who puts God to the test? James says we don't receive answers to prayers because we want to satisfy our own selfish desires (Jas 4:3). Pray for charismatic empowerment so that you might glorify God, strengthen his church, and help your neighbor.

✦ Do I believe in miracles or magic? We must be ever mindful that the Holy Spirit is a person, not just a power. As a person, the Holy Spirit can think, speak, make intercession, be grieved, etc. (Rom 8:26-27; Eph 4:30). When we seek to genuinely know the person of the Spirit, we are in the domain of miracles. When we try to manipulate and control the Spirit to meet our own selfish desires, we are in the realm of magic.

✦ In making room for the movement of the Spirit, am I vulnerable to persons who are insincere and exploitive? Do I have the spiritual maturity to "test the spirits" to see if they are of God (1 John 4:1)? If they are not of God, do I have the courage to confront error for the strengthening of the church (Acts 5:1-11)?

As you pray and seek the Spirit, recall that from beginning to end, Jesus realizes the kingdom by the power of the Holy Spirit. As his disciples, we too can enjoy this extraordinary presence of the Spirit: the hallmark of the kingdom.

2

The HOLY SPIRIT
in MARK

AUTHORITY AND OBEDIENCE

"By what authority are you doing these things?" they asked.
"And who gave you authority to do this?"

MARK 11:28 NIV

AS WE ENTER MARK, a familiar pattern emerges. For Mark, nothing of God's kingdom is established apart from the Holy Spirit. This holds true even for the Son of God. Thus straightaway, Mark opens his Gospel with two dramatic statements about the Holy Spirit. First, as with Matthew, John the Baptist prophesies that Jesus will baptize his followers in the Holy Spirit. Unlike Matthew, however, Mark has omitted the phrase "and fire" (compare Mt 3:11 and Mk 1:8). Second, Jesus receives the Holy Spirit after being baptized by John in the Jordan River.[1] It is clear that for Mark the ensuing ministry of Jesus is empowered by the Holy Spirit.

It is generally conceded that Mark writes to Romans. In connecting with his audience, he translates all Aramaic terms (Mk 5:41; 7:34; 14:36; 15:34) and explains Jewish religious practices (Mk 7:3-4). Mark

---

[1]Matthew, Mark, and Luke have the Holy Spirit descending upon Jesus "as a dove" (Mt 3:16; Mk 1:10; Lk 3:22). Are the evangelists simply describing the motion of the Spirit (descending slowly like a dove when landing) or are they describing the shape of the Spirit (the Holy Spirit looked like a dove)? All three synoptic Gospels use the same verb—*katabainō*, "to come down from above"—to describe the direction of the Spirit. Yet Luke adds *sōmatikos*, meaning "bodily," to indicate the visible shape of the Spirit. Altogether, the Spirit *looked* like a dove and *settled* on Jesus like a dove.

makes sure that the last person to testify that Jesus is the Son of God is a Roman centurion (Mk 15:39). So Mark is addressing a highly militarized culture that respects authority and obedience. That's why the question posed in the key verse is so critical for Mark's portrayal of the Lord. Mark has Jesus ministering and acting in the supreme authority of the Holy Spirit. For a Roman, the only appropriate response in the presence of such authority is unquestioned obedience. That is why Mark skips the birth narratives altogether and enters directly into the dynamic and forceful work of the Spirit in the life of Jesus.

Jesus' temptation in the wilderness is a case in point. Matthew states that Jesus was "led up" by the Spirit into the wilderness. Mark uses the more forceful *ekballō* (that is, "to cast out") and so Jesus is "thrust" into the wilderness to be tempted by Satan. In so doing, Mark accomplishes two things. First, he demonstrates that the Spirit is in sovereign control of Jesus' ministry from beginning to end. Second, the unidirectional action of the Spirit in driving Jesus into the wilderness implies some degree of reluctance on the part of the human Jesus (see also Mt 26:39). Yet Jesus intentionally submits to the dictates of the Spirit in obedience to the will of the Father. The resultant victory of Jesus over temptation is of cosmic proportions, prevailing amid earthy creatures (wild animals) and heavenly hosts (angels) (Mk 1:13).

Mark is the only Gospel that pairs "wild animals" and "angels," suggesting that the animals are not hostile to Jesus but commune with him who is their Creator. For Mark, Jesus has transformed the wilderness of sin into the Garden of Eden, reflecting God's eventual transformation of all creation (see Rom 8:18-21).

Departing the wilderness in the power of the Spirit, Jesus initiates a relentless campaign of spiritual warfare against Satan and his minions. Mark uses the word *demon(s)* fourteen times but also employs the more curious phrase "unclean or impure spirit(s)" eleven times.[2] In fact, both Jesus and his disciples perform some type of exorcism no less than

---

[2]For *demon(s)*, see Mk 1:34, 39; 3:15, 22; 5:12, 15; 6:13; 7:26, 29, 30; 9:38; 16:9, 17. For "unclean or impure spirit(s)," see Mk 1:23, 26, 27; 3:11, 30; 5:2, 8, 13; 6:7; 7:25; 9:25.

twelve times in Mark. Clearly, victory over the devil is important for Mark. When Jesus gives a number of signs that identify true believers, the first of these signs is that they will cast out demons in his name (Mk 16:17). True to Mark's theme of authority, the unclean spirits recognize Jesus' identity and obey his commands. Ironically, the religious experts in Israel reject their own Messiah in rebellion.

Since most Romans would not have known the Hebrew Scriptures, Mark cannot appeal to the fulfillment of prophesy. Rather, Jesus' exorcisms and healings are evidence that the kingdom is being established in power. This does not mean that Mark ignores prophecy altogether (see Mk 11:1-10; 13:10; 14:9). The so-called Little Apocalypse in Mark 13 is an extended prophecy concerning the end times.

Unexpectedly, those who are delivered from the devil and disease are commanded not to tell anyone. Jesus' command not to share his identity constitutes the so-called "Messianic Secret" and occurs no less than six times in Mark.[3] Much debate surrounds its meaning, but clearly Jesus does not want others to set the agenda for his own kingdom vision. His rule is unlike the powers of this world, especially the power of the Roman Empire.

Relatedly, Jesus taught that the kingdom of God is not defined by the conventions of this world. It is the domain of the Spirit (see Rom 14:17). Thus Jesus repeatedly challenged the conventional understanding of the Sabbath, what is clean and unclean, and tithing (see Mk 2:23-28; 7:1-8; 12:38-44). Jesus is the supreme authority over everything. He is Lord over the Sabbath because he made the Sabbath. He is the source of all holiness. His presence brings all things and persons into the realm of the divine. As the true object of worship, Jesus defines true worship.

As supreme authority, Jesus legitimates all other authorities, particularly civil authority. Although branded and executed as an insurrectionist, Jesus was not an anarchist. His kingdom is essentially spiritual, apolitical, and nonviolent. He certainly subverted the values of this world but did not raise an army to fight the kingdoms of this world. Much of this is encapsulated in his teaching about paying taxes to

---

[3]See Mk 1:34; 3:9-12; 7:36; 8:30; 5:39-43; 9:9.

Caesar (Mk 2:14-17) and his repeated counsel that the greatest in the kingdom of God will be the servant of all (Mk 10:42-45).

In sum, it is the Holy Spirit who testifies to and undergirds the high Christology found in Mark. Moreover, it is the Holy Spirit that transfers this Christ-affirming power to those who truly believe.

PAUSE FOR PRAYER

As one reads through Mark, the power of the Spirit in Jesus can be overwhelming, even terrifying. On occasion, the disciples are scared speechless in the presence of Christ's power. To think that this power is promised to all who believe! To command a mountain to be thrown into the sea is heady stuff indeed (Mk 11:23)! Yet Mark reminds us that even as we are regaled by the extraordinary power of God in Christ, the kingdom is entered by those who become as a little child (Mk 10:15). We must remember that there is a divine inversion in Mark. Those who are first in the power structures of this world will be last in the kingdom of God, and those who are last in the estimation of this age will be first in the kingdom (Mk 9:35; 10:31). We have power by way of privilege; our greatness is measured by our gratitude.

THE PRESENCE OF THE HOLY SPIRIT IN MARK

The Holy Spirit and spiritual warfare (Mk 1:23-27; 5:1-20; 9:14-29). The Romans of the first century enjoyed a good fight, especially when they won. Consequently, the Holy Spirit is a warrior in Mark. Through the power of the Spirit, Jesus is taking territory for God. The triumph of the Spirit in Mark is set forth by a series of exorcisms. For example, the very first miracle in Mark is an exorcism and occurs immediately after the Spirit comes upon Jesus at his baptism. Similarly, the devil is defeated after the Spirit thrusts Jesus into the wilderness. Mark's message is clear. To all those who oppose the Spirit-empowered Christ, resistance is futile. Although spiritual battles occur throughout Mark, their outcome is never in doubt.

An intriguing quality of Mark's cosmology is that demons and impure spirits recognize Jesus as the Holy One of God (Mk 1:24). Additionally, and in some ways even more fascinating, the unclean spirits are surprised to see Jesus. They are shocked (and terrified) that Jesus has appeared so soon. They know that they will inevitably face the judgment of God, but can this really be happening now?

This first exorcism in Mark is written to impress. Jesus commands that the unclean spirit "be muzzled" and to come out of the oppressed person. The unclean spirit sends the person into a spasm and shrieks as it leaves its victim.

The vividness of this account is matched by its theological content. First, there is an awareness in the spirit world that is not shared by our world. The repeated use of *us* in verse 24 indicates that the spirits who oppose Jesus are well aware of the Father's plan. Second, the story graphically conveys Mark's understanding of the end times. Although a more sophisticated "realized eschatology" will be left to subsequent writers, Mark lets us know that the last days have arrived in Jesus. Final judgment has been powerfully brought forward in Christ. The kingdom of God is being realized even now in God's Son. Finally, Mark makes it clear that Jesus is the sovereign and unquestioned authority of God in the world. There is but one option in the face of such authority: complete and utter obedience.

The second exorcism of Jesus' career occurs in Mark 5 and is even more intense than the first. The importance of this event can be seen in that Mark devotes nearly an entire chapter to this story. However, it is space well spent, for the exorcism in Mark 5 reveals a lot about Jesus and his kingdom work.

Once again, Mark's Roman audience plays a critical role in interpretation. His hearers must know that just as the Romans vanquish their foes, Jesus also conquers all opposing forces to his kingdom. That is why for Mark's audience, this exorcism would have been viewed as a military engagement on the field of battle.

Matthew states that Jesus was sent *only* to the lost sheep of Israel (Mt 10:6; 15:24). Yet Mark's exorcism took place in the region of the Gerasenes, which was in the Gentile territory of Decapolis (Mk 5:1, 20). There is a not too subtle message that Jesus' domain is not limited to Israel but extends into Gentile territory as well.

Mark's record is both confrontational and full of pathos. The man with the unclean spirit had been banished to live among the tombs, a forbidden zone in the ancient world. He was clearly viewed as a public menace, for "many times" he had been clapped in irons, but to no avail. The afflicted was able to break the fetters into pieces, and like a wild animal, was "untamable." Unlike the previous exorcism, this account brings an extraordinary sense of despair. All throughout the night and day, the person is "shouting out loud" in agony (from the Greek *krazō*, "to cry out in a loud voice") and cutting himself with sharp stones (Mk 5:4-5).

An adversarial note is struck in Mark 5:6. From a great distance away, the man starts running toward Jesus. For a Roman soldier, this would have signaled an attack. But then Mark adds a single word that changes everything: *proskyneō*. This word can either mean to kneel before an enemy in surrender or to fall down and worship as a god. For a Roman soldier, an enemy kneeling in surrender is a good thing but does not command honor and respect for the vanquished. On the other hand, to worship someone as a god would be the highest form of veneration. Perhaps Mark is employing a double-entendre here. The man possessed with an unclean spirit is both surrendering to the authority of Jesus *and* worshiping him as divine. Yet a victory does not come without a fight and so Mark continues with his story.

As in the exorcism of Mark 1:24, the presence of Jesus means that Judgment Day has arrived for all demons and unclean spirits. Again in Roman military fashion, the vanquished spirit pleads for Jesus not to torture him (Mk 5:7). Mark's grammar adds intensity to the scene. Jesus and the man are shouting over one another as the scene unfolds. To gain control over the situation, Jesus demands to know the name of the unclean spirit. The possessed person ominously responds "Legion" (Mk 5:9). Since a Roman legion was composed of up to six thousand soldiers, this was an extreme case indeed. Oddly, the unclean spirits are terrified of being sent out in a disembodied state. They implore Jesus to send them into a herd of swine. As the Master of their fate, Jesus grants their request with stunning effect (Mk 5:10-14).

This account enhances Jesus' stature even more than the first exorcism. There is the added element of Jesus ministering crossculturally among Gentiles. Also, the reader is drawn into the suffering of the demon-possessed man. He is literally being driven by a legion of demons into a life of exile and self-harm. Tragically, he is also driven to confront Jesus, his only hope for help.

Yet all is not lost to him. He is able to worship Jesus and place his fate in Jesus' hands. Once delivered, he desires to join Jesus in ministry. As his new supreme commander, Jesus denies his request and gives him standing orders.[4] Jesus silenced the unclean spirits (Mk 1:34; 3:11-12), but the man has a mission. He is to return to those who had placed him in irons and tell them of God's great mercy toward him (Mk 5:18-20).

Although Jesus gave his disciples power over demons (Mk 3:14-15), it did not always go well. In Mark 9:14-29 his disciples were unable to drive out a harmful spirit from a young boy. The spirit was *alēlos*, or "voiceless" (Mk 9:17). In typical fashion, Mark spares no effort in relating the horrifying effects of this speech-robbing spirit. When the spirit attacked, the child was dashed to the ground, foamed at the mouth, ground his teeth, and then became stiff as if dead. The whole thing was exasperating to Jesus. He commands that the boy be brought to him.

From this point on, the story echoes main features in Mark. The spirit recognizes Jesus, reacts violently, and brutalizes the child. Jesus is unflappable and inquires how long this sort of thing has been happening. In contrast, the father is beside himself, rattling off the torment this spirit has put them through. He then utters a single word that introduces a new element to Mark's exorcism accounts. When responding to Jesus, the father says *if*.

Jesus had previously described the disciples and their generation as "faithless." Their lack of faith failed to cast the demon out. The father's statement, "*If* you are able . . ." implies that perhaps Jesus is also unable to help his son. Jesus retorts, "*If* able to . . ." and then follows by saying that all things are possible to the one who believes. Sensing that the

---

[4]Jesus is consistent but not necessarily predictable. He cast seven demons out of Mary Magdalene, but unlike the Gerasene, he allows her to follow him (Mk 15:40, 47; 16:1, 9; Lk 8:2-10)

onus to believe now squarely rests on him, the father breaks down emo-tionally and speaks in contradictions. "I believe . . . help my unbelief." Simply put, "My spiritual and emotional resources are exhausted. Jesus, you have to do this."

In classic fashion, Jesus first rebukes and then commands for the spirit to come out of the boy and never to enter him again. With a shriek and a spasm the boy collapses as dead but is soon restored to his father, hale and hardy.

One final element arises in this account. In the realm of spiritual warfare, the enemy may be the same, but all battles are not equal. Jesus confides in his disciples that this kind of spirit can only be cast out by prayer.

In closing, Mark includes the words about Beelzebul and the blas-phemy of the Holy Spirit (Mk 3:22-30). However, he adds an inter-esting, if not disturbing feature. Mark brackets this whole section with some troubling words about Jesus' mother and brothers. Apparently they judge him to be insane and in need of their supervision (Mk 3:21, 31-35). Jesus issues an astonishing reply, especially for a first-century Jewish family. As far as one's relationship to him is concerned, family bonds are inconsequential when compared to doing the will of God. What's worrying about this account is that his family, because of their unbelief and false appraisal of him, are counted among the enemies of the Lord.

The Holy Spirit and the transvaluation of values (Mk 10:13-45; 12:38-44). Mark is writing to a people who fully endorse hierarchical power structures. Beginning with the emperor at the top and de-scending to the lowliest enslaved person at the bottom, the Romans cultivated a highly stratified society. The whole arrangement was fueled by a patron/client system whereby the largess of one (the patron) was carefully meted out to those in need (the clients). The latter were be-holden to the former, and so it went in a never-ending cycle of benevo-lence and indebtedness. Money, political power, and social standing defined what was honorable and anything less moved in the direction of shame. Everything was done to enhance honor and avoid shame.

Jesus' vision of the kingdom ran headlong into this imperial model of life and relationships. He promoted those qualities of the kingdom that, in time, would be described as "fruit of the Spirit" (Gal 5:22-23). If there is anything unlike the culture of Rome, it is the fruit of the Spirit.

Mark's challenge was to convey this radical message of the kingdom in terms that made sense to his audience. He does so by using the signs and symbols of Roman hierarchy even while subverting that hierarchy. He selects those words and deeds of Jesus that echo imperial hierarchical concepts yet move in the opposite direction. In so doing, he affects a transvaluation of values that is in accordance with the Spirit of God.

The greatest concentration of this kind of transvaluation is in Mark 10. Here Mark records three important teachings of Jesus that effectively undermine the values of this fallen world. The first is the childlike quality of the kingdom. In first-century Rome, women and children literally had no place in public life. Similarly, an onerous kind of patriarchy was present in Judaism. The disciples tacitly endorsed such views by speaking harshly to those who brought little children to Jesus. Jesus was outraged at their boorish behavior. In contrast to the bombast and bluster of the Roman Empire, the kingdom of God is like that of little children. For those who refuse to receive the kingdom with the simple, sincere, and unpretentious heart of a child, there is absolutely no chance for them to enter it (Mk 10:13-16; see also Mt 19:13-15; 18:1-9).[5] Consequently, anyone who would wound the heart of a child is subject to the most severe judgment (Mk 9:42; see also Mt 18:6-7).

The second example is an expansion and application of the first. A wealthy man approaches Jesus and essentially demands a checklist for inheriting eternal life (Mk 10:17-22). His take on faith is achievement oriented, almost mechanical. If you do these things, then this result must follow. Jesus realizes that this person might be religious in practice,

---

[5]English grammar does not permit the use of a double negative. However in Greek, strong negation is conveyed in this very way. The *ou mē* ("no not") in Mk 10:15 means that unchildlike persons will certainly not, in no way, enter the kingdom of God.

but he's a materialist at heart. His false sense of values is skewing his understanding of God, his relationship to neighbor, and even how he views himself. Jesus' remedy is threefold. First, he must sell all his material possessions. In this way, the man will deconstruct the false value system he has created. Then, he must express love for his neighbor by giving to the poor. Only then will he truly understand God's true purpose for material blessings. Finally, he must render total and unreserved devotion to God. In a spirit of supreme self-possession, Jesus frames devotion to God in terms of following him.

In the end, the man departs crestfallen. He has failed the childlike criterion of the kingdom as set forth earlier (see Mk 10:14-15). A child's heart allows for no conflicting values. In like manner, authentic faith, the kind that is at home in the kingdom, cannot simultaneously endorse the values of this world.

In light of the uncompromising demands of the kingdom, the disciples are stunned. Their bewilderment opens the door for Jesus to address the heart of the issue. The greatest miracle of all is to escape the relentless, downward tug of this fallen age and to be born again. Salvation only comes from God (Mk 10:24-27).

Shockingly, Jesus raises the stakes even higher. Devotion to God does not only involve forsaking material possessions but also a willingness to leave one's family members. Also, to be counted worthy of the kingdom is to welcome persecution, a point not lost on the early church.[6] The first in this age will be last in the kingdom and those considered least in the eyes of the world will be first in the kingdom (Mk 10:28-31). All of this reflects the heart of the Spirit. The Spirit serves others, graces others, empowers others.

The church is not immune from valuing the things of this age. Even as Jesus speaks of his impending betrayal and crucifixion, two of his disciples (James and John) seek to advance their personal fortunes just

---

[6]In contrast to an honor/shame society, Jesus links one's eternal destiny to the issue of shame (Mk 10:38). Consequently, the disciples rejoiced to be counted worthy to suffer *shame* for Jesus' name (Acts 5:41). Paul says he is not *ashamed* of the gospel of Christ (Rom 1:16). It appears that Timothy struggled with owning the shame of the gospel (2 Tim 1:8).

before he dies! Basically, they want to secure a coregency with Jesus when he comes into his kingdom. Jesus informs them that they are acting like unredeemed Gentiles. He then reiterates that the greatest in the kingdom will be the servant of all.

Perhaps most annoyingly, worldly power structures can surface in worship contexts as well. The religious leaders of the day made a grand display of their piety, all the while perpetrating injustices on the poor and powerless. Jesus counsels that those who appear to do the least in worship are in fact doing the most for God (Mk 12:38-45).

All these examples convey the same thing. The Spirit of the kingdom is radically opposed to the spirits of this world. All of this is supremely set forth in the paradigm-setting life and death of Jesus. As Mark explains, the stone that the builders rejected as worthless was in reality God's choice cornerstone for his whole plan of salvation (Mk 12:10-11).

The Spirit of holiness (Mk 2:15–3:6; 7:1–8:13). Several renewal movements were underway during the time of Jesus, with the Pharisees being the most prominent. Their name literally means the "Separated Ones" because they sought holiness by being separate from everyone and everything they deemed as unclean. A major aspect of Jesus' ministry was to challenge this understanding of holiness.

For Jesus, holiness is a quality of the Most High God. For him, true holiness is realized by the *Holy* Spirit and is not a fragile something that needs to be protected by innumerable religious rules and practices. As such, holiness is not easily overcome but rather overcomes. Holiness takes in and transforms everything that can be redeemed and makes it fit for the kingdom of God.

That is why Jesus can touch a leper, and rather than being made unclean, Jesus makes the leper clean (Mk 1:40-45). In what must have appeared as a sacrilege to the Pharisees (for they only ate with persons who were in a state of ritual purity), Jesus consistently and deliberately ate with tax collectors and sinners (Mk 2:15-22). Also, Jesus' disciples ate without washing their hands in ritual cleansing (Mk 7:1-5). When the Pharisees confronted Jesus about this, he spoke forth the most profound teaching on holiness that has ever been uttered. He taught that the innumerable traditions of the Pharisees have nothing to do with holiness.[7] For Jesus, holiness is not material but spiritual. That is, holiness concerns the purity of one's heart, not the cleanliness of one's hands (Mk 7:14-23).

According to the Pharisees, proper observance of the Sabbath was another requirement for holiness. To their consternation, Jesus healed on the Sabbath and his disciples picked grain on the Sabbath as well. Again, their opposition creates an occasion for Jesus to speak the deep things of God. First, humanity was not created to serve the needs of the Sabbath, but the other way around (Mk 2:27; 3:4). Second, the one who made the Sabbath is Lord over the Sabbath (Gen 2:1-2; Mk 2:28).

Immediately after these controversies about purity, Mark has Jesus encountering Gentiles. Many Jews, especially the Pharisees, considered Gentiles sinners by nature, even dogs. Yet Jesus answers the Gentiles' prayers and commends their faith (Gal 2:15; Mk 7:27-37). The Spirit of holiness is inclusive and affirms every person, regardless of one's social, moral, or ethnic identity in this world (Acts 1:8).

SUMMARY THOUGHTS

Mark conveys a single, powerful message. The Roman Empire is no match for the kingdom of God. Caesar is not Lord; Jesus is Lord. Those who are in the know—and in Mark's case this includes demons and unclean spirits—fear his power and honor his person. The strictures of Pharisaic Judaism are too narrow and unyielding for the expansive reach of God in Christ. Like old and brittle wineskins, all must yield to God's Spirit-empowered Christ. There are no barriers, whether they be religious, social, or political, that can stop the redemptive campaign of the Lord. Nothing can withstand his holiness. Nothing can make him impure.

---

[7]Not only did the Pharisees keep the 613 commandments contained in the Hebrew Scriptures, they also held to the teachings of the fathers (Mk 7:3, 7-10; see also Gal 1:14). It is believed that the oral law of the Pharisees was written down in the Mishnah (ca. 200 AD) and contains over 4,000 individual laws governing Jewish religious practice.

What Does It Mean for Me?

Mark has written an action-packed, hope-filled Gospel. His constant refrain is, Victory is assured! It is a joy to apply Mark's message to our lives. We are weak, but Jesus is strong. We lack faith, but he is faithful. We need a miracle, and with God, nothing is impossible.

Yet for Mark, Jesus is not to be trifled with. Jesus is described as "indignant" three times in Mark (Mk 1:41; 3:5; 10:14). He rebukes his disciples and even calls one of them Satan (Mk 8:33; 16:14). With respect to devotion to God, if you are thinking "family first," then think again. Jesus answers prayer, but he is not at our every beck and call. Before you can be servant of all, you need to serve him first.

All these issues address the ongoing challenge of spiritual growth and discipleship. Prayerfully consider the following as you endeavor to grow in grace.

+ Much of Jesus' ministry in Mark involved casting out demons and unclean spirits. Jesus grants this power to his disciples no less than three times in Mark. As a person of the modern age, what do you think about demons and unclean spirits? Was Jesus simply reflecting the thought forms of his day, or was he accurately portraying a truth that few accept today?

+ If Jesus was right about demons and unclean spirits, how might this relate to your personal calling? According to Mark, if you are not a person of prayer, the question is moot.

+ Recall that Jesus' exorcisms happened "along the way," so to speak. If his path crossed that of a demon, the Lord took care of business. On the other hand, he did not go hunting unclean spirits. Keep this in mind when claiming the promises in Mark 16:9-20. Although known to the church by the second century, these verses are absent from our earliest and most complete manuscripts. In any case, they are promises for protection (see Acts 28:1-5), not instructions to deliberately enter life-threatening situations. To do so is to put God to the test, inviting deadly consequences.

✦ Throughout Mark, the disciples express a somber respect for the Lord, even a touch of fearfulness at times. In our modern penchant for celebration in worship, have we become too familiar with Jesus?

✦ With regard to the "transvaluation of values," Mark can be hard hitting. What areas of your life could undergo transvaluation in the Lord? How might our modern tendency to compartmentalize shield certain sectors of our lives from being transvalued in Christ? After all, business is business.

✦ Jesus' words about childlikeness are both charming and alarming at the same time. To what extent have we allowed the hardness of life to destroy a childlike trust in God? Sometimes a "second childhood" can be a good thing.

✦ How do you understand the holiness of God? Is holiness just a factor of religion that you can manipulate to your own satisfaction? Or is holiness that living, dynamic indwelling of the Spirit that not only transforms you but also has a positive effect on whatever context you might find yourself in?

✦ In Mark, Jesus commends persons for having great faith, is astonished at the lack of faith and chides others who have little faith. In an age that quantifies everything, we can easily misunderstand Jesus here and be tempted to order faith by the yard. If we've got enough faith, we can make God do what we want. When this happens, a true knowledge of God begins to go awry.

As you pray and seek the Spirit on these points, allow the character of Mark to have its way in your life. Mark is simple, honest, vulnerable, and real. Embracing these qualities will go a long way in developing spiritual maturity.

3

The HOLY SPIRIT *in* LUKE

GOOD NEWS FOR THE POOR AND FREEDOM FOR THE CAPTIVES

The Spirit of the Lord is on me, because he has anointed me to proclaim
good news to the poor. He has sent me to proclaim freedom for the prisoners
and recovery of sight for the blind, to set the oppressed free, to proclaim the
year of the Lord's favor.

LUKE 4:18-19 NIV

LUKE CAN RIGHTLY be called a "theologian of the Spirit." He intuitively joins any thought about God with the person and work of the Holy Spirit. In fact, Luke mentions the Holy Spirit nearly as much as Matthew and Mark combined. When one considers the number of times the Spirit appears in the book of Acts, the companion volume to Luke, Luke references the Holy Spirit over seventy times in his writings.[1]

Yet it is not the number of references that is important here. What really matters is how exceptional the Spirit is for Luke. Simply put, there is no presence of God without the Holy Spirit. For example, the birth narratives in Luke, the longest and most complete in the Bible, are permeated with the work of the Spirit. John the Baptist was filled with the Holy Spirit before he was even born (Lk 1:15)! The last words

---

[1]Matthew and Mark have the *Holy Spirit* or *Spirit* nineteen times while Luke has eighteen references (see Lk 1:15, 35, 41, 67; 2:25, 26, 27; 3:16, 22; 4:1 (2×), 14, 18; 10:21; 11:13; 12:10, 12]. The book of Acts references the Spirit over fifty times and is a study in its own right.

of the exalted Christ are for the disciples to receive the promise of the Spirit (Lk 24:49).

For Luke, no person or event has any constructive role in the kingdom apart from the Spirit. The birth narratives are replete with references to persons filled with the Spirit and prophesying. Once Jesus receives the Spirit at his baptism, he is the sole locus of the Spirit in the world. Up until the Day of Pentecost, no one else operates in the Spirit except Jesus. So the Spirit is both programmatic and paradigmatic for the life and ministry of Jesus. The Spirit not only sets the agenda for Jesus' actualization of the kingdom, the Spirit establishes the pattern of how God now works in the world. This program and pattern in the Spirit began with Jesus and will continue by way of his church.

As such, the first great event of Jesus' ministry was not an exorcism or healing as was the case in Matthew and Mark. Rather, what would determine the quality and content of Jesus' ministry were the words he spoke in the synagogue in Nazareth. When Jesus said, "The Spirit of the Lord is upon me," he determined the entire basis of his ministry. Isaiah's prophecy inaugurated the Spirit-anointed ministry of Christ, together with all of the charisms of his ministry (Lk 4:18-19; Isa 61:1-2).[2] It meant that the word and work of Jesus is good news for the poor, deliverance for the captives, healing for the infirmed, and freedom for the oppressed.[3] Now is the time for the Lord's good favor to be realized on earth. All of this happens through the person and power of the Holy Spirit.

Indeed for Luke, the manifold nature and gifts of the Spirit are pre-eminently set forth in the life and ministry of Jesus. The Spirit is a Spirit of joy who welcomes those who are outside the boundaries of Judaism. The Holy Spirit in Luke is the Spirit of justice who cares for the poor and oppressed. Overall, the Spirit in Luke is extraordinarily positive. When the Spirit is present, there is praise, singing, and prophecy. On the other hand, to speak and act contrary to the Spirit invites judgment.

---

[2]The reference to Isaiah 61 is unmistakable. One wonders, though, considering the words about freedom and release, how much the Jubilee of Leviticus 25 and 27 might relate here.

[3]It should be noted that the word "prisoners" in Luke 4:18 is *aichmalōtois*, which literally means "those taken with the point of the spear." Jesus is talking about prisoners of war, not hardened criminals or lawbreakers.

Luke's vision of the Spirit has come down to us through the ages. His record of the Spirit is something to cultivate, to pray about, and to receive.

PAUSE FOR PRAYER

Luke has quite a bit to say about the Samaritans in his Gospel (see Lk 9:52; 10:33; 17:16). Bad blood had existed between the Jews and the Samaritans for hundreds of years (see Ezra 4:1-4).[4] That is why when Jesus and his disciples were traveling to Jerusalem, some Samaritans barred them from passing through their village. Indignant, James and John, the "Sons of Thunder," want to call down fire and destroy the Samaritans in the manner of Sodom and Gomorrah. Jesus rebuked them and then chose another path (Lk 9:52-56). Some later manuscripts have Jesus saying, "You do not know what kind of spirit you are of; for the Son of Man did not come to destroy men's lives, but to save them."

Racial prejudice had poisoned the spirits of James and John. Yet Jesus' rebuke gets the point across. The Spirit always helps, never harms. We must build others up in the Spirit and be conduits of God's grace. Anything less is "to grieve the Holy Spirit" (Eph 4:29-30). Pray now that you will always seek the leading of the Spirit to help and not to hurt. Such prayers become especially important when you feel slighted or mistreated, as James and John apparently felt.

THE PRESENCE OF THE HOLY SPIRIT IN LUKE

The Holy Spirit and two extraordinary births (Lk 1:1–2:40). If Mark completely skips the birth narrative of Jesus, and Matthew records everything from Joseph's perspective, Luke doubles down on the subject.

---

[4]The animosity that existed between Jews and Samaritans was due to a long and sad history. In 597 BCE, Nebuchadnezzar, king of the Babylonians, overran the southern kingdom of Judah and captured Jerusalem (2 Kings 24:10-16; 25:1-4). Only the best and brightest of Israel were taken into captivity in Babylon. The rest were left to fend for themselves and soon began to intermarry and adopt the ways of their non-Jewish neighbors. When King Cyrus of Persia released the Jews from exile in 538 BCE (Ezra 1:1-6, 6:1-5; 2 Chron 36:20) the returnees found a "mixed multitude" abiding in Israel (Neh 13:1-3). More than likely, these persons came to be known as the "Samaritans." From this point on, a rift developed between the Jews and Samaritans (Ezra 9:1-2, 10-12; 10:18-44; Neh 13:23-29), a schism that would last until the time of Jesus and beyond.

He not only records the miracle of the virgin birth, but he alone records the birth of John the Baptist. Perhaps because he is a physician, Luke records everything from the perspective of the mothers.

The Spirit is intensely active in Luke's birth narrative. John the Baptist was full of the Holy Spirit while still in his mother's womb. When Mary greets Elizabeth, the yet unborn John moves suddenly in the womb, and his mother is filled with the Spirit. Once born, John's father Zechariah is also filled with the Holy Spirit and prophesies. When describing the role of the Spirit in the virgin birth, Luke uses the word *episkiazō* or "overshadow" (Lk 1:35). The image of the Spirit overshadowing Mary is reminiscent of the Spirit hovering over the waters in creation (Gen 1:2).

Everyone associated with the birth of Jesus and John is influenced by the Holy Spirit. Zechariah is filled with the Spirit and prophesies. The Spirit guides the aged Simeon to the temple so that he can meet the holy family. Simeon prophesies in the Spirit, who reveals to him that Jesus will be a light to the Gentiles (Lk 2:25-35).

Luke wants his readers to know that the Holy Spirit effects the birth of Christ and inaugurates the messianic age. It is the Spirit who reveals, fills, overshadows, conceives, moves, and prophesies.

The Holy Spirit and the charismatic ministry of Christ (Lk 4:1-21; 7:17-23). Luke is the only Gospel to say that Jesus was full of the Holy Spirit *before* and *after* his temptation in the wilderness (Lk 4:1, 14). Moreover, Jesus predicates his entire ministry on the words, "The Spirit of the Lord is upon me" (Lk 4:18-19). When the disciples of John the Baptist inquire whether Jesus is the Christ (Lk 7:19-20), Jesus rehearses a litany of divine works recalling his words in Nazareth (see Lk 4:18-19). The blind are made to see, the lame can walk again, lepers are cleansed, the deaf hear, the dead are raised, and most importantly for Luke, the gospel is preached to the poor. In sum, the proof that Jesus is the Messiah is seen in his Spirit-anointed deliverance ministry that empowers the poor and heals the infirmed.

Some of the spiritual warfare so evident in Matthew and Mark is also present in Luke. In Luke, Jesus states that he drives out demons "by the finger of God" (Lk 11:20).[5] When threatened by Herod Antipas, Jesus responds that he casts out demons on an ongoing basis (Lk 13:32). In every case, it is the Holy Spirit that defeats the powers of darkness.

The Holy Spirit and social justice (Lk 1:53; 3:1-17; 6:20-38; 12:14-21; 14:12-24; 16:1-13, 19-31). God's care for the poor is a constant refrain in Luke. Mary is thankful that God has filled the hungry and sent the rich away empty. Luke describes the ministry of John the Baptist as caring for the poor and powerless. Those who have a surplus should share with those in need. Those in power should enact fair taxes. No one should use power to extort money from the innocent. For Jesus, the kingdom has drawn near when the good news is preached to the poor (Lk 4:18; 7:22). Matthew has "Blessed are the poor *in spirit*," but Luke simply says, "Blessed are you who are poor" (Mt 5:3; Lk 6:20). Twice in Luke, Jesus commands someone to sell everything and give to the poor (Lk 12:33; 18:22). On the other hand, the rich should mourn because judgment is coming. You simply can't serve God and money.

Only Luke has the parable of the rich fool and the pitiful yet terrifying story of the rich man and Lazarus. Material riches mean nothing if you're spiritually poor (Lk 12:21). Those who hoard wealth and have no care for the poor can expect judgment. Where one's treasure is, there one's heart will be also (Lk 12:34). We should give to persons who cannot afford to repay us.[6] It is the poor and powerless who will sit at God's banquet table. For Luke, benevolence to the poor fulfills all the purity regulations (Lk 11:41).

In sum, Luke empowers the poor and turns the values of this world upside down (Lk 9:57-62). What people hold in high esteem is repugnant to God. Jesus has come to set this earth on fire. Allegiance to him takes precedence over family ties (Lk 12:49-53). The only answer to materialism is to make Jesus your sole possession.

---

[5]The "finger of God" is a divine circumlocution, or roundabout way of saying the "Spirit of God" (compare with Matt 12:28). For additional accounts see Lk 4:33-35, 4:41; 8:2, 27-39; 9:38-43; 11:14. As was the case in Matthew and Mark, Jesus gives his disciples power to cast out demons (Lk 9:1, 10:17).

[6]Jesus' words are diametrically opposed to the all-important patron/client system of the Roman Empire. For the Romans, a good patron only gives to those persons who can repay.

The Holy Spirit and crosscultural mission (Lk 2:32; 4:26-27; 7:2-9; 10:27-37). The Holy Spirit in Luke is expansive and welcoming. The redemptive power of God in Christ bursts through the confines of Judaism and reaches out to Gentiles. The aged Simeon prophecies that Jesus will be a light of revelation for the Gentiles. The widow of Zarephath and Naaman the Syrian are commended for their faith. The same holds true for centurions and Samaritans—often they alone are thankful to God. The soul of every person, even a despised Samaritan, is precious to God.

The Holy Spirit is the Spirit of joy (Lk 1:46-55, 67-79; 2:13-14; 6:22-23; 15:1-32). Compared to the empty frivolity of the world, the kingdom can appear severe. In the main, however, the Spirit of God is a Spirit of joy. In Luke, people on earth and angels in heaven are singing for joy. Even when persecuted, the disciples are to rejoice and leap for joy. Upon return, the seventy-two disciples are full of joy (Lk 10:17). Jesus is full of the joy of the Holy Spirit (Lk 10:21). Moreover, the parables of the lost sheep, lost coin, and lost son, all unique to Luke, are full of joy and rejoicing. And finally, after the ascension of Christ, the disciples return to Jerusalem with great joy (Lk 24:52). Outside of the kingdom it may be dark and dire, but within there is unspeakable joy.

The Holy Spirit is the promise of the Father (Lk 11:1-13; 24:49-52). Prior to his ascension, Jesus makes an extraordinary promise to his disciples. He will send "power from on high," the promised Holy Spirit of the Father (Lk 24:49). This prediction of Pentecost forms a perfect segue to the book of Acts (see Acts 1:8; 2:1-4). Luke's message is clear. What Jesus began to do in the Spirit during his earthly ministry, he will continue to do through the Spirit in the church.

The Lord's Prayer forms the immediate context for the promised gift of the Holy Spirit. In that prayer, all the provision of the Father, both spiritual (the forgiveness of sins) and material (the granting of daily bread) comes by way of God's ultimate provision, the indescribable gift of the Spirit. It is God's benevolent will to give the Holy Spirit to all who ask him.

SUMMARY THOUGHTS

Luke is a theologian of the Spirit. The Spirit is prophetically active before Jesus is born, indwells John the Baptist while still in the womb, and empowers Jesus from the time of his baptism in water until the moment he is taken up into heaven at the ascension. The Spirit directs Jesus to preach the gospel to the poor, set free those who have been taken captive, heal the infirmed, and deliver those who have been oppressed. Through the Spirit, Jesus is realizing the kingdom in joy. The unmatched benevolence of the Father assures that through Jesus, the person and power of the Spirit will be gifted to the church. The gift of the Spirit is the source of all spiritual gifts and ensures that the kingdom will proceed in power until the Lord's return.

WHAT DOES IT MEAN FOR ME?

For Luke, the Holy Spirit is not some distant theological abstraction. The Spirit is the genuine and personal presence of God that is experienced in everyday life (Lk 1:5-8; 2:8-11; 3:1-3). It is a comfort to know that the Spirit provides an unfettered communion with the Almighty. It is a challenge to realize that the voice of God is an ever-present reality to be heard and obeyed. The imminence of the Spirit behooves the sensitive believer to pray without ceasing (1 Thess 5:17).

✦ The Spirit in Luke clearly reaches out to persons on the fringes of society. Pray now that you might truly sense the longing of the Spirit for the marginalized and by that same Spirit be used to alleviate their suffering.

✦ The Holy Spirit in Luke is a very positive Spirit. However, along with this positivity, Luke has interwoven an element of judgment. Everything that agrees with the Spirit is affirmed. Everything that conflicts with the Spirit is rejected. In this regard, we are to "step in the same footprints" as the Spirit (2 Cor 12:18). If we claim unrestricted communion with the Spirit, we should pray that our steps be ordered by the Spirit.

✦ The heart of the Holy Spirit is a joyful heart. Does your heart reflect the joy of the Spirit? A preeminent fruit of the Spirit is joy. Paul says that bitterness and harmful speech grieve the Holy Spirit (Eph 4:30-31). Pray that the Holy Spirit will reveal the deep recesses of your heart and expose those areas in need of joy-filled grace.

✦ It is the Father's good pleasure to give the Holy Spirit to all who ask. In one sense, we should keep on asking. Paul welcomed the prayers of the Philippians concerning the "provision of the Spirit" in his life (Phil 1:19) Pray that you might always be asking the Father to grant you a continual supply of his Holy Spirit.

4

The HOLY SPIRIT in JOHN

THE SPIRIT OF TRUTH

And with that he breathed on them and said, "Receive the Holy Spirit."

JOHN 20:22 NIV

JOHN DOES NOT FOLLOW the structural pattern of Matthew, Mark, and Luke. Rather, he speaks of the Logos or the Word existing from eternity past. Such a concept would have been very familiar to the Greeks, John's target audience. For them, the Logos was that Divine Reason that granted symmetry and sense to all of creation. From here, in characteristic fashion, John covers a lot of theological ground with a few simple words. The Word was God, through whom all things were created, the very light of God, the source of all life and the sole pathway into the family of God. He then comes to the incarnation but frames it very differently than the Synoptics. He simply yet pointedly states that the Word became "flesh" (Jn 1:1-14).[1] Although a good number of translations say this "in-fleshed" Word *dwelt* among us, John uses the verb *skēnoō*, which literally means "to pitch a tent." This language would have struck a chord with Jewish readers. They would have recalled the tabernacle of Exodus 25 and understood that the tent of meeting was a mere shadow of the Incarnate Word, Jesus Christ.

---

[1]John's use of the somewhat stark term *flesh* may be a strike against an early form of Gnosticism. The thought of God becoming "flesh" would have been abhorrent to the Gnostics (1 John 4:2-3).

John's unique approach holds true for his understanding of the Spirit as well.[2] The baptism of Jesus is a case in point. Like the Synoptics, John says the Spirit descended upon Jesus like a dove. Yet John makes a critical addition. He says that the Spirit *remained* on Jesus (Jn 1:32-33). For John, the Holy Spirit is an abiding presence in the life of Jesus who ushers in the kingdom of God in power. God grants the Spirit to Jesus without limit (Jn 3:34). Yet the Spirit in John is not intended to wow people. For example, unlike Mark, John's Gospel does not contain a single exorcism. Although Jesus heals many people (Jn 4:48; 6:2; 7:31; 12:37), in place of the conventional word for "miracle," John employs *sēmeion* or "sign." The Spirit performs *signs* through Jesus that speak to his divinity (Jn 10:24-25). Although Jesus did many signs, John chooses only seven signs, but these signs convey the structure and meaning of his entire Gospel (Jn 20:30-31).[3]

These seven signs show that Jesus is very God of very God, the sovereign Lord over all creation. Jesus has power over the quality and quantity of anything (Jn 2:1-11; 6:5-13). Space and time cannot contain his power (Jn 4:46-54; 5:1-9). His person takes precedence over the laws of nature, for he is the one who created these laws (Jn 6:16-21). The misfortunes of life must yield to his healing presence (Jn 9:1-41). Finally, the last great enemy, death, is no match for the source of all life (Jn 11:1-46). All of this is possible for Jesus has an unlimited presence of the Holy Spirit (Jn 3:34).

John has more of Jesus' teaching on the Holy Spirit than any other Gospel. In John, Jesus teaches that one must be born of the Spirit to enter the kingdom of God (Jn 3:3, 7). It is the Spirit who gives life; hence, his words are full of the Spirit and life (Jn 6:63). True worship only comes through the Holy Spirit (Jn 4:23-24). The Holy Spirit is that

---

[2]The words *Holy Spirit* or *Spirit* appear nineteen times in the Gospel of John: Jn 1:32, 33 (2×); 3:5, 6, 8, 34; 4:23, 24; 6:63 (2×); 7:39 (2×); 14:17, 26; 15:26; 16:13, 15; 20:22. Additionally, John uses the unique term *Comforter* or *Advocate* four times: Jn 14:16, 26; 15:26; 16:7. All total, John makes more references to the Holy Spirit than any other gospel.

[3]When Jesus is challenged in the Synoptics, he points to the sign of Jonah (Mt 12:39-42; Lk 11:29-32). But in John, Jesus challenges his opponents to destroy the Temple, and he will rebuild it in three days (Jn 2:18-22). Though very different, both challenges make the same point. For the obstinate and insincere, the only sign for them is the resurrection of the dead.

inexhaustible supply of living water flowing from the innermost being of every believer (Jn 7:37-39). The Holy Spirit is that truth-filled Advocate whom Jesus and the Father will send. The Advocate is that inner witness who teaches the believer all things. The Advocate always grants a stalwart testimony for Christ (Jn 14:17, 26; 15:26). The Spirit will prevail in the courtroom of this world, condemning its flawed understanding of sin, righteousness, and judgment (Jn 16:8-15). Lastly, Jesus utters those matchless words, "Receive the Holy Spirit" (Jn 20:22).

John teaches the deep things of the Holy Spirit, albeit by employing very simple words. The modest phrase, "born of the Spirit," carries us to an entirely new dimension, one not of this world. John's assurance that the Spirit will be "with you" and "in you" ravishes the thoughtful reader. If there ever was a Gospel that invokes an unbroken season of prayer, it is the Gospel of John.

PAUSE FOR PRAYER

Pilate asked Jesus the haunting question "What is truth?" The moral vacuum of the Roman Empire had bred a cold cynicism in Pilate that despaired of truth. The crushing irony was that the Truth was standing right before him. This is the constant witness of the Spirit in John. The Truth does not consist of facts or the lofty thoughts of philosophy or even in the Holy Scriptures per se (Jn 5:39). Rather the Truth is a person; the person of Jesus Christ. He is the way, the truth, and the life and is the sole access to the Father (Jn 14:6). Hence the Spirit of truth always leads one to Jesus. Pray now as you enter the Spirit-filled world of John, that in every instance and at every turn, you draw nearer to the Truth, that is, to the person of Christ.

THE PRESENCE OF THE HOLY SPIRIT IN JOHN

The Spirit grants new birth (Jn 1:12-13; 3:1-16). For John, salvation is solely the work of God, accomplished through his Son and enacted by the Holy Spirit. Salvation is not a matter of becoming familiar with God, but rather becoming family with God. God's family is diverse and all inclusive. The family of God is not determined by one's ethnicity, nor the result of human adoption procedures, nor does it come about in the natural way. No, to be part of the family of God, one must be born from God. Through faith in Jesus Christ one is given the rightful privilege to be called a child of God.

This new birth is accomplished by the Spirit and lies beyond the scope of human experience and will. This is precisely the predicament of Nicodemus. As a Pharisee and member of the Sanhedrin, he came to Jesus at an odd time (at night) for an odd talk (one that is totally directed by Jesus). After a few pleasantries, Jesus cuts him off and abruptly lays down the nonnegotiable for entering the kingdom: you must be born again.[4] Jesus' curt yet incisive pronouncement leaves Nicodemus both stymied and confused. Thinking on an entirely human level, Nicodemus utters nonsense about reentering the birth canal to be delivered a second time. His crude imagery does not dissuade Jesus. Nicodemus may want to speak of the flesh, but Jesus speaks only of the things of the Spirit. As a spiritual leader in Israel, Nicodemus should know these things, but he does not.

Jesus does not make it easy for Nicodemus, for he speaks obliquely about how the Spirit works in one who is born again. It is like the wind blowing. There is empirical evidence (you can hear it and feel it), yet the Spirit is beyond human comprehension (you don't know where it came from or where it's going).[5] One can sense the Spirit's power, but his ways are sovereign and ultimately inscrutable.

Keeping the pressure on, Jesus recalls the remedy for the venomous snake bites recorded in Numbers 21:4-9. A bronze snake was lifted up on a pole, and whoever looked upon it would be healed. Jesus indicates that this whole episode was really about his impending death on the cross. What follows is one of the golden verses of the entire Bible,

---

[4]The word "again" is *anōthen* and can also be translated "from above." Since Jesus is contrasting being born of the Spirit with being born in an earthly way, the idea of being "born from above" makes some sense. Jesus may be employing a double-entendre that encompasses both meanings. That is, to be "born from above" through the Spirit means that you have been "born again."

[5]Again, Jesus may be intentionally using dual meanings when talking with Nicodemus. The word for "wind" is the same word for "Spirit," and the word for "sound" is the same word for "voice." Could Jesus be telling Nicodemus that since he is in the flesh, he is not able to hear the voice of the Spirit?

John 3:16. Although Nicodemus fades from view, he was positively affected by Jesus' words, for he becomes a help to Jesus both in his life and in his death (Jn 7:50; 19:39).

There are at least three things that can be gathered from this account. First, one must be born again to enter the kingdom of God. This does not involve turning over a new leaf or giving renewed attention to religious practices. Rather, a completely new start of a totally different kind is required. Second, this essential transformation lies beyond the scope of human effort. This new birth is completely the work of the Holy Spirit. Finally, the basis for all of this is the love of God as evidenced in his Son's death on the cross.

The Holy Spirit gives life (Jn 6:30-69). As Jesus rounds out his discourse with Nicodemus, he reiterates that regarding God and his kingdom, the flesh profits nothing; it is the Spirit that gives life. He goes on to say that his words are full of the Spirit and of life. Since the Spirit grants new birth, then the Spirit must sustain and nourish that new birth. Jesus' words about the life-giving Spirit appear amid his miraculous feeding of the five thousand (Jn 6:1-13) and the bread of life discourse (Jn 6:26-69). In these contexts, Jesus exhorts the crowds not to seek the food that spoils but to seek the food that lasts unto eternal life. His challengers want bread like the manna Moses gave in the wilderness. Jesus redirects their thoughts to the true spiritual nourishment that only he can provide. As was the case with the bronze snake in the wilderness, the manna was simply a shadow of Jesus who is the true bread of God that gives life to the world (Jn 6:33). To underscore his point, twice Jesus states, "I am the bread of life" (Jn 6:35, 48).

Then Jesus says something that was quite disturbing. He began speaking about eating his flesh and drinking his blood. The thought of cannibalism was so upsetting that many forsook Jesus and did not follow him anymore. Shockingly, Jesus invites the Twelve to leave as well (Jn 6:51-61, 67). They stick with him because, regarding eternal life and the promised Messiah of God, there simply is no alternative to Jesus.

For John, the life-giving work of the Spirit is predicated on the life-sacrificing work of Jesus. An inherent Trinitarianism emerges here. The Father has life in himself, the Son has life in himself, and the Spirit gives life (Jn 5:24-26; 6:63).

The Spirit of truth and revelation (Jn 4:7-24; 12:20-23). On several occasions, Jesus refers to the Spirit as "the Spirit of truth." Also, the disciples will not be orphaned in the world, for he will pray to the Father and he will send *another* Advocate.[6] This is the Spirit, who will be with them and in them (Jn 14:16-18). So the Spirit's mission is to testify about Jesus (Jn 15:26) and guide believers into all truth.

The epistemological implications of these statements are enormous. A prophetic or revelatory work is inherent to the Spirit (Jn 16:13), for he grants all truth, not only in the present but also in the future.

Jesus' encounter with the Samaritan woman at the well reveals important aspects about the Spirit. Jesus' care for her deconstructs centuries-old racial and gender barriers.[7] Intriguingly, the phrases "gift of God" and "living water" are the same phrases used to describe the gift of the Holy Spirit. Is Jesus implying that he would have given her the gift of the Spirit if she had asked for it? Speaking prophetically, Jesus discerns her past and present marital status. Her response reveals how nationalized and politicized religion had become. The Samaritans had their own temple on Mount Gerizim and the Jews had their temple in Jerusalem. Jesus informs her that true worship is expansive and inclusive. True worship is not the sole domain of any single ethnic group, nor can it be confined to any one place. Even now, the Father seeks those who worship him in Spirit and in truth.

The crosscultural element inherent to this story is found in another unique portion of John. Some Greeks approach Philip and request an audience with Jesus. When Jesus hears the request, he makes a dramatic

---

[6]The word for "another" is *allos* and means another of the same kind or quality. So the Advocate of the Spirit, though different in person, is the same as Jesus in essence.

[7]The precise manner and time of the emergence of the Samaritans is open to question. The conflict that arose between those Jews who had returned from the exile and the Jews who had stayed behind and intermarried with "the people of the land" no doubt played some role in the emergence of the Samaritans (Ezra 4:1-5; Neh 13:1-3, 23-24).

and unexpected response. Jesus says that the hour has come for him to be glorified. Clearly the interest of Gentiles in meeting Jesus marked an important turning point in the plan of salvation.

The Spirit as Advocate (Jn 14:16-18, 26, 15:26, 16:7-13). The word for "Advocate" in John is *paraklētos* and allows for various translations such as "Helper," "Comforter," and "Counselor." In the first century, *paraklētos* referred to one's defense lawyer in a court of law. The fact that the Paraclete will witness or testify on behalf of Jesus lends support here. The word "witness" is *martyreō* and meant to give testimony in court. It is from this word that we get our word "martyr," for in time Christians were killed for testifying for Christ. The legal aspect of the Spirit continues when Jesus says that the Spirit will *convict* the world of its distorted view of sin, righteousness, and judgment. The fact that the Paraclete is often mentioned in contexts of fear and persecution makes sense as well. The court of this world is hostile to Jesus and his followers, yet the Holy Spirit will give a strong defense for the gospel.

In John, the hostility directed toward Jesus is formidable and relentless. In several places John notes that the Jewish leadership was out to kill Jesus (see Jn 5:18; 7:1; 8:40; 10:31).[8] They hurled some of the most outrageous accusations against him. They branded him a demon-possessed Samaritan, one who may well commit suicide (Jn 8:22, 48, 52). They judged him to be raving mad (Jn 10:20). Even his own brothers taunted Jesus to show himself publicly, knowing full well that he would probably be killed (Jn 7:1-5). Thus, Jesus taught his disciples that they would be hated by the world and he earnestly prayed for their protection (Jn 17:12-17).

Such animosity cast a chill over those who would follow Jesus. The fact that Nicodemus came to Jesus at night may be an indication of his unwillingness to be seen with Jesus in public. Indeed, John says that many rulers actually believed in Jesus but would not openly acknowledge their faith for fear of being excommunicated from the synagogue. The reason for their hesitancy is that they loved the praise

---

[8]Jesus and everyone associated with him were under the constant threat of betrayal and death (Jn 7:19, 20, 25; 8:37, 40). As time would tell, their fears were not unfounded.

of men more than the praise of God (Jn 12:42-43). So in the midst of the hostile courts of this world, the informed and powerful defense of the Spirit, our Advocate, was sorely needed then and certainly welcomed now.

The Spirit as sent gift (Jn 14:16, 26; 15:26; 16:7). There is an extraordinary futurity associated with the Holy Spirit in John. John states that the Spirit had not yet been given. He teaches that those who believed in Jesus would receive the Spirit *later*. He *will* pray to the Father and he *will* give the Advocate to the faithful. The divine order is that Jesus must first be glorified and then the Spirit will be given. When this happens, the Spirit is likened to living waters continually flowing from within (Jn 7:37-39; see also Jn 16:7). Jesus tells the disciples that the Spirit is *with* them now but will be *in* them later. The transition from *with* to *in* may point to a more intrinsic and intimate presence of the Spirit, one that will be enjoyed at some future date. When this time comes, the Spirit will remain with believers forever (Jn 14:16-17). Just as Jesus reveals the Father, the Spirit reveals Jesus to those indwelt by the Spirit.

The Spirit has a shepherding role in the lives of believers, guiding them into all truth. The word for "guide" is *hodēgeō* and literally means "to guide along a road or path." The image is of an ongoing journey whereby the Spirit takes the lead all along the way. As the faithful follow the leading of the Spirit, "all truth" is constantly unfolding before them. The word for "truth" is *alētheia*, which means "un-covering." As believers are guided along their journey by the Spirit, there is an accompanying "un-covering" of God and the things of God. Nothing will take believers by surprise because the Spirit reveals the *ta erchomena*, or "things that are to come."

In all of this, the Spirit is not self-promoting nor does he generate wisdom from himself. Rather the Spirit conveys only what he has already heard from Jesus, and what the Spirit hears from Jesus originated from the Father (Jn 16:8-15). So the indwelling of the Spirit engenders a living conversation about Jesus and, by extension, an intimate communion with the Father.

Finally, when the resurrected Lord appeared to his disciples still prior to the ascension, he breathed on them and pronounced those blessed words, "Receive the Holy Spirit" (Jn 20:22). Just as the prophets of old, Jesus signaled not only in word but also in deed what was soon to come. The word *receive* is in the imperative or command mood. The Spirit is a gift that comes with an expectation. Cooperation and submission are required to receive the Spirit.

John's favored theme of regeneration is not mentioned here. The Spirit is not granting new life to the disciples. Rather, a Johannine version of Luke 24:49 and Acts 1:8 is presented. The disciples are not to wait for regeneration but for the promised reception of the Holy Spirit.

SUMMARY THOUGHTS

What can be gleaned from John's promise of the Holy Spirit? First, Jesus taught that the gift of the Spirit was yet future. Yet once given, the Spirit would be a constant presence in the life of the believer. There is a didactic role of the Spirit—he teaches and reminds us about Jesus. There is a legal aspect of the Spirit—he witnesses to Christ and convicts the world of its skewed values. The Spirit guides the faithful to all truth. Yet this truth is not an artifact from the past but the living revelation of things to come. There is a trinitarian quality to all of this. Working backward, if you will, the Spirit conveys what he has heard from the Son, but the content of this wisdom is traced back to the Father. However, with the actual granting of the Spirit, the conceptual flow works the other way around. The Father grants the Holy Spirit in response to the prayers of the Son, who in turn breathes the Spirit onto his disciples.

John has done a masterful job of portraying the person and work of the Holy Spirit. By way of simple words and imagery, John has revealed the deep things of the Spirit. The continual abiding of the Spirit is what empowers Jesus' entire ministry. There can be no continued work of Christ apart from the Spirit.

What Does It Mean for Me?

For the believer, everything hinges on the constant indwelling and guidance of the Holy Spirit. Our love of the Father, our witness for the Son, and our fellowship in the Spirit are made possible through prayer.

+ Embrace this wonderful truth in all of its far-reaching consequences: there is no entry into the kingdom unless you are born again by the Spirit. Pray now that you never depart from this foundational truth of salvation. Pray that by his grace and through his Spirit, you might lead others to Christ.

+ The flesh profits nothing. Only the Spirit grants life. Pray for that continual guidance of the Spirit that grants a life of maturity and grace.

+ The prime directive of the Holy Spirit is to point us to Christ. Pray that your life be a continual abiding witness to Christ, a witness that is birthed and empowered by the Holy Spirit.

+ Jesus wants everyone to receive the gift of the Holy Spirit. That is why he is interceding to the Father on your behalf. Pray that you not only receive the Spirit but also receive everything the Spirit might have for you. Pray that the Spirit leads you into all truth. Pray to be submissive and open to the Spirit's mentoring hand in your life.

+ Every believer is being tried by the corrupted courtrooms of this world. Pray for the Advocate, the expert witness of the Holy Spirit, to argue your case for Christ in a world that is dull to the reality of sin, devoid of righteousness, and in need of justice.

+ Realize that in all of these things, it is the Spirit who leads and directs, not us. Unbroken submission to the sovereign control of the Spirit is like living waters deep within welling up and without end. Joyful yielding to the winsome person of the Spirit is like a refreshing breeze, of which the origin and final destination are unknown, but its presence is wonderfully felt and gladly experienced.

5

The HOLY SPIRIT *in* ACTS

A PROMISE KEPT

On one occasion, while he was eating with them, he gave them this command: "Do not leave Jerusalem, but wait for the gift my Father promised, which you have heard me speak about. For John baptized with water, but in a few days you will be baptized with the Holy Spirit."

ACTS 1:4-5 NIV

NOTHING BUILDS CONFIDENCE in another like a promise kept. The book of Acts builds confidence in God. All four Gospels contain the blessed promise that Jesus will baptize believers in the Holy Spirit (see Mt 3:11; Mk 1:8; Lk 3:16; 11:13; Jn 1:33; 14:26; 15:26). The central message of Acts is that Jesus followed through on that promise. On the Day of Pentecost, the Holy Spirit was poured out on the assembled believers, and the church and the world were never the same again. Just as Jesus began his ministry *after* the Holy Spirit came upon him at baptism, so too the church begins its ministry *after* they were baptized in the Holy Spirit. Just as the Spirit remained on Jesus and realized the kingdom of God in power, in like manner the Spirit remains upon the church and sustains God's charismatic ministry in the world. Believers are now the duly appointed, Spirit-filled emissaries of the Lord. The witness of the Spirit in the life of Christ, so critically emphasized in the Gospels, is now testifying through the church in power.[1] Through the Spirit, the charismatic deliverance and healing ministry of Christ that majestically rolled back the effects of the fall has now been transferred to the Spirit-empowered, Spirit-gifted people of God. In this sense, the church now becomes the exceptional locus of the Spirit in the world. The Spirit-filled church is the "body of Christ" made present (1 Cor 12:27). As such, there is no clearer, more powerful, or more effective witness for Christ than his Spirit-filled church as it ministers for him in the world.

The living presence of God, the redemptive power of Christ, the hope of glory, in sum, every good and perfect gift comes by way of the Holy Spirit. All of this is dramatically unfolded in the book of Acts. All of this began on the Day of Pentecost.

For these reasons, the book of Acts is especially precious to Spirit-focused believers. It is the only book of the New Testament that even mentions Pentecost in any substantial way.[2] Also, Acts draws together Pentecostal themes like no other book in the New Testament. It frames the Day of Pentecost as an eschatological or end-time event that perfectly fulfills the ancient prophecy of Joel 2:28-32. The prophecy of John the Baptist about Jesus being the Spirit baptizer is also fulfilled. The prayer of Jesus to the Father to send the Holy Spirit to the church is answered. The Great Commission in Matthew, with its inherent witness to and inclusion of Gentiles, is realized through the Holy Spirit. The promise of Jesus to send out believers in power actually comes to pass at Pentecost. The assurance that the Advocate would grant believers the words to say when faced with opposition and persecution was realized time and time again in Acts. The knowledge that the witness of the Spirit will not only be in word but also be in miraculous signs and wonders—this is the legacy of Acts for the church.

---

[1] Jesus tells his disciples not to worry when they are persecuted, for the Holy Spirit will give them words to speak (Mt 10:19-20; 13:11; Lk 12:11-12). This promise was fulfilled when the apostles stood before the Sanhedrin and gave an effective testimony through the power of the Holy Spirit (Acts 4:8; 5:32).

[2] Apart from Luke's extended treatment in Acts 2, the word *Pentecost* is only mentioned in two other places in the New Testament, and that in passing (Acts 20:16; 1 Cor 16:8).

In sum, what we see in Acts is simply what the church *is*, not what the church *was*. These are the signs that follow believers (Mk 16:17). The empowering presence of the Holy Spirit is a generational promise that transcends time and place. It is only limited by the effectual call of God, a call that will go forth until the end of time (Acts 2:38-39).

The claims of the book of Acts are bold and consequential. The spiritual burden of Acts is a call to prayer. The beauty of Acts is an open invitation to inquiring supplication and receptivity of heart.

PAUSE FOR PRAYER

"Did you receive the Holy Spirit when you believed?" This is the question that Paul posed to some dozen disciples in Ephesus (Acts 19:2). It is a haunting question. It is an unsettling question. Indeed, these disciples are nonplussed when they first hear it. They don't know what Paul is talking about. But Paul does. He knows that even though one has come to faith, hence the words, "when/since you believed," this does not exhaust everything the Holy Spirit has to offer.

Paul's question can be a bit off-putting for us as well, especially if we feel we have all that God has to offer. But what if we don't? What if there are dimensions and experiences of the Spirit that we do not yet enjoy? Dare we embrace that humble transparency that prays, "God, I want everything that you have for me"? As you study through Acts, why not continually present this bold petition as an open-ended prayer before the Lord?

THE PRESENCE OF THE HOLY SPIRIT IN ACTS

The book of Acts: God's manifesto of the Spirit (Acts 1:1-8; 2:1-47; Joel 2:28-32). As the companion volume to Luke, Acts reflects Luke's passion for the Spirit. The Holy Spirit is mentioned fifty-six times in Acts alone.[3] On average, one cannot read a chapter in Acts without encountering the words "Holy Spirit" or "Spirit" at least twice. The Spirit-anointed Christ, who was so central to Luke's Gospel, serves as a bridge

---

[3]For a comprehensive list of the references to the Spirit in Acts, see Acts 1:2, 5, 8, 16; 2:4, 17-18, 33, 38; 4:8, 25, 31; 5:3, 9, 32; 6:3, 5, 10; 7:51, 55; 8:15-19, 29, 39; 9:17, 31; 10:19, 38, 44-45, 47; 11:12, 15-16, 24, 28; 13:2, 4, 9, 52; 15:8, 28; 16:6-7; 19:2, 6; 20:22-23, 28; 21:4, 11; 28:25.

to the Spirit-anointed church in Acts. As Luke opens Acts, he is careful to note that the exalted Christ gives authoritative instructions to the apostles *through the Holy Spirit*. It is noteworthy that from this point on in Acts, the Eleven are never referred to as disciples again, only as apostles. These Spirit-filled disciples have now taken on a new role in the book of Acts. They are now apostles and are responsible for leading the church and establishing its doctrines and practices *through the Holy Spirit*.

When addressing the apostles, Jesus explicitly harks back to the promise of the Father concerning the baptism in the Holy Spirit. Setting aside their interest in the end times, Jesus utters what arguably is the key verse for the entire book of Acts. In Acts 1:8, Jesus says that they will receive power when the Holy Spirit comes upon them, and they will be witnesses not only in Jerusalem but to the farthest reaches of the earth. The word for "power" in this instance is *dynamis* and refers to the enabling energy to accomplish something. Conceptually, Jesus says that his followers will be Spirit-empowered witnesses and their impact will be on a global scale. What is interesting is that the apostles did not preach the Word first and then demonstrate the power of the Spirit. Rather, in what would become a familiar pattern throughout Acts, the miraculous power of the Spirit was made evident first, and then the Word of God was preached. Luke's message is clear. It is the manifest power of the Spirit that testifies to the risen Lord, which in turn creates the context for Spirit-inspired preaching. Just as Jesus prophesied, it is this kind of witness that will change the world for God. Indeed, the ministry started in the holy city of Jerusalem and by the time Luke's record comes to an end some thirty years later, the gospel is being preached in Rome.

Acts 2 opens with a detailed account of the gift of the Spirit at Pentecost. Pentecost was one of the three great feasts in Judaism, the other two being Passover and the Feast of Tabernacles (Lev 23:34-44; Deut 16:13-22). The word *Pentecost* means "fiftieth" because it was celebrated seven full weeks after Passover ($7 \times 7 + 1 = 50$).[4] For this reason, it

---

[4]If the Lord's Supper occurred about the time of Passover and the Lord appeared to his disciples for forty days after the resurrection (Acts 1:3), then the disciples would have waited in the upper room for about ten days (Acts 2:1).

is sometimes called the "Feast of Weeks" (Ex 34:22). Pentecost was also an agricultural feast that celebrated the first ingathering of the grain harvest. Thus Pentecost is sometimes referred to as the "Feast of First Fruits" (Ex 23:16-19). All of this means that Pentecost was a joyous time of plenty for the Jews. It was a time to celebrate the abundant provision of the Lord. For Luke's purposes, the disciples were about to experience that abundance in a profoundly spiritual way.

The outpouring of the Holy Spirit was accompanied by the sound of a strong wind and the appearance of flames of fire. The visible apparition of fire rested over each of the 120 believers that were present (Acts 1:15). A long-standing tradition of the Jews was that the law was given to Moses on Pentecost. Indeed, the theophany of wind and fire in the upper room has been likened to the fire and smoke that appeared on Mount Sinai (Ex 19:18). Could Luke be saying that an entirely new way of living before God and neighbor is being inaugurated on the Day of Pentecost? Could he be indicating that life in the Spirit has now replaced life under the law of Moses?

Acts 2:4 represents the "golden verse" for Pentecostals and charismatics. Luke says that every believer present began to speak in "different kinds of tongues" (*herterais glōssais*). A central question here is whether this phrase represents known foreign languages of the day (*xenolalia*) or whether the expression refers to an ecstatic, Spirit-inspired heavenly language (*glossolalia*)—one that requires the gift of interpretation (1 Cor 12:10, 28; 14:6). Those that opt for *xenolalia* point to the varied nations that were present in Jerusalem on the Day of Pentecost (Acts 2:9-12). The crowds needed different languages so that they could understand the message spoken by the disciples. The Spirit spoke those different languages through the believers.

One wonders, though, how persons from thirteen different nations could pick out their own language from 120 people speaking simultaneously. Since it was normal for multiple languages to be spoken in Jerusalem during the festival season, one wonders too why this was judged to be so astounding, even a sign of drunkenness (Acts 2:13). All in all, the people are literally "shocked out of their skins"—*existanō*—Luke's favored word for those who witnessed a miracle (Acts 2:7, 12; 8:9, 11, 13; 9:21; 10:45; 12:16).

In response, it is interesting that Luke carefully says that *each one* of the people in the street heard *them all* (the entire 120) speaking in *their own* indigenous dialect. Could it be that the astounding thing was as much a miracle of hearing as it was a miracle of speaking? That is, as the crowd chatted about, each one claimed that the whole group of disciples was speaking in their hometown language. Moreover, each one was hearing the entire group of disciples speaking in a Galilean twang (Acts 2:7; Mt 26:73)! If this were the case, the Holy Spirit inspired the ecstatic speech of glossolalia, but it was heard in each person's own dialect.

We may never be certain of the details of the Day of Pentecost, but some things are clear. It was a miracle. The people heard the mighty things of God in their own tongue. Peter realizes two things: that he must interpret the event and that what has happened is a fulfillment of prophecy on a cosmic scale. They had experienced and witnessed the last days outpouring of the Holy Spirit as spoken by the prophet Joel. The Day of the Lord was at hand, the promised Messiah had come, and the only option now was to repent and accept Jesus as savior.[5] Jesus is the Lord who was confirmed by miracles, wonders, and signs. The authenticity of his unique and irreplaceable calling was that God raised him from the dead. Pentecost is a sign that the resurrected Lord is presently at the right hand of the Father and has secured the promised gift of the Holy Spirit.

This last point is an important one. For Luke, the genuine presence and work of the Spirit is always accompanied by empirical evidence. Something is always heard, seen, or felt. Whether it be the sound of

---

[5]Pentecost was a time of joy and excitement for the disciples. When quoting Joel 3:4, Peter quotes from the Septuagint or LXX, the Greek translation of the Hebrew Scriptures. Here it speaks of the "great and glorious day of the Lord" (see Acts 2:20). Yet the Hebrew text contains the idea of "fearful" or "dreadful" (*yare'*) and thus speaks of "the great and terrible day of the LORD" (Joel 2:31). This is a reference to Judgment Day. This is why some of Peter's hearers were "cut to the heart" and cry out, "What shall we do?!" They sense they are facing impending judgment.

wind or the appearance of fire, glossolalia, scales falling from Paul's eyes, or even a corrupt sorcerer like Elymas wanting to buy the power of the Holy Spirit, some tangible evidence is always present (Acts 9:8; 13:8-9). Perhaps the most dramatic example of this was when Peter and John had survived an interrogation by the Sanhedrin. Upon their release, the believers lifted their voices in prayer and were all filled with the Holy Spirit. What was the tangible sign of this infilling? The place of prayer was physically shaken by the power of God (Acts 4:31).

The Holy Spirit is a person (Acts 10:19; 11:12, 28; 21:4). In spite of Luke's focus on the miracle-working power of the Holy Spirit, the Spirit is a person not a power. As a member of the Holy Trinity, the Spirit possesses all the attributes of divine personhood. As a person, the Holy Spirit can be lied to and conspired against (Acts 5:3, 9). The Spirit can be resisted, and he can speak (Acts 7:51; 8:29; 10:19). The Holy Spirit can encourage and be encouraged (Acts 9:31; 15:28). Oddly enough, the Holy Spirit can prevent the gospel from being preached in an area (Acts 16:6-7). On the other hand, the Spirit can call into ministry and direct in ministry. At times the Spirit can even give warnings during the course of ministry (Acts 13:1-2; 20:22, 23, 28; 21:4).

All of this means that in our ongoing love of God, we should be ever mindful that the Spirit, the third member of the Trinity, is a real and living person. As a person, we can enter a genuine relationship with the Holy Spirit, one that is living and dynamic. The Spirit can hear from us and we can hear from him. This relationship, like all relationships, can be cultivated or neglected.

The Holy Spirit as a second definite work of God (Acts 1:4-5; 8:5-24; 9:10-19; 19:1-8). As an equal member of the Trinity, the Holy Spirit plays a critical role in redemption. Just as the Father sent his Son to carry out the plan of salvation, the Holy Spirit actualizes that plan in the lives of those who humbly receive God's grace by faith. However, unlike John's theme of being born again by the Spirit, Luke emphasizes that the Holy Spirit empowers and equips those who are already born again and committed to the kingdom. As such, Luke describes the Spirit as affecting a second definite work in the lives of the redeemed.

Recall that in Acts the disciples are not told to go to Jerusalem and be born again. No, they are to wait for the promised gift of the Father and be baptized in the Holy Spirit. Similarly, in the wake of Philip's charismatic ministry among the Samaritans, Peter and John do not pray for the Samaritans to be saved. Rather, they prayed for these believers to receive the Holy Spirit because, as Luke explains, the Spirit had not yet "fallen upon" them. This post-conversion reception of the Spirit by the Samaritans is so dramatic that Elymas, also known as Simon Magus, wants to buy the power to convey the Holy Spirit. Peter sharply rebukes this sorcerer and proclaims that the gift of the Spirit is not for sale. Similarly, when the Lord spoke to Ananias in a vision, he did not send Ananias to witness to Saul so that he might be saved. Rather Ananias was commissioned to pray for Saul so that he might receive his sight and be filled with the Holy Spirit. True to form, Luke says something like scales fell from Saul's eyes. The so-called Cornelius Event follows suit. While also responding to a divine vision, Peter found himself in the household of Cornelius, a Gentile centurion. As he shared about how God had anointed Jesus with the Holy Spirit and power, even while he was speaking these uncircumcised Gentiles received the gift of the Holy Spirit and began to speak in tongues (*glōssais*) just like the first disciples did on the Day of Pentecost. In the same manner, upon meeting some disciples of John in Ephesus, after Paul wins them to the Lord, they begin to speak in tongues and prophesy.

The Holy Spirit is the Spirit of prophecy (Acts 9:1-20; 10:1-48; 11:3-18; 16:9-10). From the initial outpouring of the Spirit at Pentecost up until the time of Paul's arrest in Jerusalem, Luke portrays the Holy Spirit as the Spirit of prophecy. At Pentecost, believers spoke forth the mighty works of God as the Spirit gave them utterance. As noted, Peter joins the gift of the Spirit at Pentecost with the prophecy of Joel. In his first sermon, Peter notes that the Holy Spirit spoke through David, prophesying in advance the doom of Judas (Acts 1:16). Peter references the Spirit-inspired David once again in his second sermon (Acts 4:25). Acts is replete with Spirit-inspired visions that have world-changing consequences. At strategic times in the church, the prophet Agabus speaks forth by the Spirit (Acts 11:28-30; 21:10-15). As a matter of course, Luke says that there were prophets in Antioch. It was here that the Spirit said to consecrate Paul and Barnabas for the first mission to the Gentiles.

The Spirit as crosscultural witness (Acts 8:1-17, 26-40; 10:1-48; 16:9-15). The last words of Jesus just prior to his ascension constitute the key verse of Acts. Jesus promised his disciples that when the Holy Spirit came upon them, they would receive power and be his witnesses unto the farthest reaches of the earth (Acts 1:8). For the most part, however, the church was confined to Jerusalem for the first eight chapters of Acts. It took the persecution of Saul of Tarsus to get the crosscultural mission of the church underway.

The target of Saul's persecution was the Hellenists of Acts 6 and 7. The Hellenists were those Greek-speaking Jews of the Diaspora who had come to have faith in Jesus.[6] Luke is careful to say that their leadership, consisting of Stephen and six others (Acts 6:5), were all full of the Spirit and wisdom. Stephen appears to have carried the radical vision of Jesus forward to the point of leaving traditional Judaism far behind. Hence Saul orchestrated Stephen's martyrdom and drove the rest of the Hellenists out of Jerusalem.

Of those scattered, Philip traveled north into Samaria and preached the gospel there. Although Luke presents the conversion of Cornelius as the first Gentile to enter the church (Acts 10), the Hellenists were moving in that direction all along. This is true because the Samaritans were only half Jewish and considered Gentiles by many Jews in Israel. Yet not only did Philip share Christ with them, but the Samaritans received the Holy Spirit through ministries of Peter and John. Furthermore, the Spirit led Philip to witness to the Ethiopian eunuch in

---

[6]The Hellenists of Acts 6 were Greek-speaking Jews who had lived in the Diaspora outside of Israel. The Hebrews, by contrast, spoke Aramaic as their native tongue and were residents of the Holy Land. Prior to his conversion, Paul knew enough about the Hellenists to target them for persecution, yet he left the Hebrews unscathed. Had the Hellenists caught the expansive vision of Jesus and were they about to welcome uncircumcised Gentiles into the church? We do know that they were the first in the church to go directly to Gentiles (Compare Acts 8:1-4; 11:19).

Gaza. This Ethiopian may well be the first full-blooded Gentile convert admitted into the church.[7]

Some of the Hellenists who had been scattered as a result of Saul's persecution began witnessing directly to the Gentiles (Acts 11:20). Fleeing the wrath of Saul, they convened in Antioch and started the first mixed Jewish and Gentile church. After Saul's dramatic conversion on the Damascus Road and his reception of the Spirit, he joins the church in Antioch. He is no longer Saul the persecutor but Paul the apostle. He soon joins with Barnabas, one full of the Holy Spirit and faith. They are both commissioned by the Spirit to evangelize the Gentiles.

Examples of the Spirit's power throughout Paul's three missionary journeys are too numerous to mention. Yet there is one Spirit-led event that demands our attention: Paul's vision of the man from Macedonia. This vision guided Paul and his missionary cohorts to take the gospel westward into Europe rather than travel east.

When summarizing his ministry, Paul says that his witness was not in word alone but by powers, signs, and wonders wrought by the Holy Spirit (Rom 15:18-19). Arguably, the charismatic ministry of Paul was used by the Spirit to dramatically change Europe, greatly influence Western civilization and by extension impact the rest of the world. History has borne out that those last, fateful words of Jesus in Acts 1:8 have surely come to pass by way of the person and work of the Holy Spirit.

The Holy Spirit and politics (Acts 5:18-25; 12:5-11; 16:26-28; 18:12-17). In the opening of his Gospel, Luke addresses Theophilus as *kratiste*, or "most excellent" (Lk 1:3). This is the same form of address that Paul afforded the Roman governors Felix and Festus (Acts 24:3; 26:25). This may mean that Theophilus occupied some kind of political office in the Roman government. As such, one can understand why Theophilus might harbor reservations about Christianity. After all, the

---

[7]Deut 23:1 prohibited eunuchs from becoming full members of the covenant. However Is 56:3-5 lifts the ban on eunuchs. For Philip, the coming of Christ and the outpouring of the Holy Spirit has, to a degree, brought the last days forward into the here and now. Therefore, as the eunuch himself implied, there was now no hindrance preventing him from being baptized and received into the church.

founder of the faith was crucified by the Roman governor Pontius Pilate. There are reports from the provinces that wherever the gospel is preached, there are riots and all kinds of social unrest (Acts 6:12; 13:50; 14:2; 17:5; 21:27; 24:5-6). Additionally, Christians are breaking out of jail on a regular basis. Theophilus would have certainly known about the edict of Claudius that expelled all of the Jews from Rome and that some Christians were caught up in the trouble (Acts 18:1-2). He would have known too that Paul was tried before the Roman governor Gallio. If Theophilus was stationed in the capital of the empire, it would have been troubling that Paul, the vanguard for Gentile mission, was in a Roman prison just down the road awaiting trial before Nero.

Luke must explain to Theophilus why Christians get into so much trouble with Roman leadership. Being the skillful writer that he is, Luke does not address the problem head on. He simply notes that, without exception, starting with Jesus, no Roman official renders a guilty verdict against a Christian. Also, as was the case with Jesus, Christians do not plot insurrection against the empire. For Luke, there is no militant, zealot movement within the church. That's why the lynchpin of the Roman army, the centurions, always have a favorable view of Christians in Luke. In Acts, centurions serve as examples of sincere faith, they are philanthropists, they fear God, and perhaps most importantly, they protect the apostle Paul.[8]

What is the conclusion of the matter? Theophilus should know that despite appearances, Christianity is not a hostile threat to the Roman Empire. For Jesus and his followers, their kingdom is not of this world. Acts has a clear message for Theophilus: do not hesitate to commit to the faith.

The Spirit grants gifts (Lk 4:14-20; Acts 3:1-11; 9:36-41). The charismatic ministry of Jesus that was announced in Nazareth continued by way of his Spirit-baptized church. Healing the lame (Acts 9:33-34; 14:8-10), raising the dead (Acts 20:9-12), and exorcisms were all part of the Spirit's work in the early church. These works were so commonplace

---

[8]Some form of the word *centurion* appears twenty times in the New Testament and always in a favorable light (see Mt 8:5, 8, 13; 27:54; Mk 15:39, 44, 45; Lk 7:2, 6; 23:47; Acts 10:1, 22; 21:32; 22:25, 26; 23:17, 23, 27; 24:23; 27:1, 6, 11, 31, 43; 28:16).

that, at times, Acts simply says *many* signs and miracles were done by the apostles (Acts 5:12). If a simple touch of Jesus' garment conveyed healing, the shadow of Peter and even sweat bands from Paul could do the same (Acts 5:15-16, 19:11-12).[9]

These extraordinary manifestations of the Spirit were not only done by the apostles. The Spirit granted such wonders to all believers. For example, Ananias was used by the Spirit to restore Paul's sight (Acts 9:17-18). Stephen and Philip were full of the Holy Spirit and performed great signs and wonders (Acts 6:8; 8:6-7). A prophetic message was spoken forth in Antioch (Acts 13:2). Agabus was among a number of prophets in the church at Jerusalem. Like Jeremiah and the prophets of old, Agabus prophesied not only in word but also in deed (Acts 11:28; 21:10-11). As Paul explains, these "gifts of grace" (*charismata*) are part of the inheritance of the redeemed. In unending fashion, they evidence the loving benevolence of a gracious God (1 Cor 12:7).

The Holy Spirit is not magic (Acts 8:9-24; 13:6-13; 16:16-40; 19:11-20). Theophilus had been taught something about the faith but was unsure of what he had heard. Luke's job was to dispel that uncertainty with an orderly account of the gospel that was based on credible sources. One area that really needed clarification was how the power of the Holy Spirit differed from the dark forces of the ancient world. This was necessary because the enemies of the gospel had tried to brand the apostles as charlatans and magicians. For example, when interrogated by the Sanhedrin, they ask Peter and John *by what power* or *in what name* did they heal the lame man (Acts 4:7).

Luke's method for instilling confidence in Theophilus is an interesting one. He records the splendor of the power of the Spirit and then follows up with a disastrous episode of magic. In this way, Theophilus would come to know that even though the work of the Spirit may look like magic, the character and goals of the Spirit are diametrically opposed to the occult.

---

[9]Luke tells us that Paul was a leather worker (*skēnopios*) (Acts 18:3). In this trade, leather remnants were often used to make sweatbands and aprons. It appears that those facecloths and aprons that had touched Paul's body were sent out to the infirmed with healing effect.

One of the first examples of Luke's pattern in combating magic is the case of Simon Magus. Simon had practiced magic in the area of Samaria for a long time. The Spirit-wrought miracles and wonders done by Philip caught his attention. Also, when Simon Magus saw that the Holy Spirit came upon the Samaritans through the laying on of hands, he wanted to buy this power. Peter's strong rebuke would leave no doubt in the mind of Theophilus. The Spirit is not for sale and it is substantially different from magic.

A similar event occurred during Paul's first missionary journey. He and Barnabas were ministering throughout Cyprus when they obtained an audience with the Roman governor, Sergius Paulus. Sergius retained the magician Bar-Jesus in his court. This shyster also went by the name of Elymas, or "Sorcerer." He did his best to undermine the witness of Paul and Barnabas. Yet Paul, filled with the Holy Spirit, confronted Elymas and the magician was struck blind for a time.

A different kind of encounter happened in Philippi. A slave girl was possessed with a spirit of Pytho, an ancient snake believed to have helped create the world. She had multiple owners who were profiting from her ability to tell fortunes. Paul exorcised the evil spirit and the girl lost her ability to predict the future. Her owners had Paul and Silas thrown in jail, but in response to their worshipful praise, the Lord sent an earthquake that burst the prison wide open. The distraught jailer was won to the Lord and once again the gospel triumphed in power.

If anything seemed like magic, it was the miracles accomplished by scraps of leather from Paul's workshop. Luke makes it clear that it was the Lord who performed these great feats, not the pieces of leather. It is no accident that Luke follows up these unusual healings with the debacle of the seven sons of Sceva. These Jewish exorcists had combined the occult with Judaism. They were now trying to exploit the name of Jesus and Paul. Somewhat comically, the demon acknowledges Jesus and Paul but can't quite place who the exorcists are. The demon-possessed man viciously attacked these charlatans and drove them out of the house. A beneficial consequence of this melee was that many believers in Ephesus came forward, openly confessed their misdeeds and burned their magical scrolls.[10]

From these instances we can see that magic in the New Testament era was self-serving and out to get money. Many magical formulas were intended to harm or even kill others. Incantations frequently used complicated spells and were very syncretistic. Ancient magicians would employ divine names, even the name of YHWH, if they thought it would help them get their way in the spirit world.

Theophilus must know that the Holy Spirit has nothing to do with the dark forces of the ancient world. The Spirit works in accordance with the perfect will of God and always brings glory to the Father. The Holy Spirit responds to sincere faith in Christ and always works to help and never to harm. Finally, the power of the Spirit cannot be bought with money. Those who sincerely operate in the Spirit don't charge for the ministry.

Clearly, Luke was very concerned that the Holy Spirit not be confused with magic. If this happened, the gospel would just be another form of the occult in the ancient world. The apostles would be quacks and tricksters out to make money for themselves. Fortunately, Luke had the wisdom to distance Christianity from magic from the very start. The Holy Spirit used Luke to safeguard the integrity of the Spirit, not just for Theophilus, but for the entire church throughout the ages.

The Spirit and worship (Acts 4:24; 13:1-2; 16:25). A peculiar aspect of the New Testament is that it doesn't say much about worship in the early church. Much of what we can learn about worship in the church can be gleaned from the book of Acts.

From the beginning, Luke makes it clear that glossolalia was part of the Spirit's work in worship. From the Day of Pentecost (Acts 2:4), to the conversion of Cornelius (Acts 10:46), and well into Paul's third missionary journey (Acts 19:6), speaking in tongues was a part of the

---

[10]Ephesus was internationally known for the occult. It was a center for the sale of written magical formulas that are presently classified as *Greek Magical Papyri* (*GMP*). Thousands of these tiny scrolls have been found in the dry sands of Egypt. During Luke's day, the value of these magical spells was thought to lie in their secrecy. So when the Ephesians recited these magical formulas out loud, they undermined the financial basis of the magic trade in Ephesus.

Spirit's work in the church. Also, prophets and prophecy were part of the norm for church life (Acts 11:27; 13:1; 15:32). Signs, wonders, and miracles were expected (Acts 4:30; 5:12; 6:8; 8:13; 14:3). The relief from lifelong suffering that the Spirit often brought was accompanied by persons leaping for joy and praising God. Believers sang hymns, fasted, and got down on their knees and prayed (Acts 13:3; 16:25; 20:36). The Spirit revealed visions and granted words of wisdom and knowledge (Acts 5:3; 9:10; 10:3; 16:9; 18:9). The Spirit worked joy among them (Acts 8:8; 13:52; 16:34). Even suffering for Jesus' name was an occasion for rejoicing (Acts 5:41). In sum, the Holy Spirit was intensely active in the worship of the church. The Spirit not only worked externally by way of signs and wonders but also internally by eliciting joyous praise, Spirit-inspired song, and heartfelt prayer.

SUMMARY THOUGHTS

Luke wants to give Theophilus confidence in the things he has been taught (Lk 1:4). The Holy Spirit's work among believers adds to that confidence. Luke informs Theophilus that Christianity is not a new religion. Jesus is the promised Messiah who fulfills all the ancient prophecies of Judaism. In short, Christianity is Judaism on the move. Theophilus should know that the same Holy Spirit that anointed and empowered Jesus during his earthly ministry is the same Holy Spirit who is powerfully active in the church. It was the Spirit who welcomed Gentiles into the church, just as they were, without being circumcised. No Gentile, including Theophilus, needs to convert to Judaism in order to be saved. Also, appearances can be deceiving. Although Christians were often victims of violence and injustice, Christianity was not a political or military threat to the Roman government. Nevertheless, the church is empowered by the Holy Spirit; it is growing and nothing can stop it. Theophilus needs to join now while he still can.

WHAT DOES IT MEAN FOR ME?

The early church was not only a place of spiritual power, but it was also a place of continual prayer. The believers are described as being constantly in prayer, breaking bread in prayer, lifting their voices in prayer, and the like.[11]

+ In the church, true greatness is measured in terms of gratitude. In Acts, gratitude is expressed in the context of prayer. Allow the Spirit to use the life of the church as a model for your life in prayer.

+ The Scriptures repeatedly refer to the Holy Spirit as a gift of grace to be received in grace. Pray now that in each of your prayers you humbly acknowledge the wonderful gifts of the Lord. Pray now that your entire life be a never-ending prayer of thanksgiving for the inexpressible goodness the Lord has granted by his Spirit.

+ The gift of the Spirit should express the fruit of the Spirit (Gal 5:22-23). The fruit of the Spirit is what draws persons to Christ. Pray now that the beauty and winsomeness of the Spirit be so evident in your life that others will crave the same.

+ Here are some hard questions. When appealing to the Spirit, do you practice magic or pray for a miracle? Do you want to access power, or do you, in submission and love, seek relationship with God? Do you want something *from* the Spirit or do you want more *of* the Spirit? As you pray to God in the Spirit, filter your requests through that veil of love that only thinks of glorifying God, doing his will, and building up the church.

+ Oh, for the Spirit of uninhibited worship, the kind of spiritual abandon that David had when he danced before the Lord (2 Sam 6:14)! He knew what it meant to worship in the Spirit and he knew what it meant to have the Holy Spirit taken from him (Ps 51:11). Jesus seeks those who worship not only in truth but also in Spirit. Pray that you might render that kind of worship in the Spirit that is pleasing to God.

+ In Acts, the Spirit not only calls, but he also gifts. The joy of ministry happens when God's call and his gifts work in perfect harmony in your life. Only the Spirit can bring these two great

---

[11]For some instances of prayer and prayerfulness see Acts 1:14; 2:42; 3:1; 4:24; 6:4; 8:22, 24; 10:9, 31; 14:23; 16:13, 16; 21:5; 26:29; 28:8.

moments together. Only in prayer can that perfect work of God be realized in your life.

✦ Jesus said that his kingdom was not of this world. Correspondingly, the arena of the Spirit's work no doubt is in this world but not of this world. As Paul taught, the kingdom of God is not in food and drink but in righteousness, peace, and joy in the Holy Spirit. Know this: as much as the Spirit might lead you to address the ills of this world, his domain is not confined to this world.

✦ Luke lacks precision when discussing the Spirit. He speaks about receiving the Spirit, being full of the Spirit, the Spirit falling upon believers, and the like. Yet all four Gospels are remarkably consistent in that they all say Jesus will baptize believers in the Holy Spirit. Acts carries this jargon forward and states that all the disciples were baptized in the Holy Spirit and adds that they all spoke in tongues. Peter explains that God had granted Cornelius and his household the Holy Spirit because he heard them speaking in tongues. Also, when Paul asked the Ephesian disciples if they had received the Holy Spirit since they believed, he followed up with a question about baptism. When they accepted Christ and received the Spirit, they began to speak in tongues. We may not have all the details we want, but one thing is for sure. Speaking in tongues is consistently linked with being baptized in the Holy Spirit. Have you been baptized in the Holy Spirit as described in the book of Acts? Pray that God's expressed will be done in your life with regard to the baptism in the Holy Spirit.

✦ We are right to cherish the fact that God has given us his Son. Yet when he came, he promised that he would give us the Holy Spirit. Let us receive that promise in all of its fullness! Let us truly celebrate all of the riches and gifts of the triune God: the Father, the Son, and the Holy Spirit.

6

The HOLY SPIRIT *in* ROMANS

THE SPIRIT OF ADOPTION

The Spirit you received does not make you slaves, so that you live in fear again; rather, the Spirit you received brought about your adoption to sonship. And by him we cry, "Abba, Father."

ROMANS 8:15 NIV

PAUL'S EPISTLE TO THE ROMANS is the first of thirteen letters attributed to him. As such, Paul's writings compose nearly half of the New Testament. Also, nearly every major Christian doctrine can be traced to Paul. This relatively large number of writings allows for a more comprehensive study of his work. Thus it can be seen that Paul is remarkably consistent in belief and practice. On occasion he wrote more than one epistle to the same church. This allows for a developmental study of Paul's relationship to these churches.

Apart from the Gospels, Paul's epistle to the Romans is perhaps the single most important document of all time. Its influence on the church and by extension on Western civilization is incalculable. Every major theologian in the history of the church, from Augustine in the fourth century to Karl Barth in the twentieth century, has been profoundly affected by this great letter. Martin Luther, the great reformer of the fifteenth century, needed but one line from Romans to shake the church to its foundations and birth the Protestant Reformation. "The just shall live by faith" (Rom 1:17) is substantially responsible for more religious, social, and political consequences than one can imagine.

For all these reasons, Paul's words about the Holy Spirit in Romans carry special weight. The apostle references the Spirit thirty times in Romans.[1] Remarkably, two-thirds of these references are found in a single chapter. In Romans 8, the Spirit appears twenty times and contains some of the most profound theological concepts in all of Scripture. This chapter occupies the center of Romans and is the conceptual fulcrum for the entire letter.

For Paul, the Holy Spirit is the authenticating power of God who raised Jesus from the dead. The Holy Spirit reveals the true meaning of circumcision and conveys the warmth of God's love in our hearts. The Spirit is the joy of the kingdom and fills us with hope that can't be contained. The Holy Spirit is the emotive heart of God that speaks to our heart and instills the peace, love, and joy of the Lord.

In Romans, the Holy Spirit constitutes nothing less than a new paradigm for living. It is a paradigm of freedom that knows no fear. Nothing in the law lies beyond our grasp. Through the power of the Holy Spirit, the righteous intent of the law is accomplished in us. The Spirit is nothing less than the living presence of God. The Holy Spirit is the Spirit of adoption who testifies to our hearts that we are indeed the children of God. In response, the indwelling Spirit cries out, "Abba, Father!"

In short, the Holy Spirit has realized in us an identity that is not of this world. The Spirit not only determines who we are in the present but who we will become in the future. It is the Spirit who mediates the tension between life in this world and the intense longing for the age to come. In the meantime, the Spirit mentors our minds, informs our consciences, and makes perfect intercession for us according to the will of God. Moreover, it is the Holy Spirit who makes us holy and wholly presentable to God. Finally, it is the Holy Spirit who empowers us to witness for Christ, not only in word but also in signs and wonders that glorify God and heal his people.

---

[1]For all references to the Holy Spirit see Romans 1:4; 2:29; 5:5; 7:6; 8:2, 4-6, 9-11, 13-16, 23, 26-27; 9:1; 14:17; 15:13, 16, 19, 30.

If there is one book of the Bible that nearly says it all, it is Paul's epistle to the Romans. Its wisdom and power are inexhaustible; practically overwhelming. Every line calls us to thoughtful reflection and prayer.

PAUSE FOR PRAYER

Whether it forms the controlling center of the epistle or is viewed as an extended theological parenthesis, Romans 9–11 has challenged thoughtful readers for centuries. These chapters are full of irony and pathos and contain disappointment as well as hope. In one poignant passage, Paul wishes himself cursed of God if that would mean the salvation of his kinspeople according to the flesh, the Jews. The word for "cursed" is *anathema* and means under the judgment of God and destined for hell (Gal 1:8-9). Paul's statement is not mere hyperbole. He would willingly swap places with those condemned if that would mean their salvation. Pray now that, if not in whole, somehow in part, you can harbor such mature love for lost souls.

THE PRESENCE OF THE HOLY SPIRIT IN ROMANS

The Holy Spirit reveals the gospel (Rom 1:4; 5:5; 8:14-16). Near the end of Romans, one encounters a peculiar expression. Paul speaks of "*my* gospel" (Rom 16:25; see also Rom 2:16 and 2 Tim 2:8). The phrase says something about the self-consciousness of Paul. He is aware that, to some degree, he possesses a unique understanding of the gospel. His gospel is a mystery that has been hidden from ages past (Rom 10:20; 11:25; see also Eph 3:3-9; Col 1:26-27), but has now been revealed (Rom 16:25-26; Eph 3:2-4) *to him*. This knowledge of the gospel of Christ has come to him specially and directly by divine revelation (Gal 1:11-12).

These words . . . *mystery . . . hidden . . . from ages past . . . revealed . . .* demonstrate that Paul understands the gospel to be an apocalyptic, end-time revelation of God. Indeed, the word that Paul uses for "revealed" is *apocalyptō*, from which we derive the word "apocalyptic." The word literally means "to unveil" and forms the first word of the most apocalyptic book in the New Testament, the book of Revelation (Rev 1:1).

All of this means that for Paul, the good news cannot be discovered by human effort or investigation. The deep things of God must be revealed to us by the Spirit of God (1 Cor 2:10). For him, the righteousness of God has been revealed (Rom 1:17). This righteousness is totally independent from the law of Moses (Rom 3:21).[2] Conversely, the wrath of God is revealed (Rom 1:18; 2:5). The notion that God justifies the ungodly is a revelation (Rom 4:5). Finally, God's end-time glory will be revealed in us (Rom 8:18-19).

The Spirit's first and last testimony: the resurrection of the dead. In the opening to Romans, Paul says that Jesus was raised from the dead by the power of "the Spirit of holiness."[3] In this way, the Spirit "designated" or "appointed" Jesus as the Son of God. The word for "designated" is *horisthentos* and literally means "to draw a circle around." So by way of the resurrection, the Holy Spirit "drew a circle around" Jesus, and everything that fell within that circle pointed to one thing: Jesus is the Son of God. Thus the Spirit's first witness for Jesus was proclaimed not in word but by the most powerful deed of all time, Christ's resurrection from the dead. This is the authenticating sign of Jonah that Jesus spoke about in the Gospels (Mt 12:39-41; Lk 11:29-32). So for both Jesus and Paul, the resurrection is the definitive sign that Jesus is the Messiah.

For Paul, this first witness of the Spirit simultaneously foreshadowed the last witness of the Spirit. The Spirit's work in the resurrection of Jesus was a dramatic intrusion of the eschaton, that last and complete coming of the kingdom of God. That is why Paul can assure his readers that if the same Spirit who raised Jesus from the dead is presently living in them, the Spirit will infuse life into their mortal bodies (Rom 8:11). Thus the gift of the Holy Spirit is the "first fruits" of something far greater to come (Rom 8:23). The word for "first fruits" is *aparchē* and is a technical term

---

[2]In Rom 3:21, Paul uses the word *chōris* in describing the complete independence of the righteousness of God from the law of Moses. This word means "having no basis in" and is crucial for understanding Paul's doctrine of justification by faith alone apart from works of the law (Rom 3:20-31; 4:13).

[3]The actual phrase used in Rom 1:4 is "the Spirit of holiness" and only appears here in the Bible. Since many Jews were hesitant to pronounce or even write the divine name (hence the tetragrammaton, YHWH), "the Spirit of holiness" is a divine circumlocution or roundabout way of saying "the Spirit of God."

to describe a special kind of sacrifice in the temple. The Jews were instructed to gather up the first ripened grain from their fields and wave it before the Lord as a thank offering (Lev 23:10-11). It was an act of thanksgiving, given in advance, expressing gratitude to the Lord for the full harvest that would surely come. In Romans 8, the greater thing that would surely come is the redemption of our physical bodies. The transformation of our mortal bodies into the likeness of Jesus' glorious body marks our full and final adoption into the family of God (Phil 3:21).

In the meantime, however, we live in the tension between the "already" and "not yet." Already the horizon of the new age has dawned in our hearts because of God's Son. Already we have the first fruits of the Holy Spirit. Not yet are we fully glorified. For this reason we groan, the Holy Spirit groans, indeed the entire creation groans, for that great and final day when the kingdom of God will be fully realized in power (Rom 8:22, 23, 26).

The Spirit of adoption. Paul shares the family of God motif with other New Testament writers (Heb 12:7; 1 Pet 1:14; 1 John 3:1, 10; Rev 21:7). Unlike John, however, Paul does not use the language of regeneration to describe how one becomes a child of God. In its place, Paul uses the imagery of adoption.

To describe salvation in terms of adoption is unique to Paul. Also, Paul is the only one who speaks of the Holy Spirit as the "Spirit of Adoption" (Rom 8:15). His word for "adoption" is *huiothesias*, which literally means "one placed as a son" (Gal 4:5; Eph 1:5). Since Roman law had very clear guidelines concerning adoption, Paul may be resorting to his Hellenistic background in his use of adoption language. Adoption in Roman society was legal, public, and binding. We normally think of adoption in terms of adopting a baby or a young child, yet in Rome, one could adopt adults into one's family. At times, emperors would adopt children to secure an heir to the throne.[4] Even slaves could

---

[4]When Julius Caesar was assassinated in 44 BC, his adopted son Octavian took his place as emperor. In short order he ended the republic and declared himself Augustus, or the "Supreme One." Augustus in turn adopted his stepson, Tiberius. Also, Claudius adopted Nero into the imperial family.

be adopted. When this happened, they were no longer slaves but free persons. They were entitled to the family inheritance just like natural born children of the family.

Often in a Roman adoption, a witness would place his hands on the shoulders of the person being adopted and physically move them into the presence of their new parents. There would be a verbal announcement that this person was now a full member of the family.

All of this perfectly fits Paul's understanding of adoption. The Holy Spirit does not make us into slaves but adopts us. We now are full members in the family of God and the Spirit inspires believers to cry out, "Abba, Father" (Rom 8:15). *Abba* was the Aramaic term that a Hebrew child would call out to his or her father. This is the very term that Jesus used to refer to his heavenly Father as well (Mk 14:36). This "Abba cry" is the direct testimony of the Spirit that we are the children of God (Gal 3:26). There was no coercion or need on the part of God to adopt us, for he already had a Son. Rather, Paul says that it was the good pleasure of God to bring us into his family (Eph 1:5). And just as an adopted child of the emperor was an heir to all the riches of the empire, so too are the adopted children of God heirs of God and joint heirs with Christ (Rom 8:17; Eph 3:6; Titus 3:7). This is why Jesus is not ashamed to call us brothers and sisters. We too can call God *Abba*, our Father (Gal 4:6).

Being adopted into God's family means we have been adopted unto freedom. Through the Spirit we have been freed from the tyranny of sin and death (Rom 8:2). The freedom-granting Spirit of God has freed us from bondage to the law of Moses (Rom 6:7, 14, 18; Gal 4:5; 5:1-2). A Spirit-indwelt child of God is not enslaved to anyone or anything.

The Holy Spirit as a new way of life. A new family mandates a new life. Thus our adoption by the Spirit constitutes a new way of living altogether. We have been released from the death-wielding letter of the law and are now led by the life-giving Spirit of God (Rom 7:6; 8:14). The controlling impulse of our lives is no longer the fallen human nature dominated by sin. Rather, it is the internal compulsion of the Spirit that guides us unto holiness. We no longer "walk" to the dictates of the flesh. Rather we "walk" in the power of the Holy Spirit. This is the path of peace and life and not the wasteland of sin and death (Rom 6:4; 8:1, 6-13). To some degree, the Holy Spirit who raised Jesus from the dead has already raised us to newness of life (Rom 6:4).

The Holy Spirit as the emotive heart of God. The Holy Spirit is a person and therefore is personable. Concepts such as "Father," "family," "adopted," and "children" speak of the emotional warmth of the household of faith. Western culture is reticent to speak of the emotions of God. This has more in common with Greek philosophers than with Hebrew prophets. A people who believe that God's banner over them is love (Song 2:4) did not take their cue from Aristotle. The Jews' portrayal of Yahweh as a young man rejoicing over his virgin bride (Is 62:5) is far removed from Aristotle's "unmoved Mover" deity. The flinty resolve of the Stoics would have branded Jeremiah, the weeping prophet, as insane. The relentless love of Hosea would have been incomprehensible to them. The Greek mind would have never conceived of divine love in terms of incarnation. Also, with regard to the emotions and pathos of the Lord, the likes of Augustine and by extension some early Reformers borrowed too much from the pantry of the Greeks and not enough from the storehouse of Israel. For them, God dispassionately runs the universe from afar and his will is inscrutable. This heartless theology has affected the church more than we care to admit.

Paul would have none of this. For him, the Spirit conveys the heartfelt emotion of God. The apostle speaks of a hope that completely banishes shame (Rom 5:5). And how is this done? It is the Holy Spirit who floods our hearts with the love of God. The word for "pours out" or "spills" can also refer to total self-abandonment in the care of another. In a culture in which the love of many has grown cold, Paul is bold in his acclamation of God. He states that in the arena of our hearts, the Holy Spirit speaks a message from God. He says, "I love you."

Weakness was despised by the ancient Greeks. For them, the perfectly honed athletes of the Olympiad were the model to attain to. Not so with the Holy Spirit. He does his best work through our weaknesses (2 Cor 12:10). When we are weak and so confused that we do not know what to say to God, the Holy Spirit passionately intercedes for us with groans that defy articulation (Rom 8:26). Whatever this might mean, one should not forget that the word for "groaning" in Rom 8:22 is the same word to describe the pangs of a woman in childbirth. The groaning spoken of in 8:23 means deep sighing and continues the theme of divine empathy.

Such sorrow, however, is atypical for the Spirit. The heart of the Spirit is love, joy, hope, and peace. The essence of the kingdom has nothing to do with earthly pleasures like food and drink. Rather, the kingdom is righteousness, peace, and joy in the Holy Spirit (Rom 14:17). If at times there is sorrow with God, there is never despair. God is the God of all hope who fills us with joy and peace and ever-abounding hope. For Paul, the love of God and the sacrificial love of Jesus are borne earthward by the love of the Holy Spirit (Rom 15:30).

SUMMARY THOUGHTS

Paul's epistle to the Romans contains some of the most insightful teaching on the Holy Spirit in the Bible. For Paul, the Spirit is the personally active presence of God in the church. The Holy Spirit is the voice of God that reveals to us the will and way of the Lord. The foundation of the faith and the future glory of the church have been secured by the Spirit's raising Jesus from the dead. Moreover, the Holy Spirit has completed all adoption procedures for those who are in Christ. Our adoption is not simply a formal process required by law. No, ours is a real, living family that enjoys rich personal relationships continually animated by the Holy Spirit. We have been fully welcomed into the family of God and have been united with the eternal family of the triune God. This is not a bleak household, cold and indifferent to its family members. On the contrary, the Spirit brings the emotional life of the Trinity to bear on our lives and fills us with love, joy, hope, and peace. The Spirit navigates the corridors of our heart while deeply penetrating the mind of God, and, with perfect clarity, intercedes on our behalf.

Prayer is the medium through which all these good graces are received and enjoyed. The depth of Paul's knowledge of the Spirit, informed more by the experience of his heart than captured by the rule of his mind, calls one to unbroken, reflective prayer. The following points represent some touchstones, spiritual suggestions if you will, that may help lead you to a deeper and more meaningful communion with God.

What Does It Mean for Me?

Paul teaches that no amount of human effort can wrest the truth from the hands of God. Certainly, we must apply ourselves and work hard to acquire those skills that make for responsible interpretation. In the end, though, the things of God must be revealed by his Spirit.

+ As Paul says, the things of God are spiritually discerned (1 Cor 2:10-11). Pray now that as you work, read, and study, you would be ever mindful to invite the revelatory presence of the Holy Spirit, without whom all our labors are in vain.

+ The tedium of this life can hem us in at times. We can allow the dustups of this world to becloud the hope of the resurrection. Pray that the Spirit will grant divine perspective that has no end. This perspective is infused with righteousness, peace, and joy in the Holy Spirit. Such is the eternal inheritance of the children of God.

+ Sadly, violence, cruelty, and hatred are all too common in the modern family. Sadder still is when these life-sapping experiences continue to harm well into adulthood. This is not God's will for any of us. That is why the Spirit of adoption woos us into the primordial family of God. Regardless of the status of your earthly family, pray that you might experience the fullness and health of God's family, which is infinitely better than anything this world can afford.

+ To what extent have you entered the emotive life of God? Is God just a theological abstraction that makes better sense of a senseless world? Jesus calls us friends (Jn 15:15). Abraham was a friend of God. Are you?

✦ These kinds of questions can make us feel uncomfortable for several reasons. First, they appear to be too familiar with God, almost flippant. But Jesus doesn't seem to mind. He is Lord, but he is also our friend. But there is another reason, perhaps more worrisome than the first. We are uncomfortable with such questions because we prefer to keep God at arm's length. It is safer that way. But this kind of "safety" lies at the heart of idolatry.

✦ What's the point of all this? The family of God is an exuberant family characterized by speaking and caring and crying out loud, "Abba, Father!" Even when words fail, sound doesn't, for there are groans of the Spirit that usher prayers into the very presence of the Father. The Holy Spirit is the Spirit of love, joy, peace, and unending hope.

✦ We are all created in the image of God. That image harbors the full range of living emotions. There is no genuine communion with God that is completely devoid of emotions. Pray that you can fully enter the emotional life of God. Pray for that vulnerability, that transparency, that grants God permission to love you in a way that he has intended from eternity.

7

The HOLY SPIRIT
in 1 CORINTHIANS

THE SPIRIT OF WISDOM AND GRACE

There are different kinds of gifts, but the same Spirit distributes them. There are different kinds of service, but the same Lord. There are different kinds of working, but in all of them and in everyone it is the same God at work.

1 CORINTHIANS 12:4-6 NIV

PAUL'S FIRST EPISTLE TO the Corinthians is especially important to Pentecostals and charismatics. In 1 Corinthians Paul says more about the gifts of the Spirit than in any other place in the Bible. For example, chapter 12 is the only place that we have a list of the charismatic gifts of the Spirit. Also, chapter 14 sets forth the most detailed description of how the gifts functioned, or should function, in the church.

In 1 Corinthians, the Holy Spirit has inspired the apostle Paul in a unique way. Critical teachings of the church can only be found here. For example, in this great epistle Paul contrasts the wisdom of God with the folly of this world (1 Cor 1:18-31). The perfect unity of the Trinity serves as the model for the church (1 Cor 12:4-6). In 1 Corinthians, Paul explains that the arrogant, self-promoting spirit of the world has nothing to do with the true ministers of God. He teaches that the people of God are the temple of God (1 Cor 3:16-17). As such, the behavior of the saints must reflect the character of Christ (1 Cor 6:15). Communion with Christ and communion with idols are mutually exclusive (1 Cor 10:21). The gifts of the Spirit meet all the needs of the church and must be employed for the common good. Since God is a God of order and peace, their worship services must reflect the same (1 Cor 14:40).

In sum, 1 Corinthians grants us so many "Paul is the only one" moments. Paul is the only one to give an extended rationale for ministerial support (1 Cor 9:1-14). He is the only one to recite the tradition of the Lord's Supper (1 Cor 11:23-26). He is the only one to write a whole chapter on the love of God (1 Cor 13:1-13). He is the only one to rehearse the witnesses of the resurrection of Christ (1 Cor 15:1-8). He is the only one to give a detailed description of the nature and purpose of the resurrected body (1 Cor 15:35-54).

Even more astounding is that all these unique and powerful teachings came from the quill of an apostle who was wrestling with a church that had gone terribly wrong. The Corinthians had managed to distort nearly every cardinal teaching and practice of the church. As we examine their struggles in this regard, we realize that for them, as well as for us, the only sure way forward is to seek the Lord in prayer.

Pause for Prayer

"I always thank God for you . . ." "I praise you for remembering me in everything . . ." These are the words of a man who had been terribly hurt by the church. The Corinthians had judged Paul to be inferior to the other apostles (1 Cor 4:3). They had ignored and insulted him. Yet Paul's very last words to them were, "My love be with you . . ." (1 Cor 16:24).

How do the Corinthians respond to his offer of love? They heap even more scorn on the one who founded their church. For them, Paul is weak and mumbling and not very pleasant to look at. He is emotionally unstable, and no one endorses him. He is a pseudo-apostle, trying to ride the coattails of church leaders who really have the Spirit (2 Cor 5:12-13; 10:10; 12:11-13).

Nevertheless, Paul does not respond in kind. He cries through a letter he does not want to write. His tears testify to his love for them. If they doubt his love, God knows otherwise (2 Cor 2:4; 11:11).

Oh for a tender heart with a thick skin! Pray now that God would grant you that mature love that, as Paul says, would "gladly spend and be spent" in the care of others.

THE PRESENCE OF THE HOLY SPIRIT IN 1 CORINTHIANS

The Holy Spirit as revealer and teacher (1 Cor 1:18-32; 2:6-16). The Corinthians had made critical missteps. Some had adopted the false values of the world in their appraisal of the cross. As in the case of the Greeks, they praised the esoteric wisdom of this world and judged the cross of Christ as *mōria*, or "foolishness." Aligning with those Jews who rejected Jesus, the cross has nothing to do with the miraculous power of God. It is a *skandalon*; a point of stumbling and confusion.

Paul claims that in either case, whether it be the extreme rationalism of the Greeks or the unbelief of some Jews, the result is the same: eternal death. In fact, God had deliberately chosen the cross to undercut the power structures of this world. The cross negates worldly values so that there is no basis for human boasting in God's sight (1 Cor 1:17-31; 3:18-20). The church in Corinth proves that God's plan is working! Neither the philosophers of the Greeks nor the religious elite of the Jews are members of the church of God. If the apparent weakness of the cross magnifies the power of God, so too does the weakness and timidity of the apostles. They are but common field hands in the work of the Lord whose weakness demonstrates the superior power of the Spirit (1 Cor 3:5-9).

For Paul, human values and demands have nothing to do with God's redemptive work. God's salvation is in Jesus and his cross. Jesus has become for us wisdom, righteousness, sanctification, and redemption. This means that no human faculty can unlock the paradox and power of the cross. Only the Holy Spirit can reveal such truths because only the Spirit of God can plumb the depths of the mind of God. Yet God has given his Holy Spirit to the humble and simple in heart so that they might know the power and promise of the cross. Not only so, but the Spirit has granted believers an entirely new speech form by which they are able to express the spiritual things of God. All of this is nonsense to unbelievers, because the deep things of God can only be discerned by the Spirit, whose home is in the church alone.

The Holy Spirit as sanctifier (1 Cor 1:11-13; 3:1-4; 4:8-16; 6:12-20; 7:1-17; 15:1-58). The Corinthians are the saints of God and only the saints can receive the lessons of the Spirit (1 Cor 1:2). The Greek word for "saints" is taken from the root *hag* and literally means "to cut." So in forming the church, God "carved out" or "separated" people who not only receive the revelation of Christ but also evidence the holiness of Christ (1 Cor 1:30; see also 2 Cor 7:1). This special identity has practical consequences. As saints or "holy ones," they do not need pagan judges to resolve their disputes. Since they have God's wisdom, they are well-equipped to handle such matters on their own (1 Cor 6:1-2). As saints, their presence has a more powerful spiritual effect than that of sinners. The very presence of the believer has a sanctifying effect on those around them (1 Cor 7:14).

The tragedy in Corinth is that the saints are not living up to their name. Strife, sexual immorality, and idolatry exist among them. How then can Paul repeatedly call them the "holy ones" of God?

The Holy Spirit, sanctification, and the saints (1 Cor 1:2; 6:11). Paul is not ignorant of their unholy past (1 Cor 6:1-11) nor of their moral failings in the present. Yet Paul views the church from two radically different perspectives. First is the perspective of being "in Christ." Although rich beyond description, being "in Christ" means that the entirety of the person and work of Christ—his holiness, his wisdom, and his righteousness—is now "owned" by the believer through faith (1 Cor 1:30). So from the perspective of being "in Christ," the Corinthians are sanctified. They are "saints" (1 Cor 1:2). Their future resurrection in glory is assured because they are "in Christ" (1 Cor 15:22). Paul can boast about their faith and send them his love because they are in fact "in Christ" (1 Cor 15:31; 16:24).

Yet Paul maintains another perspective on the Corinthians. This perspective takes into account their personal conduct as lived out in this world. It is this second perspective, the one that has been colored and corrupted by the decadent culture of Corinth, that Paul engages so fiercely throughout Corinthians. Because they have allowed their old sinful nature to inform their present conduct, Paul cannot speak to them as people of the Spirit but as people of the flesh (1 Cor 3:1).[1]

Herein lies the challenge for Paul. Through the power of the Spirit, the Corinthians must bring their personal conduct in the world into line with their spiritual identity in Christ. Paul meets this challenge by following a simple yet consistent method. First, he clearly exposes their failures for all to see. Next, he presents the flawless and unified character of God as the model for them to copy. To the extent that their behavior reflects the character of Christ, it is to this extent that they have been sanctified by the Holy Spirit.

Indeed, the sinful practices of the Corinthians are disheartening. One is tempted to disenfranchise them from the body of Christ. Paul does not yield to this temptation. In spite of his direct and sometimes harsh words toward them, Paul is full of hope and good will. Because of the work of Christ and the power of the Holy Spirit, the Corinthians have been washed, they have been sanctified, and they have been justified (1 Cor 6:11). In spite of their moral failings, their bodies are still the temple of the Holy Spirit and God is continually present among them (1 Cor 3:16–17; 6:19).

The Holy Spirit, the end times, and ethics (1 Cor 4:8; 5:1-5; 6:13-20; 7:1-7; 11:11-16; 13:1; 14:27-33; 15:12). In some way, the Corinthians have fused together their love for the gifts of the Spirit with their belief in the eschaton or the end time. For them, the Spirit's power in their midst means that *already* they reigned as kings, *already* they have the riches of the kingdom, *already* they have the complete fullness of the promised inheritance. In the Spirit, they have escaped the strictures of this world. The freedom of the Spirit means that the conventions of this age no longer apply to them. Even the physical functions of the body are no longer a factor in the life of the Spirit. This means that they can consort

---

[1]The Corinthians have accused Paul of being a simpleton who has only one, artless message: Christ crucified. They judge him to be unpolished, capable of only the coarsest of speech. In writing to them, Paul does not stray from the singular message of the cross (1 Cor 1:17). Nevertheless, he employs the literary devices of Greek rhetoric in order to undermine the value of Greek rhetoric. For example, in 1:18-25, Paul uses rhyme, alliteration, antithetic parallelism, and hyperbole to hold the cross high in the minds of the Corinthians.

with prostitutes and still be in the Spirit. Even a case of incest in the church is of no concern for them. Marriage is for the unspiritual who are still bound to this age. Didn't Jesus say that the saints are as the angels in heaven, neither married nor given in marriage? Being carried away by the Spirit has made them like the angels. They speak in tongues of angels, don't they? Everybody knows that an idol is a nonentity that cannot hurt someone who is truly spiritual. Although the world may require it, their women do not need to wear a covering on their heads. Who needs the resurrection of the dead when you have been transported by the Spirit into the kingdom? And yes, it is important to evidence the gifts of the Spirit by incessantly speaking in tongues and out prophesying your neighbor in church.

What a cauldron of chaos! Yet Paul stays the course. With biting sarcasm, he deflates their overblown view of themselves.[2] He chides that compared to the Corinthians, God had appointed the apostles last. His play on the word "last" or *eschaton*, is a swipe at their false view of the end times. Their haughty triumphalism is contrasted with the apostles being paraded around as a laughing stock to the world. Yes, angels come into play, but the real angels are puzzled about what God is doing with his servants! The apostles are not rich. They are poor, hungry, and dressed in rags. From the world's perspective, the apostles are no more than scum and rubbish.[3] Oh that the apostles knew the secret of the Corinthians! Then they could escape this morbid existence and reign in pleasure with them!

Those in Corinth who think they know it all need to think again. Their faith union with Christ is more substantial than they realize. His identity has become their identity. This means that their carnal conduct in the world can negatively implicate Christ. Dare any of them take the

---

[2]When confronting the Corinthians, Paul uses the verb *fysioō* (1 Cor 4:6; 8:1), literally meaning "inflated with hot smoke." Its figurative meaning is one of arrogance and false pride. The Corinthians had so filled themselves with false wisdom and the illusion that they had arrived at the highest state of spiritual life that they have become windbags whose voice and conduct had nothing to do with the sanctity of the Holy Spirit.

[3]In dispelling the false image that the Corinthians have of some ministers, Paul describes the apostles as *perikatharma*, or the pile of trash accumulated after sweeping out a room. The apostles are as the *peripsēma*, or the putrefying liquid resulting from scouring out a dirty vessel.

members of Christ and join them to a harlot? The sex act is not as cavalier as they might suppose. Sex is not just another biological function of the body on the order of eating and digesting food. No. From the beginning God has ordained a "one flesh" dynamic to this unique and important aspect of human relatedness. For the believer, Jesus is sacramentally present in the physical bond of husband and wife (Eph 5:24-33). All of this means that marriage is sacred even when a believer is married to an unbeliever. In the providential care of God, such marriages are valid and binding. The sanctifying presence of the believer has a positive effect on the whole family. For these reasons, marriage is not to be dismissed or neglected, even for the sake of spiritual devotion.

Similarly, communion with Christ and communion with idols are mutually exclusive. Indeed, "all things are lawful" for those who enjoy the freedom of the Spirit, but not everything is helpful (1 Cor 6:12; 10:23).[4] Just as Paul commanded them to flee fornication, he now commands them to flee idolatry (1 Cor 6:18; 10:14).

Their gaffe concerning the resurrection may well be fatal. The physical resurrection of Christ is the lynchpin of the faith. If they truly have the Spirit, then they must know that Christ was raised by the Holy Spirit (Rom 1:4).

If the Corinthians were confused, the apostle was not. He charts a clear path forward. In the midst of the unduly complicated world that they have created, Paul simply says, "Just do what I do." They are to copy him. The word for "copy" is *mimētai*, from which we derive our word "mimic." The Corinthians should not hesitate to mimic Paul because Paul is imitating Christ (1 Cor 4:16, 11:1).[5]

The gifts of the Spirit: general overview (1 Cor 12:1–14:40). The Holy Spirit is consistently linked with bestowing gifts throughout the New

---

[4]The Corinthians have adopted a number of slogans such as "I am of Paul," "I am of Apollos," etc. (1 Cor 1:12). Another slogan was "All things are lawful," which Paul quotes twice, first in regard to sexual immorality (1 Cor 6:18) and then in the context of idolatry (1 Cor 10:23).

[5]The imitation motif occurs often in Paul's writing (see Eph 5:1; 1 Thess 1:6; 2:14). For Paul, Christianity is a way of life that is energized by the Holy Spirit and expresses the ethos of the Spirit. God has provided living models of the faith that we can "copy."

Testament. In the book of Acts, the Spirit grants power to all the disciples so that they might witness on a worldwide scale. An important aspect of this witness came in the form of Spirit-inspired gifts. These gifts included glossolalia, prophecy, healing, words of wisdom, and even raising the dead. It is important to note that these supernatural gifts were not confined to the apostles. On the contrary, lay persons like Ananias, Agabus, Stephen, and Philip all evidenced powerful manifestations of the Spirit. Similarly, Paul's record in 1 Corinthians, especially chapters 12–14, is evidence that the Spirit continually granted gifts throughout the life of the church.

In some respects, these chapters contain more about the gifts of the Spirit than the rest of the New Testament combined. This is both exciting and daunting. The material is so rich that it nearly defies interpretation. Yet there is another factor that proves particularly vexing. From our perspective, Paul's description of the gifts lacks precision. For example, in 1 Corinthians 12:10 Paul speaks of "energies/works of miracles" but in 12:28 he simply has "miracles." Do these two expressions represent the same gift or is Paul referring to two different things? Similarly, how much overlap exists between the gift of prophecy in 12:10 and the presence of "prophets" in 12:28? Is the "gift of discerning of spirits" in 12:10 the same as the gift of "interpretation" in 12:30? Also in 12:8 Paul pairs "a word of wisdom" with "a word of knowledge." But in 13:2 Paul joins "knowing all mysteries" with "knowing all knowledge." Does this mean that "a word of wisdom" in 12:8 is the same thing as "knowing all mysteries" in 13:2, or is the latter a separate gift altogether?

Even determining the total number of gifts is a challenge. There are nine separate gifts of the Spirit in 12:8-10. Yet in 12:28 Paul seems to add two additional gifts—the gift of "helps" and the gift of "administrations." If one counted "knowing all mysteries" and "interpretation" (1 Cor 13:2) as two separate gifts, then the total number would then be thirteen. Do the three types of gifted persons in 12:28 now make a total of sixteen spiritual gifts?

Also Paul provides a descriptive title to the gifts but does not define the content of the gifts. For example, is there a substantial difference between "a word of wisdom" and "a word of knowledge"? Since two different words for "interpretation" appear in 12:10 and 12:30, is Paul speaking of two separate gifts here?

The sum of the matter is that as much as we would like clear and precise information on the gifts of the Spirit, it's just not there in Scripture. We are left to rejoice in the rich array of gifts and live with the ambiguity.

The gifts of the Spirit and problems in Corinth (1 Cor 13:1-2; 14:9, 23). Rather than understanding the gifts as *charismata*, literally "things given on the basis of grace," the Corinthians viewed the gifts as their own special possession (see 1 Cor 4:7). As such, they exploited the gifts for their own self-aggrandizement. They were attracted to "speech gifts," particularly speaking in tongues and prophecy. To demonstrate their power in the Spirit, some in Corinth spoke in tongues *ad infinitum* and *ad nauseam*. Continuous glossolalia without interpretation had rendered their services incomprehensible. Similarly, prophetic words went forth in number, with one prophet trying to outshout the other. Their worship services had devolved into chaos that could only appear as madness to outsiders.

Paul employs a number of literary devices to restore order and orthodoxy to the church in Corinth, one of which was the metaphor of the human body (1 Cor 12:12-27). His point is that a body is an organic unity composed of many parts that work together in harmony. In the same way, the many and diverse members of the church are to complement, support, and cooperate with one another to form one perfectly functioning body of Christ. The value of each individual member is measured in terms of its appropriate contribution to the whole. The point of many members composing one body is a repetitive, cyclical theme occurring throughout the entire chapter. Upon close inspection, important details emerge that speak to the mindset of the Corinthians and what was actually happening in their worship services.

The common experience of being baptized into one Spirit carries with it the inherent necessity of being unified in the Spirit (1 Cor 12:13).

This is the only place outside of the Gospels and Acts that mentions being baptized into the Spirit. Here Paul adds the image of drinking in the Spirit. Not only are believers immersed in the Spirit, but they also imbibe the Spirit. For Paul, believers are literally surrounded by the Spirit, both inside and out.

The dynamic power of a body stems from the numerous parts that make up the body. For a properly functioning body, diversity is not a weakness but a necessary strength (see 1 Cor 12:17, 19).

Difference in function does not mean less in value. In 1 Corinthians 12:15-17, an apparent lesser member of the body (a foot, an ear) is comparing itself to a supposed grander part of the body (a hand, an eye). In verse 21, assumed superior parts of the body (an eye, a head) reject supposedly inferior parts (a hand, a foot). Tragically, some less gifted members thought that they were not part of the body at all.

Once again it appears that the Corinthians have transferred the aesthetics and values of their culture into the church. The sad result is that some members have been made to feel that they are not members of the church.

God's values and ways of relating to the world are diametrically opposed to the ways of fallen humanity. Yet the Corinthians affirm and grandstand the values of their pagan culture. What they deemed beautiful, strong, and gifted gets center stage while everything else gets pushed to the background. Paul notes that this is not how the Corinthians relate to their own bodies. Those parts that are never seen in public are extremely vital to their bodies and are deserving of special attention (1 Cor 12:22-23). Paul maintains that God relates to the church in a similar way. God has granted special honor to those parts of the body of Christ that need affirmation. So the handiwork of God and his careful superintendence of each part means that there should be no division in the body.

Following on, just as the Holy Spirit was sovereign in distributing the gifts throughout the body of Christ, so too is God sovereign in the placement of each member in his church. His divine assignment for each member is according to his sovereign will (compare 1 Cor 12:11

with 1 Cor 12:18). To denigrate another member of the body is to call into question the sovereign will and wisdom of the Lord. If the Corinthians heed Paul's counsel, their church will be like a unified, healthy body in which every member is equally valued and cared for (1 Cor 12:25).

The factor of mutual care highlights the sympathetic unity of the body. The inherent interconnectedness of all the members of a body means that each member is in touch with all other members and vice versa. If one member experiences pain, it is impossible for the rest of the members to live in detached isolation, having no regard for the suffering of that member. The opposite is also true. The wellbeing of any one member is communicated to the rest of the whole body. This is how the church should be in Corinth. As the body of Christ, they should care together, feel together, and work together.

The gifts of the Spirit and the unity of the church. Paul clearly wants the Corinthians to have reliable knowledge concerning matters of the Spirit.[6] In 1 Corinthians 12:2, he briefly alludes to the problem of syncretism in the church at Corinth. He notes that prior to becoming Christians they were led astray by "voiceless" idols.[7] Here Paul picks up on the classic Jewish polemic against idols and idolatry (see Is 2:6; 44:9-20; Hab 2:18-20). Paul's somewhat awkward expression that they "were led while being misguided" (1 Cor 12:2) gives us some indication of why the Corinthian services were in such disarray. The ecstatic frenzy so characteristic of their former pagan worship is being carried over into their church services now. The direct quotes in 12:3 may have been included in the oral report that Paul received from Corinth (1 Cor 1:11).

---

[6]The operative word in 1 Cor 12:1 is *pneumatikos* and can be translated as "spiritual people" or "spiritual things." Since Paul says so much about spiritual gifts in 12–14, some translate *pneumatikos* as "spiritual gifts." Yet Paul does have a special word for spiritual gifts (*charismata*) and he does not use it in 12:1. Also, Paul does include examples of spiritual people in 12:28. Perhaps some phrase like "spiritual matters" would make room for Paul's discussion on spiritual gifts and spiritual people.

[7]Paul's description of the idols as "voiceless" no doubt contrasts with the loquacious nature of the Spirit. The Holy Spirit speaks through a word of wisdom, a word of knowledge, prophecy, tongues, and the interpretation of tongues (1 Cor 12:8-10). Paul has many descriptors for the Holy Spirit. "Voiceless" is surely not one of them.

These quotes may reflect actual prophetic utterances that were made during their church services. Why else would Paul include the absurd, "Jesus is cursed," quotation? Some early Christian Gnostics would have rejected the man Jesus because he was made of flesh. For them, Jesus was cursed. It is disturbing to think that the gift of prophecy might have been used to promote heresy in the church. John certainly indicates that this was happening among his congregations (1 Jn 4:1-3; 2 Jn 7).

More positively, we can learn that Paul has a trinitarian understanding of the gifts, for he sets the gifts of the Spirit within the context of the Father, Son, and Holy Spirit (1 Cor 12:4-6). His purpose is to show that the unquestionable unity of the Trinity must carry over to the manifestation of the gifts in the church. Paul's extraordinary emphasis on unity is seen in that he includes the words *one* or *the same* twenty times in chapter 12. Also, just as the diversity of persons in the Trinity exists in perfect unity, diversity in the church must be expressed in unity as well. Paul's threefold contrast between the diversity of gifts with the one God speaks the same (12:4-6). Finally, Paul's model of the church as the body of Christ perfectly reflects the diversity of the gifts promoting the unity of the church.

Verse 7 sums up the central theme of the entire chapter. The manifestation of the gifts in every believer is to work for the good of the whole church. The grammar of verses 8-11 reveals a lot about the gifts of the Spirit. The governing verb for these verses is *given* and it appears in the passive voice. The Holy Spirit graces believers with gifts that are to be received with thanksgiving. The directional nature of Paul's words is made clear by his careful use of prepositions. The gifts come "through" the Holy Spirit. They operate "according to" the Holy Spirit. The gifts are "by" the Holy Spirit and "in" the Holy Spirit. Any notion that the gifts originate from the believer is excluded by Paul. Furthermore, the distribution of the gifts occurs "just as the Spirit wills" (1 Cor 12:11). So the Spirit is not only the divine source of the gifts but is also the sovereign distributor of the gifts. The members of the church are simply humble recipients of God's *charismata,* unmerited gifts bestowed on the basis of grace.

The gifts of the Spirit: a brief description. *A word of wisdom.* The word *logos*, as used in the phrase "a *word* of wisdom," can be translated as "message." So "a word of wisdom" is a message full of or characterized by wisdom. This gift conveys the wisdom of God and brings it to bear on the life of the church. So there is a utility to a word of wisdom. Through the Spirit, God's wisdom is realized in our real-life context.

A word of knowledge. This gift may communicate specific information or facts that, apart from the Holy Spirit, could not be known. For example, Agabus knew that there would be a famine in the land. The Spirit also showed him what would happen to Paul if he went up to Jerusalem (Acts 11:28; 21:10-11). The Spirit told Peter that Ananias and Sapphira had conspired to deceive the Holy Spirit (Acts 5:1-11). The Spirit told Paul that many souls would come to Christ in Corinth (Acts 18:9-10), but also informed him that suffering and imprisonments await him in every city (Acts 20:23).

The gift of faith. This gift, mentioned in 1 Corinthians 12:9, cannot be referring to saving faith. This is true because Paul is speaking of extraordinary gifts that are granted by the Spirit to persons who are already saved. So this gift may entail a special kind of faith that can believe God for astonishing things. Perhaps this gift is alluded to in in 13:2 where Paul speaks of a faith that can move mountains.

The gifts of healings. The Greek, *charismata iamatōn*, leaves no doubt that both words are in the plural. Perhaps this gift of the Spirit enables one to heal various diseases.

The gift of miracles. The unusual expression "energized things of powers" or "powerful deeds of miracles" is found in 1 Corinthians 12:10. All words are in the plural. One can only guess what Paul means by this gift, for any miracle evidences the power of God. Perhaps he is referring to those astounding types of miracles such as raising the dead to life.

The gift of prophecy. The word *prophēteia* can either mean "to speak forth" or "to announce beforehand." Thus prophecy can refer to a public proclamation performed in the name of God or it can mean to announce things that are yet to come. More than likely Paul is referring to a Spirit-inspired prophecy the likes of which are set forth in 1 Corinthians 14 (see also Acts 13:1-2).[8]

The distinguishing of spirits. This likely speaks of a gift that can critically determine whether a message or teaching is from the Holy Spirit. The word *diakrinō* means to judge thoroughly and Paul seems to have given an example of this gift in 1 Corinthians 12:3. Whatever this gift is, it is probably akin to what John speaks of in 1 John 4:1.

The gift of different kinds of tongues. From what follows in chapter 14, it appears that speaking in tongues was the Corinthians' favorite gift. It also was the gift that caused the most trouble in the church. To take "tongues" here as known foreign languages of the day is to invite a host of problems with regard to the text. For example, the tongues spoken are unintelligible to the speaker and to all others present (1 Cor 12:10). In fact, these tongues are spoken to God and are not directed to people at all. Paul instructs that the utterance of these tongues comes from the Holy Spirit. As such they constitute mysteries that are only understood by God (1 Cor 14:2, 4). They are not human languages, but rather the "tongues of angels" (1 Cor 13:1). As such, if these angelic tongues were spoken by all in mass, an outsider would think the church had gone mad. Paul continues to write that glossolalia builds up the one who is speaking in tongues (1 Cor 14:4). Yet for these tongues to ever make sense to anyone, another gift of the Spirit is required: the gift of interpretation. If the gift of interpretation is present and operative, tongues become equivalent to prophecy (1 Cor 14:5). It is of interest that the one who has the gift of tongues may also receive the gift of interpretation to make sense of it, not only for the congregation, but also for himself or herself. The gift to interpret these tongues comes in answer to prayer (1 Cor 14:13).

---

[8]To confine this gift of the Spirit to simply preaching the word is questionable. Various words for preaching and for the content of preaching are used in the New Testament (Lk 4:18-19; Mt 12:41; 1 Cor 2:4; Gal 1:16). None of these words are used here. When preaching, Paul never says he is prophesying. Similarly, to equate prophecy with teaching is doubtful for the same reasons. Also, there is strong evidence that the Corinthians were prophesying incessantly, seeking to outperform their fellow worshipers. The idea that several sermons were being presented simultaneously is incredulous. Also, the notion that Paul wants the first preacher to sit down midsermon if another stands up to preach is untenable.

In addition to *speaking* in tongues, Paul mentions *praying* in tongues (1 Cor 14:14). He adds that when he prays in tongues, his mind is unfruitful. Thus, as was the case with speaking in tongues, praying in tongues is also unintelligible. The apostle indicates as much because he is not praying through the rational faculty of the mind but by way of his spirit. The implication here, one that has been present all along, is that the Spirit-inspired gift of tongues works through his human spirit and not by way of his human mind.

As quickly as Paul transitioned from speaking in tongues to praying in tongues, he now speaks of singing in the Spirit. He doesn't explicitly say "singing *in tongues*" but the parallelism is so strong it is difficult to think otherwise.

Summarizing, Paul says that the gift of speaking in tongues is unintelligible and is in need of interpretation. Praying in tongues is praying by way of his spirit and not his mind. It too is unintelligible and his mind is unfruitful. In a parallel way, he will sing by way of the Spirit and he will sing by way of the mind. The implication is that singing by the spirit is also unintelligible. Why? Because as was the case with speaking in tongues and praying in tongues, when singing in tongues, his mind is also unfruitful.

The interpretation of tongues. As indicated, this gift of the Spirit is required to render glossolalia intelligible to humans. Paul's words do not necessarily indicate translation but rather interpretation. That is, the gift of interpretation renders the conceptual meaning of the tongues and is not a point-for-point translation of each word or syllable.

The gift of helps. Since Paul has included specially gifted persons in 1 Corinthians 12:28 (apostles, prophets, and teachers), it is suggested that the word *antilēmpsis* or "helps" is not a supernaturally endowed gift of the Spirit. Rather, "helps" simply refers to persons who have a natural inclination to be of service to others. On the other hand, Paul explicitly retrieves the word *charismata* or "gifts" in verse 28 and lists "helps" as among these gifts (see also 1 Cor 12:9, 30, 31). Perhaps what we have here is a parallel with the gift of faith mentioned in 12:9. Just as the gift of faith speaks to an extraordinary faith given by the Spirit, "helps" speaks of an extraordinary ability to serve that is granted by the Spirit. The Holy Spirit supernaturally endows a variety of people to render a plethora of services to meet the many needs of the church.

The gift of administrations. The word for "administrations" is *kybernēsis*, from which we derive our word "government." For this reason, "administrations" or "governments" is often not viewed as a gift of the Spirit. Yet it too is included in the list of *charismata* in 12:28. In God's providential care for his church, there are persons who guide and serve with such fruitfulness that they truly enjoy a divine appointment, one granted and empowered by the Holy Spirit.

Paul closes chapter 12 by commanding the Corinthians to "fervently seek" the greater gifts. His use of *zēloō*, meaning "to boil with fervent heat," reflects the intense appeal of the apostle. Nevertheless, he follows this command by saying he will show the Corinthians a more excellent way.

The Holy Spirit as God's ode to love (1 Cor 13:1-13). First Corinthians 13 is unique to the New Testament. It is the only place that gives an extended oration on what the love of God really is. Technically, only the opening of the chapter contains hymnic elements. However, the overall effect of the chapter is magnificent. Structurally, this chapter is an indispensable link joining chapters 12 and 14. Conceptually, what we find in chapter 13 harks back to Paul's teaching on the gifts in chapter 12 but also anticipates important guidelines in chapter 14. For all of these reasons, any treatment of the gifts of the Spirit in 1 Corinthians cannot neglect Paul's discourse on the love of God.

In rehearsing the gifts of the Spirit in the context of God's love, Paul accentuates three main points.[9] The first is intelligibility, a point already made in chapter 12 and one that will be emphatically repeated in chapter 14. The second is the matchless quality of God's love. Finally, Paul differentiates what is temporal from what is eternal.

With regard to Paul's first point, intelligibility, tongues that are not interpreted are just an annoying noise (1 Cor 13:1). This irritation is made more irksome when God's love is absent.

---

[9]Tongues, prophecy, knowledge, and faith are all referenced in 1 Cor 13:1, 2, 8, 9. However, verse 3 brings in the new element of sacrificial giving. Here Paul seems to be alluding to Jesus' words about selling all of one's possessions and giving to the poor (Mk 10:21; Lk 18:22).

Paul's second point is that God's love is the baseline for all ministerial endeavors. It is the all-encompassing answer to the problems in Corinth. Only love can dispel the arrogant boasting of the Corinthians that perversely delights in the promotion of the self at the expense of others (1 Cor 13:4-8).

The double-entendre of Paul's phrase "love never fails" introduces the third major point. Since love is so integrally part of God's eternal character—so much so that it can be said that God *is* love (1 Jn 4:8, 16)—love outlasts everything. Everything else, even the gifts of the Spirit, will pass away. Yet love lives on in God (1 Cor 13:8). Paul extends his temporal versus eternal dialectic by way of his partial versus complete rhetoric. *Everything* is partial when compared to the all-encompassing love of God. Just like childhood gives way to adulthood and an imperfect reflection is no match for seeing face-to-face, everything fades away when God's fullness is realized on earth.

The thought that the "completion" or *telos* of 1 Corinthians 13:10 refers to the end of the apostolic age misses the mark. The passing of human apostles is simply not grand enough for what Paul has in mind. No doubt Paul would have scoffed at the notion that the charismatic benevolence of the Spirit, and even knowledge itself, would come to an end at his death. No, it is the "face-to-face" reality of the second coming of Christ that brings all things temporal to an end. It is the full presence of the kingdom of God that sweeps away all time-bound entities of this age. That is when the "now" must give way to the kingdom "then" and God becomes the all in all (1 Cor 13:12; 15:23-24).

The Holy Spirit: respectful and orderly. The harmony that exists between the love of God and the gifts of the Spirit is reiterated in 1 Corinthians 14:1. The fact that Paul brings over the imperative of "zeal" from 13:31 shows that his passion for the gifts has not been diminished by the incomparable love of God.[10] Yet the powerful dynamic of the

---

[10]Paul's repeated exhortation for the Corinthians to fervently seek the best gifts is noteworthy. Any thought that the apostle is sidelining the gifts of the Spirit in favor of love is misplaced. Divine love is the wellspring for all of who God is and everything that he does. That is why, in that great trilogy—faith, hope and love—the greatest of these is love (1 Cor 13:13). Also, the

Spirit requires structure and order. In chapter 14, Paul presents his clearest and most practical guidelines for the operation of the gifts in the church.

Paul teaches that prophecy is preferable to uninterpreted tongues. His reasoning has to do with intelligibility. Prophecy is understandable by all who hear it and needs no interpretation. This is not the case with tongues. Without an interpretation, tongues are nonsense (1 Cor 14:5-12). Tongues are not primarily directed to people but rather are addressed to God. From a purely human perspective, tongues convey mysteries that are only understood by God. On the other hand, prophecy is intended for people. Prophecy edifies, exhorts, and comforts. Tongues do edify but only for the one who speaks in tongues. Prophecy has the effect of building up the whole church.

Paul does not want to be misunderstood. His stark comparison of tongues and prophecy is not intended to diminish tongues. He would wish that they all speak in tongues. However, the generally positive effect of prophecy for the whole church justifies Paul's preference for prophecy.

If the gift of tongues is accompanied by the gift of interpretation, then tongues also edify the whole church. That is, interpreted tongues are the same as prophecy. Through prayer, the one speaking in tongues may also receive the gift of interpretation (1 Cor 14:13). If this happens, that person functions like a prophet.

The gift of tongues can be evidenced in the form of speaking, praying, or singing. All of these manifestations are inspired by the Holy Spirit. They operate in the realm of the human spirit and not the realm of the rational mind. That's why, without some gift of interpretation, all these expressions of tongues remain incomprehensible, even to the one who is speaking in tongues. In 14:16 and 23, Paul imagines a worship setting in which every believer speaks in tongues and there is no interpretation. He posits that if an unlearned person or an unbeliever should enter the service, they would conclude that the Corinthians have lost their minds (14:23).

---

first element of the fruit of the Spirit is love (Gal 5:22). So "the more excellent way" does not displace the Spirit's granting of gifts to the church.

The word for "unlearned person" in 14:16 and 23 is *idiōtēs*. It has none of the harsh connotations of our modern word *idiot*. When Peter and John appeared before the Sanhedrin (Acts 4:13), they were labeled *idiōtēs*. In that context, the word meant something like "an unskilled layperson." Since the Corinthians are definitely not part of the religious elite (1 Cor 1:26), the word *idiōtēs* here probably refers to someone who is unfamiliar with charismatic church life. What is interesting is that in 14:23 *idiōtēs* is contrasted with the word *apistos*, or an "unbeliever." Could this mean that the one who is *idiōtēs* is actually a believer, just one who has never witnessed the charismatic gifts of the Spirit?

In any case, such persons are convicted by prophecy because it is intelligible by all. Through the inspiration of the Holy Spirit, the sins and secret things of their hearts are exposed. As was the case with the Samaritan woman who spoke with Jesus at the well, they will acknowledge the real presence of God and be moved to repentance and worship (Jn 4:7-19)

First Corinthians 14:26 grants us with a rare glimpse into the nature of worship in the early church. Apparently the first churches were charismatically active, with various members contributing hymns, teachings, revelations, tongues, and interpretation. Paul's words sound as if he takes such lively worship for granted. However, such a multi-gifted church could get messy. What is needed are guidelines that restore order to the church

Paul's hope of restoring order is a real hope. Unlike the chaotic frenzy of some pagan religions, in Christianity the spirits of the prophets are subject to the prophets (1 Cor 14:32). The plural of the word *spirit* ensures that Paul is talking about the assembled human spirits in the worship services and not referring to the Holy Spirit. The phrase "the spirits of the prophets are subject to the prophets" means that the Holy Spirit respects the relative autonomy of the human spirit. So when the Spirit moves upon a believer, the power of the Spirit is not some uncontrollable impulse. The work of God's Holy Spirit is not like the frenzied and uncontrollable effect of the spirits in pagan worship. God has empowered humanity to have control over one's own spirit, even when moved upon by his Holy Spirit. This is what legitimates Paul's issuance of guidelines for worship. The Corinthians have the ability to follow his guidelines and still fully honor the move of the Spirit in their midst.

With this established basis for governing worship services, Paul now addresses three areas in need of regulation. They are tongues, prophecy, and women talking during the worship services.

Paul's counsel is that if speaking in tongues occurs in a worship service, it should occur by two, or at the most three, speaking one after another, and then there must be an interpretation. That seems clear enough. Yet, what does Paul mean by "two or the most three"? Does he mean that only two or three persons can speak in tongues during a worship service? Or does he mean that there can only be two or at the most three messages in tongues, after which someone must interpret?

Again, ironclad certainty escapes us. Since they all may prophesy (1 Cor 14:31), Paul is not limiting the number of persons who can speak in tongues in a service. Also, the main problem in Corinth seems to have been extended seasons of glossolalia with no interpretation. For this reason, limiting the number of messages in tongues that can occur without interpretation seems to make sense. Finally, the expression "one after another" appears to point to a series of tongues that must stop at three; then there must be interpretation.

Paul has already stated that the presence and operation of the gifts are subject to the sovereign will of the Spirit (1 Cor 12:11). Yet he allows the possibility that no one might have the gift of interpretation. In this case, speaking in tongues is not to continue in the absence of interpretation. The person is to cease speaking in tongues and quietly commune with himself and God in prayer (1 Cor 14:28).

The exact same guidelines are given for those with the gift of prophecy. Since prophecy is understandable without interpretation, no gift of interpretation is needed. After two or three prophets speak, others are to judge what was said. The word for "judge" is built on the same root as the "discerning of spirits" mentioned in 1 Corinthians 12:10. Just as the gift of interpretation is required for tongues, a gift of discernment is needed for prophecy.

The gift of prophecy is a supernatural gift and must come by divine revelation (1 Cor 14:30). As was the case with tongues, Paul affirms the sovereign spontaneity of the Spirit in regard to prophecy. If a prophecy is underway, and the Spirit reveals something to another who is sitting down, the first speaker is to stop prophesying.

One can hardly resist commenting on these peculiar words of Paul. His counsel seems counterintuitive. One would think that Paul would have said that if a prophecy is being uttered, no one else should interrupt that divine pronouncement until that prophecy is finished. Perhaps Paul felt that this kind of directive would infringe on the sovereign move of the Spirit. Also, Paul specifically speaks of a revelation coming to another who is *sitting down*. Does this mean that the person who initially started prophesying was standing up?

The final category of instructions, and perhaps the most controversial, is directed toward women. In Corinth, there has been some type of disorder by some women in the worship services. The problem is so disruptive that Paul feels he must address it.

Upon first reading, Paul appears to be giving a categorical prohibition against women speaking in church (1 Cor 14:34-35). In this case, however, Paul would be contradicting his instructions in 11:1-16. There, Paul gives guidelines for how a woman should pray or prophesy in church. He explains the condition under which a woman is to pray or prophesy, not whether she can pray or prophesy. So Paul acknowledges that women can speak in church and publicly express charismatic gifts of the Spirit. How, then, are we to understand his words in 14:34-35?

In answer, there are at least two factors that must be considered. First, the entire context of chapters 12-14 is one of discipline. Second, the problem of over-realized eschatology comes into play again.

Since Paul demands uncontrolled tongues and prophecy to come to an end, it's prudent to assume that he is addressing a special disciplinary case when commanding women to be silent. A plausible scenario is that the exhilarating freedom of the Spirit has led some women in the church to ignore accepted social conventions of the day. One such convention was the wearing of a head covering in public. Since the gifts meant that they were already in the kingdom, the customs of this world don't apply. They have become like the angels, beyond the confines of earthly marriage, and are abandoning their spouses, who, being less than angelic, are consorting with prostitutes. Finally, some of these women may have adopted an intrusive and disruptive habit of talking out loud during the worship services. He explicitly cites their asking of questions in church, which ostensibly only added to the chaos already so prevalent in their worship. So Paul's command to be silent is one aspect of a whole host of problems in Corinth.

SOME CONCLUDING THOUGHTS

In spite of all their problems, Paul does not question the authenticity of the Spirit's presence among them. Also, he could have simply commanded the Corinthians to cease and desist from their use of spiritual gifts. He did not do this. Instead, he steadily untangled the mess the Corinthians had made for themselves. In the end, Paul finishes up this section with an extraordinarily balanced conclusion. For the third time, he exhorts the Corinthians to fervently pursue the gifts of the Spirit, especially the gift of prophecy (see 1 Cor 12:31; 14:1; 14:39). Finally, the very last thing he says concerning the gifts of the Spirit comes in the form of a command. Do not forbid speaking in tongues. Yet this, as well as everything else in their worship services, must be conducted decently and in order.

WHAT DOES IT MEAN FOR ME?

Paul's presentation on the gifts of the Spirit in Corinthians is both exciting and exasperating. It is exciting to think that the God of all power and graces shares his gifts with us. It is exciting to know that God is so aware of the needs of his church that he has designed an entire palette of gifts to meet those needs. Moreover, in his sovereign wisdom, he has distributed these gifts in precisely the right place in the church and for precisely the right purpose. Perhaps the most exciting thing to know is that we too are the recipients of God's special gifts and callings. It is this knowledge that gives meaning to life and ministry. It means that each of us have been ordained to occupy a specific place in the body of Christ and to make a positive and vital contribution to that body.

On the other hand, Paul's words in Corinthians are exasperating. It is exasperating to see how easily the values and practices of a fallen world can seep into the church. It is exasperating to watch the seamless garment of Christ's church be torn to shreds by the petty and egotistical aims of a few. It is exasperating to witness the more extroverted members of the church intimidate and demean the more reserved members into thinking that they are unimportant, or worse yet, that they do not even belong to the body of Christ.

So here we have it in 1 Corinthians. There are many points that elicit praise. Yet there are equally as many points that call for prayer. Before moving on from this great but challenging epistle, why not reflect on the following topics in prayer? Why not really listen to the voice of God in this wonderful text and in accordance with his perfect will for your life, heed his voice both in word and in deed?

+ It's peculiar to think that one's geographic and cultural factors could negatively affect one's spiritual life, but that is exactly what happened in Corinth. To what extent have cultural factors affected how you relate to God in the Spirit? More pointedly, to what extent has a postmodern culture influenced your interpretation of Scripture? What kinds of pressure has an increasingly secular, post-Christian society had on your faith? Take a moment to step back and identify the cultural currents that make up your world. Then go to the Lord in prayer and seek his will, the only will that is truly transcultural. Pray for a renewed spiritual sensitivity concerning the unseen pressures that come your way each day.

+ The name of the people of God, the saints, means "the separated ones." That is, the distinctive identity of the redeemed is that they are holy unto the Lord. In an increasingly pluralistic and morally indifferent world, being distinctively separate from the world has fallen out of fashion. Yet the precise command, "Be holy for I am holy," appears six times in the Bible. Certainly this command did not come with an expiration date. Another oft-repeated command in the Scriptures is that we are to worship God in the beauty of holiness. Pray that God will reveal to you what his holiness means for your life. Pray now that he will grant you that special blessing that through all of your life, you might worship him in the beauty of holiness.

✦ I have heard it said that the church is a wonderful place . . . if it were not for the people. The point is that all of us can be difficult at times. The Corinthians were difficult. Yet Paul's love for them never wavered. He had a love that was totally committed to the welfare of the church, regardless of the cost. Pray now that as you expend your heart in the service of others, God will preserve your heart for him.

✦ If Paul's teaching on the gifts of the Spirit tells us anything, it is this: we all have been gifted by God. God has placed each of us in the body of Christ exactly where he wants us. Furthermore, he has granted us gifts so that we might make a unique and vital contribution to the church. Pray that God would clarify the wonderful gifts that he has given you as a unique child of God. Pray that you have the openness and sensitivity to receive all that the Spirit desires to pour into your life.

✦ In modernity, we have lost sight of the eternal dignity of our physical bodies. There is so much to say here. The part of humanity that God created first was the physical body. The last redemptive work of God in our lives will be the glorification of our bodies. In between these two great moments of God, creation and glorification, how do you view the place of the physical body? It is clear that God highly esteems our physicality. Of all the places in the universe that he could claim as his temple, he chose to indwell our physical bodies. Pray that by God's great grace and through his Spirit, the very Spirit that resides in your body, he will reveal to you the inestimable value of your body.

✦ Without hesitation, Paul exhorted the Corinthians to copy him as he copied Christ. How comfortable are you with the idea of people copying you as their model for faith? None of us are perfect and we never will be. But pray that each day you might clearly model some grace of Christ that by his grace you can say with confidence, "You can copy that."

✦ We all tend to define God in terms of our own experience. In some cases, that can become a very narrow definition of God. This kind of narrowing can easily happen with regard to the gifts of the Spirit. We can say things like: "That's not like me," "I have never experienced anything like that before," "That's so out there," "That's outside of my comfort zone." Of course, all of these things are true. After all, these gifts are *from God.* They are from "the other side of the fence" so to speak. As such, God's gifts are unlike worldly gifts. Don't allow your horizon of the Spirit to be narrowed by the strictures of this world. Rather, pray for an expansive, ever-receptive spirit that fervently seeks all the gifts that God would have for you. Don't pray for a roadmap. Pray for an ever-unfolding pathway, one that presents new opportunities for giftedness at every turn.

8

The HOLY SPIRIT *in* 2 CORINTHIANS

THE SPIRIT OF THE NEW COVENANT

He has made us competent as ministers of a new covenant—not of the letter but of the Spirit; for the letter kills, but the Spirit gives life.

2 CORINTHIANS 3:6 NIV

SECOND CORINTHIANS provides us with a rare opportunity. We have two letters, 1 and 2 Corinthians, which were written by the same person and to the same group of believers. Both were penned within a relatively short period of time.[1] This allows for a close comparison between the letters. Also, the sequential outlay of these letters reveals a line of development in how Paul and the Corinthians related to each other.

There is a remarkable degree of continuity in Paul's teaching on the Holy Spirit. The Spirit is a full member of the Godhead, eternally existing alongside of the Father and the Son (1 Cor 12:1-3; 2 Cor 13:14). In both epistles, Paul commends the Corinthians on their reception of the gifts of the Spirit (1 Cor 1:5-7; 2 Cor 8:7). Finally, in both epistles the Spirit is described in terms reminiscent of the fruit of the Spirit (1 Cor 13:4-8; 2 Cor 6:6. See also Gal 5:22-23).

---

[1]In 1 Cor 16:5-9, Paul shares that he is writing from Ephesus. He says that he will stay on until Pentecost, and then visit Corinth. If all of these references fall within the same calendar year, 2 Corinthians could have been written within six months of 1 Corinthians. Yet if the references in 1 Cor 16 encompass a full calendar year, 2 Corinthians could have been written eighteen months after 1 Corinthians.

This kind of continuity is present throughout Paul's writings. For example, Paul's description of the Spirit as God's seal and down payment in 2 Corinthians 1:22; 5:5 is also found in Ephesians 1:13. Similarly, the concept of walking in the Spirit in 2 Corinthians 12:18 is seen in Romans 8:4-5.[2] In 2 Corinthians 5:1-9, Paul associates the Spirit with the glorification of our bodies as he does in Romans 8:11. Even the eschatological groaning for our new bodies is present in both these passages (Rom 8:23; 2 Cor 5:4). Just as Paul reflects a consistent understanding of the Father and the Son in his epistles, he also has a steady and reliable portrayal of the Holy Spirit.

With regard to the unfolding relationship between Paul and the Corinthians, things could have gone better. Second Corinthians reveals that considerable tension still exists between Paul and some members in Corinth. Why is this?

In answer, we need to literally read between the letters. In 1 Corinthians, Paul references a "previous letter" he had already written (1 Cor 5:9). Though lost, this letter addressed the chronic problem of sexual immorality in Corinth. For the most part, the majority in Corinth heeded Paul's counsel. Yet problems remained. Shortly after his first letter, Paul visited the Corinthians and things didn't go well. Thus in 2 Corinthians 2:1, Paul says that he was determined not to make *another* painful visit to them, which would actually be his third visit (2 Cor 12:14; 13:1). It's likely that a very resistant subset had blocked Paul's access to the church. Paul withdrew and fired off a very stern "tearful letter," which also has been lost. He wept when he wrote it and they wept when they received it (2 Cor 2:1-4; 7:8).[3] Although repentant, some troublemakers remained (2 Cor 7:6-7; but see 12:20–21), hence the need for 2 Corinthians.

This scenario allows us to enter the emotional world of Paul and this difficult congregation. In this context, some of the firm and at times

---

[2] The phrase "walk according to the Spirit" is taken from the Pauline expression *peripateō . . . kata pneuma*. The word *peripateō* literally means "walk around" and is used metaphorically for one's entire conduct or behavior. For this reason, some versions of the Bible, such as the NIV, translate *peripateō . . . kata pneuma* as "live according to the Spirit" (see also Gal 5:16).

[3] If this scenario is correct, and there is strong evidence that it is, then 1 Corinthians is really the second letter that Paul wrote to Corinth and 2 Corinthians is really the fourth.

caustic remarks of Paul become more comprehensible. They are not thoughtless, insensitive statements. They are heartfelt expressions of the pain and frustration Paul has endured.

All of this reveals the central importance of the Spirit in 2 Corinthians. For Paul, the centrality of the Holy Spirit stands firm despite the whirling vortex of problems in Corinth. When confronting the obstinate, Paul regards the Holy Spirit as the fulcrum on which the whole argument turns. Because of the Spirit, the hopeless mess in Corinth is met with hope. Their rejection and ingratitude are met with love and reconciliation.

The spiritual resilience of Paul is astounding. His enduring love is superhuman. Let us pray that such mature, selfless love, the kind which can only come by the Holy Spirit, can also be ours as we minister for Christ.

Pause for Prayer

In 2 Corinthians, Paul says he "robbed" other churches so that he would not be a financial burden to the Corinthians. Yet somehow this had lessened his status in their eyes (2 Cor 11:7-8). It seemed like the more he cared for them, the less they cared for him (2 Cor 12:15). In spite of their churlishness, Paul refuses to respond in kind. Admittedly, his ire flares up at points, but these are but a few sharp notes in the symphony of love he has for them. He hopes. He believes. He loves. Though their conduct be deplorable, he seeks every opportunity to speak well of them (2 Cor 1:14; 7:4; 8:24). What we see in Paul is a depth of faith, a greatness of heart, and a maturity in the Spirit. These qualities are desperately needed in the church and come only through the empowerment of the Spirit. They can only come in response to heartfelt prayer.

The Presence of the Holy Spirit in 2 Corinthians

The Holy Spirit and the "super-apostles." Paul dubs the troublemakers as "super-apostles" (2 Cor 11:5; 12:11), a phrase only found here and certainly coined by Paul. Although they claim to be Hebrews, Israelites, and Abraham's descendants (2 Cor 11:22), they are "fake apostles" who have poisoned the church at Corinth. They make superficial judgments that are based on external appearance and not based on the hidden matters of the heart (2 Cor 5:12-13). Their abuse of the Mosaic covenant has so misconstrued the faith that the ministry of the Holy Spirit is nowhere in sight (2 Cor 3:1-18). They preach a different Jesus and a different gospel other than what Paul had first preached to them (2 Cor 11:4; Gal 1:8-9).

Furthermore, these impostors have judged Paul to be inferior in every way. For them, Paul is mentally unstable and compounds his weakness by being a thief. He is not really spiritual but rather walks according to the flesh. Despite the fact that he is a coward, homely in appearance, and can't speak very well, Paul has the nerve, in their opinion, to be boastful (2 Cor 10:1-14). The bottom line, according to the super-apostles, is that Paul is really not an apostle at all (2 Cor 12:11-12).

The net result is that the Corinthians have received a different spirit from the Holy Spirit they received in the beginning. It is the spirit of the super-apostles that is at large in the world (2 Cor 12:20). This spirit is completely opposite from the Holy Spirit after whom Paul and Titus have ordered their steps (2 Cor 12:18).

This is why Paul does not respond in kind. Although no way inferior to the super-apostles (2 Cor 11:5; 12:11), he counters, not by boasting in the flesh, but by pointing to his weaknesses and suffering for Christ (2 Cor 11:22-33). In the midst of incredible hardship, Paul shows forth the understanding, kindness, and love of God. These graces are not inherent to Paul but come from the abundant supply of the Holy Spirit (2 Cor 6:4-6).

The Holy Spirit: the Spirit of the new covenant (2 Cor 3:1-18). In the midst of all the carnal proceedings in Corinth, someone asked if the church had received a letter of recommendation on Paul's behalf (2 Cor 3:1). In a technical sense, the answer was no. Since letters of recommendation always accompanied persons of good standing in the church, there could be but one conclusion. No one wrote for Paul because he was of poor character and didn't merit endorsement.

The whole thing was ludicrous. A person needs a letter of recommendation if they are unknown to the church (Rom 16:1-2). Yet Paul is the one who founded the church in Corinth. He was their pastor for a year and a half (Acts 18:1-18). He doesn't need a letter of recommendation to visit his own converts!

Yet again, rather than enter into a dog fight with the Corinthians, Paul pens some of the most beautiful words that have ever been written. He writes that the Corinthians are his open letter of recommendation inscribed upon his heart and available for everyone to read. They are the living proof of his competency in the ministry, a visible proof from Christ, not written with perishable ink on paper, but with the indelible witness of the Holy Spirit. This is the redemptive power of Christ, incised onto the tables of the human heart, which is much more powerful than carving letters in stone.

In drawing together words such as *letter, ink, stone, hearts, Christ,* and *Holy Spirit,* Paul pens words that would forever define the faith and change the world. He explains that the arena for judging ministerial competency is not the local church, as important as that is, but rather the context of the new covenant. The new covenant can't be confined to ink and paper, or even carving in stone. On the contrary, the new covenant is totally infused with the Holy Spirit of God.

It becomes clear that Paul is not really defending himself. Rather, he is contrasting the new covenant, which is empowered by the Holy Spirit, with the old covenant of Moses that was carved in stone. Paul continues that the living can only be sustained by that which is living and anything less leads to death. That is why the living Spirit of God grants life while the lifeless letter of the law of Moses kills.[4]

All of this means that the super-apostles, who boast of being Hebrews and Israelites, are the ones who are blinded to God's glory, not the apostle Paul. They have not even entered into the new covenant of the Holy Spirit, the only covenant that gives life. They are bound to lifeless letters of the old covenant and are on the path toward death.

---

[4]Here Paul employs the Greek rhetorical device of arguing *a minore ad maius* or "from the minor to the major." If dead letters carved in stone were accompanied by the glory of God, how much more of God's glory will accompany the life-giving ministry of the Holy Spirit? If the temporary ministry of the law, which resulted in condemnation, radiated the glory of God, how much more will the eternal ministry of the Spirit, which brings righteousness, show forth the resplendence of God?

The Holy Spirit as God's seal and deposit (2 Cor 1:16-24; 5:5).
Paul had made plans to visit the Corinthians but then changed his
mind. This change was not due to any fickleness on his part. The
relationship between him and the Corinthians had deteriorated to
such an extent that a visit at this time would do more harm than
good. Paul's enemies pounced. They claimed he was unstable, non-
committal, and unreliable.

Once again Paul rebounds off an unwarranted charge and makes an
extraordinary contribution to the faith. Their libel of instability, though
unfounded, has caused Paul to think of the steadfastness of the Lord.
He then frames the reliability of the Lord in terms of the Holy Spirit.
Paul says that God has "sealed" us with the Holy Spirit. The word for
"sealed" is *sphragizō* and is a commercial term of the first century. It
referred to a special mark, as in an embossed figure on a signet ring,
representing great wealth and power. The presence of that mark signaled exclusive possession by the one who owned the ring. For example,
anything that bore the seal of the Roman Empire was now the exclusive
property of the caesar. The implication is clear. The presence of the Holy
Spirit is the authoritative sign that the believer belongs to God.

The image of being sealed unto God is enhanced by Paul's use of
arrabōn. Also a commercial term, *arrabōn* conveys the idea of an advanced deposit. As such, the term corresponds to our contemporary
notion of earnest money. So the *arrabōn* reserved an item in the present
for full purchase in the future. *Arrabōn* was also used to describe an
engagement ring. Similarly, the ring points to an exclusive relationship
in the present yet promised a more intimate and binding relationship
in the future.

So the meanness of the Corinthians has once again brought forth the
beauty of Paul. He assures the Corinthians that God has demonstrated
his covenant of faithfulness by sealing them unto himself. The King of
kings has placed his mark on every believer proving that they belong
only to God. The unmistakable mark of God is nothing less than his
Holy Spirit. The Holy Spirit is an in advance deposit of the kingdom of
God. The Holy Spirit is the engagement ring of the Lord, establishing

an inviolable relationship with the redeemed in the present and a token of a more intimate and final relationship in the future. When full redemption comes, as it surely will, and the engagement is consummated in marriage, this present home of our bodies will be transformed into a glorious, eternal dwelling that is fit for the kingdom of God.

The Holy Spirit: God's sign of true apostleship (2 Cor 11:1-33; 12:1-12). The super-apostles have disenfranchised Paul from *their* apostolic community. Compared to the apostles who actually saw Jesus during his earthly ministry, Paul is a fraud. He should not be listened to. He should not be admitted into the church.

Paul counterpunches in a "one . . . two" fashion. First, he exposes the deceit of the super-apostles. They are like Satan who deceived Eve and wrecked the world for God. Satan back then and the troublemakers even now have nothing to do with the Holy Spirit. They are "pseudo-apostles" who "shape shift" and masquerade as true apostles. Their dark master has granted them power to radiate false light, as if they were the very angels of God (2 Cor 11:13-15). Second, he sets forth the true signs of an apostle. They are Spirit-empowered signs, wonders, and miracles that have nothing to do with one's appearance, elocution, or personal charisma (2 Cor 12:12). They come from the beyond and transport one into a realm that could only be described as "heaven."

Stopped being duped, Corinthians! The power of God is not manifest through sham apostles. Rather, God's power abides in the weakness and suffering of his saints. They are but earthen vessels that continually wear away. Yet these fragile frames have been seized by God and contain his glory (2 Cor 4:14-16).

With the mentioning of "weakness," Paul's second punch amounts to an odd kind of backhanded slap. Rather than focusing on power, the apostle relates the suffering he has endured for the gospel (2 Cor 11:22-28). He welcomes such suffering because this is the locus of the true power of God in the world. This is this place of humility and weakness that God has chosen to set his indelible seal of approval. In fact, this is the only place where God's supernatural signs, wonders, and miracles are effected. This is the place of a true apostle.

It is at this confluence of human frailty and divine empowerment that the incomprehensible can happen. God can snatch one up and out of this world. God can transport an apostle to his very throne in heaven (2 Cor 12:2). This is what happened to Paul. He was "caught up" by God into the "third heaven."[5] The word for "caught up" comes from *harpazō* and literally conveys a violent snatching away. It is the same word Jesus used to assure his disciples that no one would wrest them from his hands (Jn 10:28-29). Paul uses this word to describe the rapture in 1 Thessalonians 4:17.

Paul continues that whatever happened to him, whether it was an out of the body experience or he was physically transported to heaven, it was all of God. In that singular supernatural experience, God revealed things Paul was not authorized to share on earth (2 Cor 12:2-4). This is the kind of thing that God does in and through real apostles.

SUMMARY THOUGHTS

A study of 2 Corinthians can make one weary. There are so many negative schemes afoot. There are so many unfair charges leveled against one who wants nothing but the will of God to be done among his people. Yet the apostle cannot allow evil to prevail. He cannot permit the hearts of the simple to be taken captive by the crafty. He is forced to say things he doesn't want to say. By entering into the hollow world of the braggarts, he's made to feel like a fool, even to the point of losing his mind (2 Cor 11:23; 12:11).

On the other hand, 2 Corinthians is empowering. Through it all, and perhaps because of it all, Paul unveils the living heart of the gospel. The new covenant is not founded on lifeless letters and exacting moral precepts, even if these were carved in stone. The new covenant in Christ is ministered and administered through the power of the Spirit of God. Through the Spirit we have been betrothed to God. In the meantime, the Spirit showers his people with gifts that make the sufferings of this world seem like a trifle.

---

[5]In Hebrew cosmology, the first heaven was earth's atmosphere, the second heaven was the abode of the moon and the stars, and the third heaven was the very throne of God.

What Does It Mean for Me?

The sum of it all is this: when the stakes are as high as heaven, you need to fight like hell. Yet it's a fight that works redemption, not destruction. This battle is not waged through the arm of the flesh but through the enabling power of the Holy Spirit. Victory does not result in a worldly fiefdom but rather advances the kingdom of God.

The voice of God in 2 Corinthians is a strong one. In this great epistle, God calls us to spiritual maturity. He calls us to suffering in the realm of his glory. He calls us to seek his will in prayer.

✦ In regard to God, what are you willing to fight for? What are those "red lines" in the ministry that simply cannot be crossed? Reflect on Paul's struggle in 2 Corinthians. Pray that God reveal those things of the kingdom that simply must remain. Pray that he will reveal what role you are to play in maintaining the boundary markers that must not be moved.

✦ In light of Paul's Spirit/letter dialectic in 2 Corinthians, are you a person of the Spirit or a person of the letter? There is something comforting about the letter of the law. It provides a guidebook that's doable. You are being successful in religion! It's a deadly attraction. The letter kills; the Spirit gives life. Pray that you will forever walk hand in hand with the life-giving Spirit. Refuse to stumble on in the letters of the law that in the end spell *death*.

✦ Thank God we have a divine stamp that reads, "This one belongs to God." We have a promise ring from God that lets everyone know we've been spoken for, engaged to God in the Holy Spirit. God will make good on the "down payment" or "earnest" of the Spirit and make full redemption, transforming our mortal bodies into a habitation fit for eternity.

✦ We naturally recoil from our weaknesses and shortcomings. Yet Paul discovered that in his weakness, he was made strong for God. Perhaps the weakness you most want to get rid of will be the place of God's power in your life.

9

The HOLY SPIRIT *in* GALATIANS

THE SPIRIT OF FREEDOM

You foolish Galatians! Who has bewitched you? Before your very eyes Jesus Christ was clearly portrayed as crucified. I would like to learn just one thing from you: Did you receive the Spirit by the works of the law, or by believing what you heard? Are you so foolish? After beginning by means of the Spirit, are you now trying to finish by means of the flesh?

GALATIANS 3:1-3 NIV

ALTHOUGH GALATIANS IS ONE of Paul's shortest letters, percentagewise, the apostle mentions the Holy Spirit more than in any of his other letters. For example, on average the Holy Spirit is mentioned 2.66 times per chapter. By contrast in Romans, his longest and arguably most theological epistle, Paul speaks of the Spirit 1.62 times per chapter. Since Paul does not even speak of the Spirit until he's halfway through Galatians (Gal 3:2), these statistics are even more remarkable!

Nevertheless, the really important thing is not word frequency but how the Spirit functions in Galatians. Galatians lets us know that every believer can experience an unbroken communion with God through the Holy Spirit. Also, the Spirit in Galatians speaks of that exciting immediacy of God that breaks into our mundane world and works miracles among us. In Galatians, covenant faithfulness does not consist of painstaking obedience to religious rules and practices. Rather, covenant faithfulness is a dynamic, liberating, Spirit-infused relationship that draws us into the joyous family of God.[1]

As wonderful as all of this is, Paul also strikes a somber note in Galatians. We can lose sight of the precious gifts of God. The gift of his Son, the free gift of salvation, the promised gift of his Holy Spirit, all of this can fade from view if we are not vigilant in faith. Life in the Spirit is indeed wonderful, but it has a serious side as well.

PAUSE FOR PRAYER

There is something in each of us that wants to count, measure, and compare. We are often driven by a relentless self-evaluation that strives to answer such questions as, How am I doing? Am I falling behind? How much am I really worth in comparison to others? On a purely human level, such questions can aid in self-improvement, goal setting, and a sense of accomplishment. Even Paul says that when compared to others, Abraham had something to boast about (Rom 4:2). Yet then he quickly adds, "*but not before God.*" Similarly, when comparing ourselves to others, we may find some bases for boasting (Phil 3:3-6), *but not before God.* In light of the infinite righteousness of God, there is absolutely no basis for human boasting. We are all in desperate need of God's gift of righteousness in Christ. Indeed, this is the core message of Galatians. We can't merit salvation; it is the free gift of God.

So why not now, in preparation for your journey through this great epistle, pray that God grant you the grace to receive his grace? Pray that you can, once and for all, stop that futile quest to "measure up" to God and simply receive the gift of God's own righteousness . . . by faith, just as Abraham did. Moreover, for Paul the life context of Abraham is not the law of Moses but rather the Spirit of God (Gal 3:6; Rom 4:3-5).

THE PRESENCE OF THE HOLY SPIRIT IN GALATIANS

Paul's personal experience of divine revelation (Gal 1:6-8, 11-24). The Galatians have clearly lost sight of the good gifts of God. They have

---

[1]The miracles of the Spirit reveal the power of God (Gal 3:5). The fruit of the Spirit reveals the heart of God (Gal 5:22-23). The freedom of the Spirit reveals the way of God (Gal 4:24-31).

deserted the grace of God in Christ and are looking to secure their salvation by religious works, circumcision, and by observing religious holidays. They are dangerously close to being under a curse. Indeed, the crisis in Galatia calls forth strong language from Paul. Their defection from grace is a "desertion" or "betrayal" of God (Gal 1:6). Even now, they are practically under a curse, condemned to hell (Gal 1:8-9; 3:10).

What's interesting is how Paul guides the Galatians back into the grace of God in Christ. He does not preach the gospel to them again. That would be futile. He had already graphically portrayed the cross of Christ in Galatia. It was as if he had created a giant billboard of the crucifixion and placed it before their very eyes. The word *prographō* used in Galatians 3:1 literally means "to write or inscribe in front of." How could they miss this?

Rather, Paul draws on his personal experience of divine revelation. His goal is to jar the Galatians out of the spell-binding lure of seeking justification on their own terms. The word for "bewitched" in Galatians 3:1 is *baskainō*. It means "to cast the evil eye." Their behavior is so inexplicable it is as if the Galatians have succumbed to black magic of some kind. That is why Paul asserts that his law-free gospel to the Gentiles was not of human origin or a matter of human tradition, nor is he a disciple of apostles who came before him. His initial persecution of the church proves as much. Nor was he a failure at Judaism and in need of a new religion. Quite the opposite was true. With regard to first-century Judaism, Paul was an "overachiever" (Gal 1:14; see also Phil 3:3-6). Rather his gospel came to him by direct revelation of Jesus Christ. The word for "revelation" here is *apokalypsis* and means "unveiling" or "uncovering." So like the prophets of old, God personally spoke to Paul, called him, and revealed his Son to him (Acts 9:1-15; 22:5-16; 26:12-18). The Galatians must know that this revelatory experience was of prophetic proportions (Gal 1:15; Jer 1:5) and authenticated Paul's calling as an apostle (Gal 1:11-12).

The charismatic presence of the Spirit: evidence of "completeness" (Gal 3:1-5). Paul joins his personal experience of revelation with the Galatians' experience of the Spirit. They may ignore the apostolic preaching they received in the beginning, but surely they can't deny their experience in the Holy Spirit. Rhetorically, Paul reminds them that they received the Spirit by faith prior to having any knowledge of the law. It was the Holy Spirit who birthed their life in Christ. How could works of the law improve on that? The charismatic work of the Spirit is an integral part of their worship services. How can they doubt God's presence in their lives?[2] Surely the miracle-working presence of the Holy Spirit is evidentiary proof that they have been justified by faith alone, without circumcision or works of the law. The powerful miracles of the Spirit indicate they are "complete" and "whole" and don't need an addendum from the law. That is why Paul radically contrasts the life-giving quality of the Spirit with the lifeless works of the law.[3]

The Spirit of promise is the Spirit of adoption (Gal 3:6-29). Paul segues from the charismatic presence of the Spirit directly into a discussion of God's promise to Abraham. For Paul, Spirit and promise go together. That's why Paul doesn't join the salvation of Gentiles to God's covenant with Moses but rather to God's covenant with Abraham.[4] The former was based on the law, whereas the latter was secured by promise. The redemption of Gentiles rests on receiving the blessing of Abraham by faith and not by works. They are saved by way of divine promise and not on the basis of law. Thus for Paul, life in the Spirit and bondage to the law are polar opposites. The Spirit is linked to faith (Gal 3:7-9) not works (Gal 3:10); to promise (Gal 3:14, 17-22) not law (Gal 3:12-13, 17-19). In this way, the Holy Spirit brings forth one grand family of God.

The correlation of the Galatians' experience in the Spirit with God's covenant with Abraham is extraordinary (compare Gal 3:6-14 with Gen 15:4-6; see also Rom 4:19). In Genesis, God promises the aged and

---

[2]It is interesting that the Greek word for "suffered" in Gal 3:4 (*paschō*) can also be translated "experienced." Since the very next verse cites Spirit-empowered miracles, Paul may be pointing to the charismatic presence of the Spirit in their worship services.

[3]In Gal 3:1-5, only "power words" are linked to the Spirit. For example, the verb *energeō*, from which we get the word *energy*, describes the activity of the Spirit among the Galatians. Also, the Spirit effects *dynameis*, or "potent miracles," that move the Galatians toward God's intended goal for them.

[4]The phrase "the promise of the Spirit" (Gal 3:14) and "the Holy Spirit of promise" (Eph 1:13) can mean, "the promise *which consists of* the Holy Spirit" (see also Lk 24:49; Acts 2:33).

childless Abraham that he will have a natural born son. Not only so, but in time, Abraham's descendants will be as numerous as the stars of heaven. Abraham believed what God had promised and God "credited" his faith as righteousness. The word for "credited" (*logizomai*) is a bookkeeping or accounting term. It conveys the idea of penciling in a figure into a ledger book. When God saw Abraham's faith, he entered "righteousness" into his account (Gen 15:6; Rom 4:19-22; Gal 3:6).

Paul concludes that everyone who believes in God like Abraham are also the children of Abraham, regardless of whether they are Jews or Gentiles. This means that, in the end, the innumerable descendants of Abraham promised so long ago in Genesis include all Spirit-filled Gentiles who have faith like Abraham.[5]

All of this feeds into Paul's "family of God" motif, a theme he will develop throughout chapter 4. In this regard, his reasoning is somewhat circular. The charismatic presence of the Spirit is experienced by faith and not by law. Faith is the effective agent for the fulfillment of God's promise to Abraham. Gentiles who have faith like Abraham are his children, and so fulfill God's promise that Abraham will have innumerable descendants.

Once a family has been born by the Spirit, Paul can speak about inheritance (Gal 4:1-5). He restates that a child has little autonomy but is under legal guardians and household managers. All of this is metaphorical for the restricting presence of the law, which Paul shockingly compares to the enslaving rudiments of the world. The phrase "the fullness of time" (Gal 4:4) marks the liberating moment of Christ's redemption. This is when complete adoption occurs and thus ends the period of no inheritance. It should be noted that *adoption* in Greek is *hiothesia* and literally means "to place as a son." This is a unique Pauline concept but was a common practice in Roman society (Gal 4:6; see also Rom 8:15, 23; 9:4; Eph 1:5). The practice of fully adopting adults into the family perfectly relates to God adopting Gentiles into his family.

---

[5]The faith/Spirit/promise connection is critical for Paul's law-free gospel to the Gentiles (Gal 3:8-9, 14; Rom 4:3, 5, 11-13, 16). It obliterates the wall that separates (Eph 2:14) and negates all factors that divide (Gal 3:28).

Paul makes the startling statement that God sent the Spirit into our hearts "crying out loud" "*Abba*, Father!" The word *Abba* is an Aramaic term that Jewish children used for "Father" (see Mk 14:36). Also, Paul does not say *praying* "Abba, Father!" but that the Spirit "cries out" Abba.[6] How could Greek-speaking Gentiles in Galatia doubt their place in God's family when the Spirit cries out, "Abba, Father!"?

The Spirit births freedom (Gal 4:22-31). Just as Spirit and promise go together in Paul, so do Spirit and freedom. Paul uses an allegory to describe this newfound freedom of the family of God.[7] The variegated nature of Abraham's family serves as the historical backdrop for this allegory (see Gen 16:1-16). He states that the two children of Abraham (Ishmael and Isaac) and their respective mothers (Hagar and the "freewoman"; Sarah is never mentioned by name) represent two covenants. Since Ishmael was born of Abraham's concubine, Hagar, in the natural way, he is the child of the flesh. Ishmael represents all those who are bound by the law. Isaac was born of the freewoman, Sarah, by way of God's promise, and so stands for all true believers. In a parallel way, Mount Sinai stands for those under the law and the Jerusalem "from above" stands for the freedom of the gospel. In sum, Ishmael, Hagar, and Mount Sinai are symbols for the false brethren who want to bring the Galatians into bondage. The phrase "those born after the Spirit" echoes the fulfillment of God's promise to Abraham to have countless descendants, as does the reference to Isaiah 54:1.

In a masterful way, Paul draws his readers to the only reasonable conclusion. No religion or cultic practice can really make one a child of God. Only the supernatural, regenerating work of the Holy Spirit has any value for the kingdom of God. It is the Spirit that makes a new creation. This in turn deconstructs the artificial and worldly

---

[6]The verb *kratzō* can mean "shout out loud" or "scream." Its grammatical form in Gal 4:6 conveys a linear or ongoing aspect. So this strong expression may signify an ongoing audible "Abba" cry occurring in the worship services of the Galatians.

[7]For the connection of the Spirit and freedom in Paul see Rom 8:2 and 2 Cor 3:17. The point of the allegory is that the Spirit has adopted the Gentiles into a family of freedom, not slavery (Gal 4:31).

categories that so often divide us. In God's family, there is neither Jew nor Greek, slave nor free, male nor female; we are all one in Christ Jesus.[8]

Walking in the Spirit means bearing good fruit and planting good seed (Gal 5:13-24; 6:1-8). The freedom of the Spirit is not to produce the works of the flesh.[9] Rather, the Spirit brings forth good "fruit" in the believer. This singular "fruit" is expressed in nine divine qualities, all of which are indicative of a true child of God. Embracing the cross of Christ crucifies the flesh and frees one to walk in the Spirit. The word for "walk" is *peripateō,* and literally means "to walk about," conveying the idea of an unfolding journey (Gal 5:16, 25). Here Paul echoes the *halakha* or "ethical way of walking" of Judaism (Lev 26:3; Deut 8:6). Yet again, for the believer, it is not walking *after* commandments but walking *in* the Spirit.

The image of walking is a beautiful metaphor for the internal impulse of the Spirit. Just as natural walking is a matter of course, so too walking in the Spirit happens quite naturally for those who are moved by the Spirit. And just as natural walking is semiconscious yet intentional, walking in the Spirit is spontaneous yet directed by God.

Life in the Spirit (Gal 5:25, 6:1-8). The intention and direction of the Spirit generates a qualitatively different life. It is a "life in the Spirit" that actualizes God's redemptive presence in the lives of others. Living in the Spirit involves mutual burden bearing, while at the same time maintaining personal accountability to God. The element of account-ability is expressed in the God-ordained principle of "sowing and reaping." If one sows to the flesh, one will reap the consequences of the flesh. If one sows to the Spirit, one will reap eternal life. The principle of sowing and reaping was ubiquitous throughout the ancient world (Mt 13:3, 27; Lk 19:21-22). The idea of investment and cultivation of the Spirit is surely present in Galatians 6:6-7. Another unquestioned

---

[8]See Gal 3:28. Although John is the only one to use "born again" language (Jn 3:3, 7-8), Paul uses several conceptual equivalents (Gal 6:15; 2 Cor 5:17; Eph 4:24; Col 3:10).

[9]The Spirit/flesh dichotomy, so regularly present in Paul's letters (see Rom 8:1-9), finds concen-trated expression in Gal 5:19-23. Also, so much of what Paul says in 5:13-26 is shorthand for more expanded treatments like Rom 6:1-22 (compare Gal 5:24 with Rom 6:6).

principle is that you get what you plant (Gal 6:8; 1 Cor 15:36-38). Finally, the very act of planting carries with it the hope of harvest (Gal 6:9). The truth of these metaphors is so apparent, to think otherwise is to regard God with contempt.

Paul has joined "fullness" and "completeness" with the person and work of the Spirit. However, aspects of God's redemption are yet future. That is why every believer needs to "wait in the Spirit" for the full consummation of God's glorious salvation.[10] In the meantime, empty religious practices don't help anything. Only a living faith expressed in love has value.

SUMMARY THOUGHTS

Paul has captured the heart of the gospel in Galatians. The good news is that religion cannot save us; only God can. Salvation is a gift, purchased by Christ on the cross, granted by grace, and received by faith. It is a supernatural work of the Spirit, whom we received by faith and by whom we are transformed into new creatures. We experience the Spirit's miracle-working power in our midst and are wondrously adopted by the Spirit into the family of God. As the promised children of Abraham, through the Spirit we joyously cry out, "Abba, Father!" The Spirit is the life of our life whereby the Spirit's fruit is produced in ever-increasing measure. We walk in the Spirit . . . We live in the Spirit . . . We wait in the Spirit.

WHAT DOES IT MEAN FOR ME?

Paul's objective in Galatia is a bold one. He is requiring nothing short of a radical reconfiguration of one's life before God. By arguing from experience, Paul calls for a totally different way of living that is thoroughly imbued with the Spirit. He has established an uncompromising fault line between lifestyles that are essentially different in makeup and practice. On one side is "law" and its associated principles. On the other side is the Holy Spirit with his empowerment and gifts. Graphically, the arrangement looks like figure 9.1.

---

[10]The idea of "waiting" for the hope of righteousness (Gal 5:5) is part of Paul's eschatological or end-time vision. *Already* we are adopted . . . *not yet* are we fully redeemed (Rom 8:23-24; Phil 3:20).

Law		Holy Spirit
sin	I	faith
curse	I	freedom
flesh	I	family
works	I	grace
guilt	I	rebirth
death	I	life

So, in responding to the question, What does it mean for me? we should also ask, What side of the line am I on?

In Galatians 6:8, Paul exhorts his readers to "sow to the Spirit." Surely this means to cultivate the presence and influence of the Spirit in our lives. The following points can help us do just that.

✦ Our culture values achieving. For some people, life is little more than a to-do list. But the kingdom of God is about receiving love, not about lists. Is your life before God an eternal love story or a never-ending list?

✦ There is something humbling about receiving a gift. We are tempted to say, "No—let me pay for that!" If our friend prevails, we depart with "I owe you one!" But God is indebted to no one. Can you receive God's unspeakable gift with a simple, "Thank you"?

✦ It is interesting that Paul doesn't say the "reward" of the Spirit or even the "works" of the Spirit but rather the "fruit" of the Spirit. To what extent can the Holy Spirit freely express himself through your life?

✦ The family is where we can be ourselves. There is no place for pretense or professional deportment, especially in the family of God. God sees through insincerity and posturing and sees us for who we really are. So relax!

Paul has used some strong language in Galatians. Yet it is language born of passion that desires only the best for them. He abhors the path of bondage that some of the Galatians are threatening to take. He exhorts them to return to Christ in faith and once again enjoy the freedom of the Spirit.

10

The HOLY SPIRIT *in* EPHESIANS, COLOSSIANS, *and* PHILEMON

THE SPIRIT OF WISDOM AND REVELATION

*I keep asking that the God of our Lord Jesus Christ, the glorious Father,
may give you the Spirit of wisdom and revelation, so that you may know
him better.*

EPHESIANS 1:17 NIV

WHY ALL THREE? A WORD OF EXPLANATION

Paul's letters to the Ephesians, Colossians, and Philemon will be studied together because they evidence a considerable degree of interdependence. For example, all three, along with Paul's epistle to the Philippians, constitute what are called the prison epistles. These letters were all written while Paul was imprisoned in Rome. Also Tychicus, Paul's fellow worker, is mentioned in all three epistles. He was with Paul at the time of writing and would deliver all of the letters to their respective destinations (Eph 6:21-22; Col 4:7). His task was facilitated by the relative proximity of the churches. Traveling east from Rome, Tychicus would have first arrived at Ephesus. Continuing east for another hundred miles or so, he would come to Colossae, and then to Laodicea. These two metropolitan areas were only about ten miles apart.

In addition to Tychicus, Epaphras helps bind all three letters together. Colossians and Philemon mention Epaphras, who was himself a Colossian. As Paul's coworker, Epaphras was with the apostle in Rome at the time of writing. The manner in which Paul describes Epaphras indicates that he might have been the pastor of the church in Colossae (Col 4:12-13; Philem 23).

The Colossian connection is made firmer still by the mention of Onesimus. As was the case with Epaphras, Onesimus was a Colossian. He was also a slave who had escaped from his master, Philemon, the patron of the church at Colossae (Col 4:9; Philem 10). His escape and subsequent meeting with Paul served as the occasion for Paul's writing the epistle to Philemon.

Finally, although Paul had never visited the churches in Colossae and Laodicea (Col 2:1), their situations were so similar, Paul advises that both churches exchange the letters he had sent to them. So even though Paul's letter to the Laodiceans has been lost, we can know something of their church by way of Colossians. At times Paul speaks to both congregations as if they are one. He does not sign off with the Colossians without also saying farewell to the Laodicians (Col 4:16-17).

The following lists some common themes of Ephesians and Colossians.

+ Paul's intercessory prayer (Eph 1:16-23; 3:14-21; Col 1:8-12)

+ The supreme exaltation of Christ (Eph 1:19-23; Col 1:15-20)

+ Christ as the head of the church (Eph 1:22-23; Col 1:18)

+ The inheritance of the saints (Eph 1:14, 18; Col 1:12; 3:24)

+ The creation of one new humanity in Christ (Eph 1:11-22; Col 1:21-22; 2:11)

+ Spiritual warfare (Eph 6:10-17; Col 2:15)

+ Exuberant worship in the Spirit (Eph 5:18-19; Col 3:16)

Why are these letters so similar? We know that Paul worked with an amanuensis, or a male scribe (Rom 16:22). Perhaps after completing

Ephesians Paul briefed his scribe on the state of the church at Colossae and gave him the freedom to draw up an amended draft for Colossae.

Perhaps this is why Ephesians gives the impression of a fresh, creative hand while Colossians seems to have borrowed and amended as the occasion required. For example, compare the length of Paul's intercessory prayer in Ephesians with what he has in Colossians (Eph 1:16-23, 3:14-21; Col 1:9-12). For this reason, Ephesians will serve as the "home base" for the present study with relevant parallels to Colossians being cited along the way.[1]

We should be reminded that the occasion for Philemon is distinct from the shared themes of Ephesians and Colossians. Yet the repeated mention of Onesimus and Laodicea draws Paul's letter to Philemon into the orbit of the other two letters. The ethos of the Holy Spirit in the church and how it might relate to the bane of slavery in the first century will serve as the basis for addressing Philemon.

What Was the Problem in Ephesus and Colossae?

The similarity between Ephesians and Colossians indicates that Paul was addressing a common problem that was vexing both communities. Although Colossians echoes much of Ephesians, it has a more detailed report on what was plaguing the churches at Ephesus and Colossae.

In Colossians 2:8, Paul speaks of a pseudo-philosophy that can deceptively lead people astray. This sham philosophy confused the saints through a complex array of *stoichea* or "elemental principles" that supposedly granted *plērōma* or "fullness" (Col 2:9-10). This is the jargon of the early Gnostics, who by way of secret wisdom, sought "fullness" of the Spirit.

A popular thought among early Gnostics was that between the realm of matter (which is evil) and pure spirit (which is infinitely good) there

---

[1]Another reason to make Ephesians the touchstone for our study is that Paul spent three years ministering and planting churches in Ephesus and throughout the region of western Asia Minor (Acts 19:8-10). Here he led about a dozen disciples of John the Baptist to the Lord and they evidenced the gift of speaking in tongues (Acts 19:1-7). Charlatan preachers were exposed (Acts 19:13-16) and the powers of the occult were broken (Acts 19:18-20). Even a hate-filled riot could not stop the gospel (Acts 19:23-41). Ephesus was a very important place for Paul and his ministry.

were many intervening levels of existence. These strata were arranged in ascending order, beginning at the bottom with a quasi-material state and moving upward to an infinitely pure spiritual realm. Inhabiting these gradients were spiritual "aeons" whose state was determined by the degree of secret knowledge they had obtained. All of this betrays troubling aspects of Greek thought that were corrupting the faith.

Yet in Colossians 2:11, Paul begins to reflect Jewish themes and practices. He speaks of circumcision, dietary laws, Jewish holy days, and the clean and the unclean. All of these elements can be found in first-century Judaism.[2]

Taken together, "the worshiping of angels" may encapsulate the crux of the problem in Colossae and Ephesus. Some type of Jewish and Gnostic syncretism seems to be at work among the churches. This amalgam of Jewish and Gnostic themes may have posited a plethora of angelic beings. These spirit-beings were viewed as a cloud of mediators that one could pray to. The net effect was that the supreme place of Christ as the sole mediator between God and humanity was being obscured.

PAUL'S COMMON SOLUTION: THE SPIRIT'S REVELATION OF CHRIST

Paul's counter to this confusing mix of Judaism and Greek philosophy is twofold. First, he exalts the absolute supremacy of Jesus Christ over all creation and praises Jesus as the head of the church. Second, Paul speaks to the church as the body of Christ and inspires every member to live a sanctified life in the Spirit. The sum of his argument is that there are no mediating angels that can escort one up and through alleged spiritual gradients into heaven. On the contrary, only Jesus is the fullness of God in bodily form (Col 2:9). By way of the incredible power of his resurrection from the dead, all

---

[2]The relationship between Judaism and Christianity was beset with problems from the start. Some Jews in the church wanted to maintain historic Judaism as the gateway to Christianity (see Acts 15:1-5; Gal 3:10-13). Others succumbed to the historical and religious weight of their faith and desired to remain in the synagogue (Heb 6:4-8). Others were simply confused about the role of the law of Moses now that they had become Christians (Rom 7:1-6).

principalities and powers, regardless of how they may be ranked in the spiritual realm, have been irreversibly subjugated to him (Eph 1:19-23; 6:11-12; Col 2:14-15). Moreover, all those who claim Jesus as their sole and exclusive redeemer are, in a sense, *already in heaven* (Eph 1:3; 2:6).[3] There is no secret knowledge or mystery that can birth a more spiritual life than the wisdom and understanding that comes from the Holy Spirit (Col 1:9). Jesus is the mystery of God that has been revealed to everyone who believes (Eph 1:9-12; Col 1:26). All of the Jewish rituals and practices, starting with circumcision and continuing on to the myriad number of purity regulations, together with the complex observance of holy days—every bit of it—is just a shadow of who Jesus truly is in the power of God (Col 2:17). It is Jesus who has gathered up both Jew and Gentile and created one new humanity. This new humanity constitutes his body, the church, of which Christ is its head (Eph 2:11-22; Col 1:18, 24).

Every mystery, even the hidden wisdom of Christ, has been revealed to the church by the Holy Spirit, for he is the Spirit of wisdom and revelation (Eph 1:17; 3:5; Col 1:26-27). Our future inheritance in Christ has been sealed by the Holy Spirit (Eph 1:18; Col 1:10-12). It is the Holy Spirit who inspires the believer to burst forth in psalms, hymns, and spiritual songs (Eph 5:19; Col 3:16). It is none other than the Holy Spirit who leads the believer into spiritual warfare, all along assuring the glorious victory of the people of God (Eph 6:17; Col 2:15).

The content of Ephesians and Colossians reflects how Paul began his ministry in Asia. Acts tells us that in Ephesus, Paul led some dozen disciples to the baptism in the Holy Spirit and they all spoke in tongues and prophesied (Acts 19:1-7). Furthermore, the ministry of the Spirit dismantled the worlds of idolatry and magic in Ephesus (Acts 19:13-41). All told, Paul's words of wisdom in these epistles are permeated with the presence and power of the Holy Spirit.

---

[3]The phrase "in the heavenly realms" or "in the heavenlies" renders the Greek phrase *en tois ouraniois* and is only found in Ephesians. This unique expression appears at strategic points in Ephesians and refers to existence beyond this world (Eph 1:3, 20; 2:6; 3:10).

PAUSE FOR PRAYER

In Ephesians 1:9-10 (NIV) Paul states, "He made known to us the mystery of his will according to his good pleasure, which he purposed in Christ, to be put into effect when the times reach their fulfillment— to bring unity to all things in heaven and on earth under Christ." The apostle has packed so much into these few words. It is God and God alone, in accordance with his own good pleasure, who has revealed to us the mystery of his redemptive power in Christ. A critical element of this revelation is that Christ is the lodestone of all creation. He is the coordinating center of all things, visible and invisible. Colossians summarizes, "He is before all things, and in him all things hold together" (Col 1:17 NIV).

In an increasingly chaotic and fragmented world, it is comforting to rest in this unchangeable truth: Jesus is holding all things together. As long as he exists, there will be a divine integrity to all of creation. Pray now that your mind and heart will find peace and stability in the one who cannot be moved, in the one who holds all things together.

THE PRESENCE OF THE HOLY SPIRIT IN
EPHESIANS, COLOSSIANS, AND PHILEMON

The Spirit of wisdom and revelation (Eph 1:17; Col 1:9, 3:16). Both the concept and experience of supernatural revelation are found throughout Ephesians. For Paul, the mind and heart of God are not passive things in our hands that can be dissected at our good pleasure (Rom 11:34-36). On the contrary, it was the Father's good pleasure to reveal the mystery of his redemptive work to everyone who believes.[4] That is why Paul brackets the entire epistle with the revelatory work of the Holy Spirit. At the very outset of his letter, Paul asserts that the Ephesians were "sealed" with the Holy Spirit (Eph 1:13; 2 Cor 1:22; 5:5).[5] Near the end of Ephesians, they are exhorted to take up the sword of the Spirit and also

---

[4]Paul's emphasis on divine revelation can be found in Eph 1:17, 18; 3:3, 5, 10. For the pairing of "revelation" and "mystery" see Eph 1:9; 3:3, 4, 6, 9; 5:32; 6:19; Col 1:25-27; 2:2; 4:3.

[5]The word for "sealed," *sphragizō*, referred to a Roman seal, the official sign of the empire. It stood for power, authority, and ownership. All of these qualities are indicative of the Lord's relationship to the saints.

to pray all kinds of prayers in the Holy Spirit (Eph 6:17-18). Indeed, the revelatory power of the Holy Spirit lies at the heart of Paul's prayers for the Ephesians. He prays that they might receive the Spirit of wisdom and revelation (Eph 1:17). Whether this involves the reception of special gifts of the Spirit such as "a word of wisdom" or "a word of knowledge" (1 Cor 12:8) is not certain. What is certain is that the reception of the Spirit of wisdom and knowledge is for a more intimate knowledge of the Father. This Spirit-granted revelation of the Father is our only hope of illumination; an illumination that plumbs the depths of God's redemptive grace, riches, and power. Colossians employs almost the exact same wording of Paul's prayer in Ephesians but adds one important feature. The Holy Spirit grants wisdom and understanding so that believers might live lives worthy of the Lord. Such a Spirit-graced life yields good fruit that is evident in every good deed.[6] Taken together, the goal of the Spirit of wisdom and understanding is to be drawn closer to the heart of the Father, to revel in the mystery of his redemption, and to live a sanctified life in the Holy Spirit.

Paul's prayer in Ephesians and Colossians parallels the messianic prophecy of Isaiah 11:1-2. Here Isaiah prophesied that the Spirit of the Lord will rest upon the Branch that springs forth from the stump of Jesse. Isaiah describes the Spirit as the Spirit of wisdom and understanding. The Spirit is also the Spirit of counsel, power, and reverential fear of the Lord. In like manner, Paul teaches the Ephesians and Colossians that the source of all gifts of the Spirit is Jesus of Nazareth, the Spirit-anointed Branch who is the promised Messiah of God.

Paul's repeated use of the word "inheritance" correlates well here (Eph 1:13-14, 18). Jesus, as the Son of God, is heir of all divine riches. Consequently, all those who are "in Christ" have received the Spirit of adoption and are thereby inducted into the family of God (Eph 1:5; see also Rom 8:15-23). As such, they are joint heirs with Christ. The gift of the Holy Spirit is the authenticating "seal" that designates every believer as a recipient of the priceless inheritance of the Lord (Col 1:12; 3:24).

---

[6]Paul uses the common but powerful metaphor of bearing fruit (*karpos*) to describe the work of the Spirit in the life of believers (Col 1:10; Eph 5:9; Gal 5:22).

The mystery of God revealed (Eph 3:4-10; Col 1:25-29; 4:3). The
Greco-Roman world was awash in various kinds of mystery religions.
These secret cults often employed elaborate initiation rites and taught
that secret knowledge was imparted only to a few. Worship practices
were often characterized by overindulgence and sexual immorality.[7] By
contrast, Paul states that the deep things of God have been revealed to
all the saints, the "holy ones" in Christ. In fact, the divine mystery that
has been hidden for the ages has now been revealed to him and, by
extension, to every believer. This revealed mystery is that uncircumcised Gentiles would become full members of the people of God
(Eph 3:1, 6; Col 1:25-27). The incredible wonder of this mystery is that
at one time the Gentiles were alienated from God, cut off from the
covenant, and virtually without hope in the world. But now, the wall
that had for so long divided the Jews from the Gentiles has been de-
molished in Christ (Eph 2:11-14). Here Paul refers to the *soreq*, that
low-lying wall in the temple that divided the court of the Gentiles from
the court of Israel (Acts 21:28). Any Gentile that dared to tread past
that wall was responsible for his or her own death. But now, the blood
of Jesus has dismantled the wall of hostility, making peace between Jew
and Gentile, binding the countless number of Jewish rules and regulations to the cross. The revelation of the mystery is that through the
cross of Christ, God has now made one new humanity, one common
citizenship, and one unified household, all of which composes the singular body of Christ. If there is any remaining significance to the
temple, it is found in the divinely crafted temple made up of God's own
people, both Jew and Gentile, rightly fitted together to be the dwelling
place of God on earth (Eph 2:11-22; Col 3:15). The practical result is that
now, through the cross of Christ, religious, racial, and social distinc-
tions have been swept aside to provide direct access to the Father for
all people (Eph 2:18; Col 3:11).[8]

---

[7]For example, the cult of Dionysius, the goddess of fertility, often resembled little more than a
drunken sexual orgy. With regard to ritual, one was initiated into the ancient cult of Mithras,
the god of light, by undergoing *taurobolium*, or baptism in bull's blood.

[8]Paul goes so far as to say that God has created an entirely new person in Christ. Taken col-
lectively, all believers constitute a new humanity (Eph 2:15; 4:24; Col 3:10).

The inherent unity of the Spirit (Eph 4:1-32; Col 1:18-24). All of this falls perfectly in line with Paul's belief in the eternal and immutable unity of the Godhead. Similar to what we find in 1 Corinthians 12, Paul anchors the newly founded community of Jews and Gentiles in the dynamic interconnectedness of the Trinity. Thus Paul exhorts the Ephesians to keep the unity of the Spirit. The measure of the Spirit's presence in the community is measured in terms of the cohesiveness of that community. Paul's majestic cadence of *one* body, *one* Spirit, *one* hope, *one* Lord, *one* faith, *one* baptism, and *one* God and Father immerses the reader in the harmonious nature of the Spirit. The phrases "*over* all," "*through* all," and "*in* all" could not enhance the organic integrity of God's person and work any better. Paul likens the unity of the Spirit to the living unity of the body of Christ and also to the structural unity of a well-built building (see also Col 2:19). Every building reflects the vision and values of the architect. Thus the organic unity and structural soundness of the church mandates moral integrity as well. The Ephesians must live in accordance with the holy character of the Spirit that binds them together into one body of Christ. To that end they must continually show forth God's love in the Spirit (Col 1:8). To act otherwise is to grieve the Holy Spirit (Eph 4:30).

Worship in the Spirit (Eph 5:18-20; 6:18; Col 3:16). The seismic shift effected by Christ was momentous and unexpected. The thought that pagan Gentiles could now become the children of Abraham *as they were* without first converting to Judaism was indeed a mystery hidden from ages past. But now, in these last days, that mystery had been revealed in the gospel that Paul preached.

How then could one know that the Gentiles have been fully incorporated into God's family? In answer, there had to be a divine imprimatur, a supernatural sign of some kind, that demonstrated that Gentiles were now part of God's family. Without such a sign, many Jews in the early church, especially those of the Pharisees, would have dismissed such a claim out of hand (see Acts 15:1-5).

Paul argues that the authenticating sign of God's approval is the seal of the Holy Spirit. The deposit of the Spirit secures the full inheritance of Christ for the Gentiles (Eph 1:13-14).[9] The dynamic presence of the Holy Spirit in the lives of Gentiles constitutes God's inclusive mark that they are full members in the church.

The concept of an authenticating sign was realized in the ongoing practice of the church. For example Peter, together with the Jews who accompanied him to Cornelius's house, was convinced that God had accepted the Gentiles *after* they heard them speaking in tongues (Acts 10:44-46). In defense of this truth, Peter explicitly links the glossolalia of the Gentiles back to the fulfillment of Joel's prophecy on the Day of Pentecost (Acts 2:16-21; 11:15-17). Similarly, Paul points to the Spirit-inspired "Abba cry" in Galatia as proof that they, as Gentiles, are also the children of Abraham (Gal 4:6). The presence of glossolalia and prophecy were abundantly evident in the Corinthian worship services (1 Cor 12-14). Paul asserts that the Corinthians do not lack any gifts of the Spirit (1 Cor 1:7). Paul's initial act of ministry in Ephesus was praying for disciples to receive the Holy Spirit. After they were baptized in the name of Jesus, Paul laid his hands on them and they began to speak in tongues (Acts 19:6). Paul would continue to minister in the Spirit throughout his entire three-year tenure in Ephesus (Acts 20:31).

This last remark brings us to the text at hand. Paul exhorts the Ephesians that they should not get drunk with wine, but rather they should be filled with the Spirit (Eph 5:18). There is little doubt that Paul is countering some of the drunkenness that was so prevalent in the mystery cults. But does this point exhaust the whole intent of Paul's counsel to the Ephesians? It is interesting that the charismatic presence of the Spirit is associated, even if by way of antithesis, with being intoxicated. The same was true on the Day of Pentecost. Some said that the Spirit-baptized disciples were drunk with wine (Acts 2:15).

---

[9]Here Paul uses the powerful image of the *arrabōn*, often translated "deposit" or "down payment." This commercial term spoke of a partial payment guaranteeing full payment in the future. It is for this reason that the KJV translates *arrabōn* as the "earnest" of the Spirit (2 Cor 1:22, 5:5). The term was also used to describe an engagement ring that promised a more intimate relationship to come. Thus the Holy Spirit is God's advance gift that seals the believer unto himself and promises the fullness of heaven to come.

In the next verse, Paul gives some content for what it means to be "filled with the Spirit." He speaks of singing to one another in spiritual psalms, hymns, and odes (Eph 5:19). What Paul meant by *psalms, hymns, and odes* is of perennial debate. A popular theory is that all three words mean the same thing and are only used for literary effect. Yet Paul is instructing the Ephesians on how to express the Spirit in a manner distinct from pagan practices. The word *psalmos* is of course related to the Psalms and may refer to sung praises that were accompanied by a stringed instrument. The word *hymnos* corresponds to our word *hymn* and simply refers to an adoration or praise that is sung. The word *ōde* of course yields our word *ode* and simply means "a song" and has no inherent religious connection. However, Paul draws this word into the realm of divine praise by adding the descriptor "spiritual." It should be noted that Colossians 3:16 has the exact same words as Ephesians and in precisely in the same order. Colossians also uses these terms within the context of Christian worship.

We may never know what Paul means by these kinds of musical references. It is clear, however, that Paul's exhortation to be filled with the Spirit included singing various types of Spirit-inspired songs in worship. These musical expressions are to be made one to another and also in praise to God. The charismatic experience of the Corinthians may shed some light on Paul's words to the Ephesians and Colossians. Paul says that he will sing in the Spirit and he will sing with understanding (1 Cor 14:15). This remark comes right after he speaks of praying in tongues, in which case Paul says his mind is unfruitful. Could singing in the Spirit in Ephesians and Colossians be of the same nature as Paul's singing in the Spirit in Corinthians? Is Paul speaking of a glossolalic expression in song in which his mind is unfruitful?

The gift of tongues; the gift of interpretation; prophecy; praying in tongues; singing in the Spirit; the "Abba" cry; singing psalms, hymns, and spiritual songs: the Holy Spirit inspired an exuberant array of praise and gifts in early Christian worship services. All of these manifestations of the Spirit served as tangible signs that the Gentiles had been "sealed" with the Holy Spirit.

The Holy Spirit and spiritual warfare (Eph 6:11-19). The Jewish and Gnostic syncretism that had infiltrated the churches speaks to the topic of spiritual warfare. In Ephesians and Colossians, Paul speaks of "rulers," "authorities," "cosmic powers of darkness," and "morally wicked spirits" "in the heavenly realms" (Eph 3:10; 6:12; Col 1:16). Paul notes that Jesus has *already* triumphed over evil powers by way of his cross. Paul borrows from Roman military tradition when describing the victory of Jesus. The Romans would publicly display captives of war at the end of their victory parades (see 1 Cor 4:9). Similarly for Paul, Jesus' victory on the cross is complete and nonnegotiable. The powers and authorities of Satan are but vanquished foes, put on public display for all to see (Col 2:15).

Although Jesus has *already* triumphed in the spiritual realm, *not yet* has all evil been swept aside in this present world. That's why believers are engaged in a battle that is not against flesh and blood but against "rulers," "authorities," "cosmic powers of darkness," and "wicked spirits" "in the heavenlies" (Eph 1:3, 20; 2:6; 3:10).

This is why Paul twice commands the Ephesians to put on the whole armor of God (Eph 6:11, 13). Paul may be alluding to Isaiah 59:17, but his illustration in Ephesians is more expansive than that of Isaiah. The word for "armor" is *panoplia* and describes a fully outfitted centurion who is prepared for battle. Paul uses this powerful imagery to describe all of the spiritual weapons that are available to the believer. It is interesting that the universally binding command for a Roman centurion was to maintain one's position regardless of the state of the battle. Similarly, Paul exhorts the Ephesians that after they have employed everything at their disposal, there is still one order that they must obey: stand your ground!

A Roman soldier must never drop his shield in battle. To do so would leave one totally exposed to the attack of the enemy. Thus a tactic of warfare was to launch flaming arrows at the enemy. The idea was not to strike a lethal blow but to lodge the fiery arrows in the wooden shield of the enemy. As the fire spread, panic would ensue, and the soldier would cast aside his shield. Once that happened, the outcome was assured. Paul's message is clear. The devil can't really hurt you. He is trying to make you panic and cast aside your faith. But the shield of faith can actually put out the flaming darts of the evil one (Eph 6:16).

The "sword of the Spirit" is the only offensive weapon mentioned in Ephesians 6. The words "of the Spirit" probably convey the idea of source. Paul is speaking of a sword that comes from the Holy Spirit. He clarifies that this sword is the Word of God. So the most effective weapon in spiritual warfare turns out to be the Spirit-empowered Word of God.

Paul's words about "praying in the Spirit" in Ephesians 6:18 may mark a transition away from the extended image of the armor of God. But his exhortation to remain watchful and alert still retains some military significance. The picture is of a soldier standing alone on guard duty through all hours of the night. In the same way, the Christian must not allow the lonely tedium of watchfulness to dull his or her dedication to mission.

Paul uses phrases like "heartfelt entreaty" and "worshipful requests" to describe the rich texture of prayer in Ephesians 6:18. All these prayers are to be prayed "in the Spirit." In 1 Corinthians 14:14-15, praying in the Spirit means praying in tongues. Although the context is different in Ephesians, it would be arbitrary to categorically exclude such prayer from Paul's words in Ephesians 6:18.

For Paul, the world of the Christian is not spiritually benign. There are hostile powers in the realm of the spirit. These powers are deployed in battle against the Christian. Yet in the heavenly realm, all evil principalities and powers have been defeated by Christ through his cross. Yet here on earth, the believer is continually engaged in spiritual warfare. Fortunately, God has supplied the believer with all the required weapons to live victoriously in the here and now. The Holy Spirit has granted to every Christian the sword of the Spirit, that is, the Spirit-empowered Word of God. The weaponry of faith is made effectual by Spirit-inspired prayers that can defuse anything the devil throws at the Christian. Once the Christian has deployed everything the Lord has provided, he or she is commanded to stand firm and not yield territory to the enemy.

The Spirit of liberty, the presence of slavery, and Paul's epistle to Philemon (Philem 4-7, 16-17). Life in the Roman Empire was harsh. Roman military oppression, rigid social stratification, and the never-ending need to curry the favor of patrons was a constant challenge. Even worse, Rome was a slave state comprising millions of persons who suffered the double tragedy of being captured in war and then being sold as slaves. It has been estimated that in Paul's day, one in every six persons was a slave. Slaves came from every walk of life and it was their life's blood that kept the empire lurching forward.

Into this sad world came the good news of the gospel. Through the anointing of the Spirit, Jesus proclaimed liberty to the *aichmalōtois*, "those taken at the point of the spear" (Luke 4:18). To the captives, Jesus' words were nothing short of electrifying. Freedom from sin . . . freedom from the fear of death . . . even freedom from the law of Moses—such was the liberating message of the gospel. Indeed, where the Spirit of the Lord is, there is liberty (2 Cor 3:17)! Moreover, the gospel affirmed the essential dignity of the individual and empowered the marginalized in an unprecedented way. Thus Paul wrote that there is neither Jew nor Greek, slave nor free, male nor female, for all are one in Christ (Gal 3:28).

Yet slavery remained both in the world and in the church. Paul's extended address to slaves in 1 Corinthians proves as much. It is all the more alarming to read in the so-called household codes of Ephesians and Colossians that Christian slaves are told to be obedient to their masters, even to those who were difficult to serve.

The church did not just accept the status quo, however. Paul admonishes Christian slave owners not to mistreat their slaves or they will have to answer to their Master in heaven. More subtle still was the reframing of slave labor in terms of Christian service. All work is to be done as unto the Lord and not simply as unto humans. Both master and slave should remember that God is no respecter of persons and will judge everyone according to their deeds. Since God does not receive the face of anyone, one's social standing means nothing to God (Gal 2:6; Eph 6:5-10; Col 3:22-25). So there are signs that the church was struggling to develop its own social ethic and emerge from the moral quagmire that was Rome.

In the meantime, the church was in a difficult position. Although slaves were full members in the church, should the church press for the complete manumission of slaves throughout the Roman world? To do so would surely invite the wrath of Roman legions. Tens of thousands of slaves would be slaughtered. This is what happened in the Spartacus rebellion little more than a century earlier. The otherworldly character of the kingdom of God would be commandeered by a hardnosed social revolution that had little chance of success.

For all these reasons, Paul's brief epistle to Philemon is especially poignant. There can be no question that Philemon, a Christian patron and slave owner, was acutely aware of the weighty issues at stake. After all, he was a powerful patron of the church in Laodicea. On the one hand, if he severely punished Onesimus for escaping, he would betray the love and grace of Christ. On the other hand, if as a powerful Roman citizen he cavalierly released Onesimus on the basis of his Christian faith, he might implicate the church and cause untold suffering.

In studying this epistle, perhaps Philemon should be remembered not for what he did but for what he did not do. If Philemon had notified the proper Roman authorities that one of his slaves had escaped, Onesimus would have been killed on sight. The fact that Paul senses the freedom to return Onesimus to Philemon in the clear light of day means that Philemon has not contacted the government. Philemon had safeguarded Onesimus from certain death. It was this expression of mercy that provided Paul with an opening to make an impassioned plea on behalf of Onesimus.

Paul masterfully navigates the social and political minefield created by the escape of Onesimus.[10] Since Philemon understands power and patronage, Paul tactfully leverages these elements in his favor. For

---

[10]Paul uses humor to reduce the tension caused by the escape of Onesimus. "Onesimus" meant "profitable." Paul notes that Onesimus had become "unprofitable," but now has once again become profitable. Onesimus is really living up to his name now and ready to make a new start in the church at Colossae.

example, he could have used his apostolic authority and demanded the release of Onesimus. Rather, Paul's appeal is based on God's love (Philem 8-9), a foundation much stronger than church authority. Regarding patronage, Paul reminds Philemon that he owes him his very life (Philem 19). Yet Paul does not demand repayment. Rather, Paul implores Philemon to receive Onesimus again, no longer as a slave but as a brother in Christ (Philem 16). Finally, Paul expresses full confidence in the Christian character of Philemon, knowing that he will do even more than what the apostle requests.

Some argue that Paul never requires the emancipation of Onesimus. While this is true in a technical sense, substantially the letter points in another direction. Paul informs Philemon that when released from prison, he plans to visit him first. Philemon must know that Paul would surely have been grieved to see Onesimus, his son in the Lord, his very heart, still in bonds (Philem 10, 12, 20, 22).

In closing, it must be admitted that the words *Holy Spirit* do not appear in Paul's letter to Philemon. Yet where the Spirit of the Lord is, there is freedom. Surely, the Spirit who gives liberty inspired Paul to write his heartfelt appeal to Philemon. Indeed, the seeds of emancipation sown in this brief but powerful letter would flourish and grant freedom to many.

SUMMARY THOUGHTS

Heresy had obscured the preeminence of Christ in Ephesus and Colossae. In response, Paul presents what is perhaps the highest Christology in the New Testament by unfolding the mystery of the gospel and the absolute sovereignty of God. No human can pry the truth of the gospel from God's hands. God must reveal his redemptive plan by granting the Spirit of wisdom and revelation. The Holy Spirit is God's seal and deposit who guarantees full redemption in the future. The Spirit reflects the perfect unity of the Trinity. The Spirit inspires lively worship among God's people. This Spirit-inspired worship takes on a number of creative forms, all of which glorify God and edify the church. God's triumph over evil has already been won in the heavenly realm, yet the battle goes on for the church in the world. God has granted the church every weapon it needs to win the fight. The battle cry for the church is the love of God. Its aim is the peace of God. Its goal is the freedom of God for everyone who calls on his name.

WHAT DOES IT MEAN FOR ME?

The majesty of Ephesians and Colossians can tempt us to lose sight of their practical appeal. On the other hand, the practical nature of Philemon can belie its spiritual significance. The following points are meant to bring the truths of these great epistles to bear on our personal lives. Prayerfully reflect on the section below. Pray that God might grant you the Spirit of wisdom and revelation so that you might come to know him better.

+ There has been so much debate about divine election and what it means to be "sealed in the Holy Spirit." Yet Paul's main point is to convey the assurance of God's love and redemption (Eph 1:13-14). Laying aside issues like foreknowledge, human free will, and the like, simply pray that God give you peace about the wonderful love he has for you in Christ.

+ Paul prays that his recipients receive the "Spirit of wisdom and revelation." Can you pray that prayer with Paul? Can you pray for God to grant you the Spirit of wisdom and revelation?

+ Ephesians 3:14-21 contains one of the most beautiful prayers that has ever been prayed. Paul prays that his hearers be strengthened in the "inner being" by the power of the Holy Spirit. He wants them to be "rooted and grounded in love." Finally, he prays that they come to know the unknowable, that is, the measureless expanse of God's love for us. Take time to "own" each part of this prayer for yourself. Make this prayer a blueprint for all your prayers so that you might grow in the knowledge of the Father, in the love of the Son, and in the fellowship of the Holy Spirit.

+ In Ephesians 4:30, Paul speaks of "putting off" the things that might grieve the Holy Spirit. Prayerfully ask the Spirit to reveal those things that might grieve him. Once the Spirit has revealed these areas, pray that he may remove them from your life.

✦ In Ephesians 5:18, Paul exhorts us to be filled with the Spirit, and then immediately follows with examples of singing and hymn making. This kind of hymnody has nothing to do with musical talents. Rather, these songs and hymns come directly from the Holy Spirit. Paul is describing a joy-filled abandon that praises the Lord. Do you want more joy in your life? Pray for those songs of the heart that only the Spirit can inspire.

✦ We are in a warzone. That is why Paul commands that we get battle ready, not once, but twice in Ephesians. God has provided us with all the spiritual weapons we need to win the victory. Read Ephesians 6:10-17 and visualize putting on each piece of God's armor. Pray earnestly about taking up the "sword of the Spirit" and committing yourself to learning more of God's holy Word.

✦ The epistle to Philemon is filled with courage. It took courage for Onesimus to escape a life of bondage. It took courage for Philemon to keep the matter to himself and not contact Roman authorities. It took courage for Paul to write such a letter in the midst of trying circumstances. Pray now that God grant you the courage to do the right thing in a world that promotes the wrong thing.

11

The HOLY SPIRIT *in* PHILIPPIANS

THE SPIRIT OF JOY

Do not be anxious about anything, but in every situation, by prayer and petition, with thanksgiving, present your requests to God. And the peace of God, which transcends all understanding, will guard your hearts and your minds in Christ Jesus.

PHILIPPIANS 4:6-7 NIV

THE HOLY SPIRIT EXPLICITLY directed Paul to evangelize Macedonia (Acts 16:9-12). Lydia was Paul's first convert in Philippi and became the founding patroness of the church there. Her hospitality came to characterize the whole church (Acts 16:14-15). Not surprisingly, the Philippians were Paul's most generous and trouble-free church (Phil 4:15-16).

When writing to the Philippians, Paul has no need to defend his apostolic authority as was the case in most of his letters. Rather, Philippians is Paul's "love letter" to dear fellow workers whom he cherishes in the Lord. Joy . . . fellowship . . . confidence . . . heart . . . longing . . . love—these are the words that describe Paul's relationship with the Philippians.

Although Paul evidences multiple purposes in Philippians, he is clearly concerned about their spiritual wellbeing. His imprisonment (Phil 1:7), the illness of Epaphroditus (Phil 2:25-30), and the arrogance of false brethren (Phil 1:15) have instilled fear and uncertainty in the church. Thus Paul desires that a healthy Christian state of mind prevail among them—one that reflects the mind of Christ (Phil 2:5-11), is free from anxiety (Phil 4:6), and finds joy and contentment regardless of external circumstances (Phil 2:18, 28; 3:1; 4:4, 11). It is the fellowship of the Holy Spirit (Phil 2:1), together with Spirit-filled worship (Phil 3:3) that replaces anxiety with humility (Phil 2:8) and grants peace beyond comprehension and joy in the faith (Phil 4:7).

All of this means that God is not only concerned about the salvation of our souls, but he also cares about our hearts, minds, and emotions (Phil 1:27; 2:2-3, 5; 4:7-8). The God of all benevolence desires that peace (Phil 1:2; 4:7, 9), love (Phil 1:9; 2:1-2), and joy (Phil 1:25; 2:18, 29) reign in our hearts. This is the "fellowship of the Spirit" (Phil 2:1), by which every saint "stands firm in one spirit, with one mind striving together for the faith of the gospel" (Phil 1:27).

PAUSE FOR PRAYER

The Word of God is not an object to be dissected; it is a revelation to be received. Indeed, we may be able to wrest some facts from the Bible, but this is not the same thing as experiencing the truth of God's Word. For these reasons, it is not enough to know *what* the Bible says, but *why* it says it, and perhaps most importantly, *how* it applies to one's life. There is a reciprocal dynamic in studying the Scriptures. As we are sensitive to the Spirit's voice when interpreting the Word, the Word in turn is interpreting us. Pray now that the Spirit would not only empower you to interpret Philippians but that you would allow the Spirit's message to interpret you.

THE PRESENCE OF THE HOLY SPIRIT IN PHILIPPIANS

The unity of the Spirit (Phil 1:12-27). Things have not turned out as the Philippians expected. Their founding pastor, the apostle Paul, is in prison (Phil 1:12-14). Some are preaching Christ out of envy and strife, hoping to add pain to Paul's bonds (Phil 1:15-17).[1] Also, Paul may be executed at any moment (Phil 1:20). To make matters worse, the person

---

[1]The word translated "distress" or "trouble" is *thlipsis* and means "pressure." It is from this word that we get "friction." Some ill-motivated preachers wanted to increase the chafing of Paul's manacles and leg irons by preaching Christ out of envy and strife.

they sent to help Paul had fallen gravely ill (Phil 2:25-26). All these setbacks were taking a toll on the church at Philippi. Anxiety and stress were wearing away at their unity in Christ.

In response, Paul assures them that everything has worked out for the furtherance of the gospel.[2] The Praetorian Guard, the emperor's personal bodyguard, has now heard the good news (Phil 1:13). Even though some preachers are ill-motivated and spiteful, the message is still getting out (Phil 1:18). Moreover, if Paul is martyred for the faith, then he will be with the Lord (Phil 1:21-23). The Philippians should already know this, for one of their own, Epaphroditus, is a great example of Christian sacrifice (Phil 2:25-30).

Paul's clear message is that the sovereign Lord is in control. They should not succumb to anxiety and fear. Rather, they should strive as one person to maintain the unity of the Spirit. As a single fighting force, they are to engage in spiritual warfare, effectively wielding the faith of the gospel (Phil 1:27).

The fellowship of the Spirit (Phil 2:1-11). The common bond of the Philippians is Christ. He is their comfort. He is their consolation born of divine love. This is what it means to be "in Christ." This is the "fellowship of the Spirit" filled with heartfelt compassion and enjoyed only by the saints.[3]

Yet being "in Christ" means being in community. So if there is one thing that can bring joy to his joyless prison cell, it is their unity in Christ as evident in their unity with one another. This kind of spiritual unity can only happen if they all have the mind of Christ. They are to think the same thing, having the same mind as one soul, expressing the same love in Christ. They are to harbor no envy, strife, or selfish

---

[2]Philippi was named after Philip of Macedon, the father of Alexander the Great (365–332 BCE). Both father and son were accomplished generals, which might explain the frequent use of military jargon in Philippians. For example, the word translated "advance" is *prokopē* and describes the steady progress of an army through hostile territory. For Paul, the gospel is cutting through enemy lines.

[3]The word often translated "tenderness" or "compassion" is *splanchnon* and literally refers to one's internal organs (Acts 1:18). For the Greeks, the seat of deep emotion was in the gut. Hence Paul longs to see the Philippians with the "bowels of Christ" (Phil 1:8; see also Philem 7, 12; 1 John 3:17).

ambition. On the contrary, they are to humble themselves as Christ did in the incarnation, appearing as a mere human being and suffering unto death. Nevertheless, there is power in this path of humility, for God greatly exalted Jesus and gave him a name above all other names.

Serving in the Spirit (Phil 3:3-10). There was a time when Paul, unknowingly, tried to serve God in the flesh. He was driven by a works-righteousness form of Judaism that arrogantly boasted in his religious achievements and Pharisaic heritage (Phil 3:3-5). Yet his misplaced zeal led him to persecute the church, imprisoning some and killing others (Acts 8:1–9:1). All of this changed on the Damascus Road. Here, the exalted Christ granted Paul an abundance of grace, conveyed a divine calling, and announced his commission to be the apostle to the Gentiles. From that time on, he no longer sought to serve in the flesh but rather to serve in the Spirit.

To serve in the Spirit is to boast in Christ and everything that comes from Christ. It is to be filled with joy, thanksgiving, and prayer. To serve God in the Spirit is to constantly seek a mature knowledge of Christ, not only in future glory but also in present suffering. To serve in the Spirit means to refuse to identify with the power structures of this world but rather to lay hold of one's citizenship in heaven.

Paul is an example of what it means to serve God in the Spirit. Timothy is an example of the same. The apostle lavishes praise on Timothy claiming that he is unequaled, unselfish, and a proven son in the Lord (Phil 2:20-22). Epaphoditus, one of their own, is also an example of one who serves God in the Spirit. He is a "brother," "fellow worker," and "fellow soldier" who represents the very heart of what it means to be a minister of Christ (Phil 2:25). The Philippians would do well to mimic (from *summimētai* meaning to "copy together") such examples and to trace the very footprints of the pattern or "type" (*typos*) of these examples (Phil 3:17).

SUMMARY THOUGHTS

The Philippians were the kind of people who wanted things to go right. But they hadn't. Their hero was in prison, their emissary was gravely ill, and false preachers were on the rise. Stress and anxiety had robbed them of their joy and threatened their unity in Christ. They had lost perspective and were paying a high spiritual price. Paul's counsel is that they should lift their gaze above the things of this world and look unto Jesus. They should break off their reliance on the flesh and avail themselves of the power of the Spirit. They are to celebrate the unity of the Spirit, cultivate the fellowship of the Spirit, and continue serving in the Spirit. Only the mind of Christ, together with joy, thanksgiving, and prayer that come from being in Christ can restore their souls, empower their witness, and bring true contentment regardless of circumstances (Phil 4:1-13).

WHAT DOES IT MEAN FOR ME?

Paul's letter to the Philippians contains some of the most encouraging words ever penned to the church. It is as if the "fruit of the Spirit" (Gal 5:22) has come to life on every page. God's sovereign hand is at work. Paul's imprisonment has resulted in an advancement for the gospel (Phil 1:12-13). Even the insincere preach the gospel in spite of themselves (Phil 1:15-18). Paul's impending death is gain (Phil 1:21) and persecution only accentuates the Philippians' faithful witness (Phil 1:28-30). The fellowship of the Spirit reproduces the mind of Christ (Phil 2:5-11), and the presumed "failure" of Epaphroditus in reality demonstrates the sacrifice of Christ (Phil 2:25-30). Joy triumphs over worry (Phil 4:4, 6), God's peace is master of our minds, and the beauty of the kingdom fills our thoughts (Phil 4:7-8).[4] Giving is not a burden, but is a form of worship that rebounds to those who are generous in heart (Phil 4:17).

Even so, Philippians presents the discerning reader with a number of challenges, all of which are intended for our spiritual growth. The following questions and suggestions may serve as "signposts" as you continue to "walk in the Spirit" (Rom 8:4-6).

+ There is a "futurity" to faith. That is why the Lord has given us the wonderful capacity to anticipate things that are yet to come. By

---

[4]As noted, Paul assures the Philippians that the peace of God will "guard" our hearts. The word for "guard" is *phroureō* and describes a Roman centurion standing guard as his post. When God is in control, no troubling thing is allowed to pass.

faith, we can lay hold of things that are not present; we can see things that are yet invisible (Heb 11:1). Yet this wonderful gift of hope can take a wrong turn. The heavenly gaze of belief can shift downward into the world of worry and anxiety. Our minds become filled with thoughts that do not edify. Our hearts are burdened with feelings of dread. Take a moment to listen to the internal dialogue of your soul. Is it speaking "faith," "hope," "trust"? Why not make it a practice to dwell on the things Paul sets forth in Philippians 4:8?

✦ Our world has become so coarse and mean-spirited. Arrogance and self-will have practically become criteria for success. There seems to be no place for humility. But the Scriptures repeatedly say that there is a mysterious power to humility. The biblical pattern is humility first, exaltation next. Why not pray that the Lord grant you a genuine spirit of humility? You might be surprise at how much success will follow.

✦ We've all heard it said that in the final moments of one's life, no one says that they wished that they had spent more time in the office, had earned more money, or had a bigger house. On the contrary, at such times persons inevitably long for things that money can't buy. In the closing chapter of Philippians, Paul teaches that contentment does not consist of earthly possessions. So why invest so much in things that you might later regret? Make up your mind to rest in the riches of the Lord and you will never be discontent again.

✦ No doubt Epaphroditus felt like a failure. He was supposed to take care of Paul while he was in prison, and now Paul was nursing him back to health! To make matters worse, word had gotten back to the Philippians that their plans had fallen through. Epaphroditus had let them down. Yet Paul does not see it this way at all. Of all the members at Philippi, Epaphroditus is the only one that Paul commends by name. He is a perfect example of Christ, for he was willing to serve others unto death. You also might feel like a failure. Yet know this: If your heart is dedicated to serve others in love, you are a great success in the Lord. You are an example of Christ.

12

The HOLY SPIRIT *in* 1 *and* 2 THESSALONIANS

ESCHATOLOGY AND ETHICS

For we know, brothers and sisters loved by God, that he has chosen you, because our gospel came to you not simply with words but also with power, with the Holy Spirit and deep conviction. You know how we lived among you for your sake. You became imitators of us and of the Lord, for you welcomed the message in the midst of severe suffering with the joy given by the Holy Spirit.

1 Thessalonians 1:4-6 NIV

PAUL'S MINISTRY IN THESSALONICA was rough going. Luke informs us that Paul did have a measure of success there. A few Jews came to the faith, but the greater success was among the God fearers. These persons were Gentiles like Cornelius and Lydia. They had claimed Yahweh as the only true God but did not fully convert to Judaism (Acts 10:2; 16:14). Paul's message that they could become the children of Abraham without first becoming Jews was especially attractive to them. Luke also adds that quite a few prominent women of Thessalonica joined the faith (Acts 17:1-4). We also know that Aristarchus was one of Paul's Thessalonian converts. He became one of Paul's coworkers and ministered with the apostle throughout Asia Minor (Acts 20:4; 27:2; Col 4:10; Philem 24).

Paul faced severe opposition in Thessalonica. Some unbelieving Jews started a riot and tried to frame Paul and his coworkers as political revolutionaries who wanted to overthrow Caesar and instate a new king called Jesus. Paul's friends were arrested and had to pay bond money to the civil magistrates. This was a pledge that they had no ill intent against the government. The situation was so grave that Paul had to slip out of town under cover of darkness (Acts 17:5-10).

In the midst of persecution, the saints welcomed the charismatic presence of the Spirit. If they were to endure the persecution of humans, they must have the power of the Spirit. That's why Paul reminds the Thessalonians that the gospel did not come to them in word only but was demonstrated by the power of the Holy Spirit. Paul assures them that the pain of suffering for the kingdom cannot dampen the overwhelming joy that comes from the Holy Spirit (1 Thess 1:6). Their experience of the power and joy of the Spirit is a sign that they have been chosen by God (1 Thess 1:4-6).

At the time of Paul's writing, conditions had become worse in Thessalonica. Living a life worthy of their calling in Christ had become increasingly difficult. Some entertained a distorted version of Christ's second coming while others had lost faith that Christ would come again. In giving both comfort and correction, Paul reminds them of the special ministry of the Holy Spirit.

PAUSE FOR PRAYER

The second coming of Christ is a powerful promise. Yet as was the case in Thessalonica, an inordinate fixation on Christ's return in the future can thwart one's spiritual development in the present. Too much thought about heaven can undermine our effectiveness on earth. When the great reformer Martin Luther was asked what he would do if he knew the Lord would return tomorrow, he replied that he would plant a tree today. What Luther meant was that his personal conduct is always being informed by the ever-present reality of the second coming. Spiritually and morally, Luther was always ready for the Lord's return. Pray now that you can receive and celebrate the joy and hope of Jesus' soon return. Yet pray also that the ever-present prospect of that hope inspires you to live a holy and pure life right now.

THE PRESENCE OF THE HOLY SPIRIT IN
THESSALONICA: SOME PRELIMINARY CONCERNS

*Two separate epistles with a common problem (1 Thess 4:13-18;
2 Thess 2:1-8).* First and Second Thessalonians will be studied together
because even though they are two separate epistles, they share a
common problem. The issue at hand for both letters concerns the parousia or second coming of Christ.[1] In Paul's first letter, it appears that
some of the Thessalonians have lost hope in the second coming. The
reason for such despair is not explicitly stated. However, many in the
early church believed that Jesus' return was imminent. He would certainly come back during their lifetime. When some members died and
there was still no parousia, a crisis of faith ensued. Many stopped believing in the second coming altogether (1 Thess 4:13-14). In response
to their despair, Paul insists that even though some have already died
in the faith, Jesus is surely coming again.

The occasion for 2 Thessalonians also focuses on the parousia but for
an entirely different reason. Some in Thessalonica had overreacted to
his first letter and were now saying that the Lord had already returned.
To make matters worse, someone claiming to speak for Paul and his
cohorts sent the Thessalonians a false report stating that the parousia
had in fact already occurred. There was confusion on all sides. Even
Paul didn't know if the false message came by way of prophecy, by word
of mouth only, or by a letter that had been forged in his name. His
advice is simple and straightforward. Don't believe it (2 Thess 2:1-2)!
Paul then goes on to explain important end-time events that must occur
prior to the second coming (2 Thess 2:3-12). Paul emphasizes the role
of the Holy Spirit in showing the correct way forward (1 Thess 4:8).

*The theological significance of the second coming (1 Thess 1:9-10;
2 Thess 1:6-11).* The despair and confusion among the Thessalonians
constitutes a larger problem than might first appear. If the authenticity

---

[1]The phrase "second coming" does not appear in the New Testament. What is normally translated as "second coming" is actually the Greek word *parousia* or, literally, "the presence." This
distinction may have some significance for the faith. That is, the return of Christ might not be
so much a movement from a distant heaven down to our earth, but rather the revealing of his
divine presence that is already here.

of Jesus' earthly ministry was demonstrated by his resurrection from the dead (Rom 1:4), then the validation of his heavenly status comes by way of the second coming (Acts 1:11). To reject either the resurrection or the parousia would have devastating consequences for the faith (see 1 Cor 15:12-19).

Basically, the problem addressed in both epistles is one of eschatology or "the study of the last things."[2] The far-reaching consequence of rejecting the second coming is established by its strategic place in God's plan of salvation. That is, the definitive "end" of all things is set forth from the very beginning of all things and is woven throughout everything in between. For example, the *protoevangelium* or "fore gospel" of Genesis 3:15 foreshadows the final defeat of Satan by the seed of Eve.[3] As God's salvation story unfolds, the prophets speak of the Branch of Jesse who will usher in the end time when the lion will lay down with the lamb (Is 11:1-16; 65:17-25). Jesus repeatedly indicated that the end-time realization of the kingdom was brought near through his presence and power (Mt 12:28; Mk 9:1; Lk 10:9; 11:20). Large portions of Jesus' teachings were exclusively devoted to signs heralding the end of the age (Mt 24–25; Mk 13; Lk 21). This end-time motif is continued by way of the many eschatologically themed parables of Jesus (Mt 13:24-43; Lk 12:36-48). Jesus' disciples were quick to discern the end-time message of the Lord. They basically asked Jesus when God was going to end this age (Mt 24:3). The disciples had invested so much of their end-time expectations in Jesus that his death on the cross proved devastating. It is for this reason that the disciples on the Emmaus road lament that they had hoped Jesus was the one who would restore Israel (Lk 24:21). The resurrection of Christ represents hope renewed but ultimately hope delayed. Just prior to the ascension, the disciples once again ask Jesus whether he will restore Israel at this time. In response, Jesus employs end-time jargon when he replies that it is not for them

---

[2]The word *eschatology* is derived from the Greek words *eschaton* (meaning "the end") and *logos* (meaning "a word, message, or study"). Hence, *eschatology* means the study of the last things.
[3]The word for "seed" in Gen 3:15 is in the singular as well as the pronoun *he*. From the beginning, Genesis envisions a singular offspring from Eve who will utterly defeat Satan at the end.

to know the "times" or the "seasons" (Acts 1:6-7). As Jesus ascends to heaven, the second coming of Christ comes to the fore again. The heavenly messengers assure the disciples that this same Jesus will come again. Finally, when the Holy Spirit is given at Pentecost, Peter interprets the fulfillment of the Joel prophecy in terms of the last days. It is interesting to note that Joel simply says, "And afterward I will pour out my Spirit," but Peter says, "*In the last days*, God says, I will pour out my Spirit" (Joel 2:28; Acts 2:17).

All of this means that the parousia is the critical component of a much broader eschatological story that begins in Genesis and ends in Revelation. Indeed the Scriptures speak of three great interdependent moments in God's plan of salvation. The first is the coming of the Messiah in the person and work of Jesus Christ. The second is the outpouring of the Holy Spirit at Pentecost. The third is the second coming of Christ at the end of the world. All of these are seen to be eschatological through and through.

To the point at hand, any despair or confusion about the second coming on the part of the Thessalonians is no small matter indeed. Failure at this critical juncture of the faith would disrupt the entire endtime schema of the Lord as set forth in the entirety of Scripture. It is for these reasons that Paul devoted so much time and space to address and clarify the parousia in his letters to the Thessalonians.

THE HOLY SPIRIT, ESCHATOLOGY, AND ETHICS

One of the constants of Scripture is that eschatology and ethics go hand in hand. So the error of the Thessalonians was not simply a matter of false doctrine but also an issue of false praxis. Thus the tumult and confusion about the second coming inevitably affected the conduct of believers in Thessalonica. Some appear to have regressed in their spiritual development and fallen back into their old sinful habits. Others seem to have disengaged from the day-to-day routine of life and stopped working for a living. For all these reasons, when trying to get the Thessalonians back on track, Paul emphasizes the sanctifying presence of the Holy Spirit.

Paul's main point is that the timing of the second coming is not the important thing. What really matters is that the parousia is a time of personal accountability for the redeemed and a time of judgment for the lost (2 Thess 1:6-12). Thus Paul's mandate for the Thessalonians is to continually appropriate the power of the Holy Spirit so that they might live worthy of their calling in Christ. Jesus might not have returned *yet* but the Holy Spirit is here *now*. The Thessalonians must commit themselves to the sanctifying presence of the Holy Spirit and let the Lord take care of the timing of the second coming.

This is why at the beginning of his first letter, Paul includes the imitation motif that is so common in his epistles (1 Thess 1:6-7; 2 Thess 3:9; 1 Cor 4:16). Paul's own life in the Spirit serves as an ethical pattern for the Thessalonians to trace out in their lives. Accordingly, the theme of holiness not only appears at the beginning of the letter but also is present at the end. Paul prays that the God of peace will sanctify the Thessalonians through and through, because the Lord is in fact coming soon (1 Thess 5:23).

Paul emphasizes that looking forward to the coming of Christ has real consequences for one's personal life right now. Belief in the second coming in the future means being sanctified in the Holy Spirit in the present.

Paul's appeal to the Spirit (1 Thess 4:1-18). One of Paul's strongest statements concerning the Holy Spirit is found in 1 Thessalonians 4:8. Here Paul admonishes that if anyone rejects his instructions, they are not simply rejecting the teachings of a human being, but are rejecting God, the very one who gave them the Holy Spirit. This statement is of interest for at least two reasons. First, it points to the high place that the Holy Spirit occupied in the minds of the Thessalonians. A warning about rejecting God is made even more binding by mentioning God's gift of the Holy Spirit.

Paul's warning would have been especially grave for the Thessalonians. The Thessalonians were presently undergoing trials and persecution. Paul sent Timothy for the express purpose of strengthening them during this time of suffering (1 Thess 3:1-4). Even near the end of his second epistle, Paul notes that they are still suffering for the kingdom of God (2 Thess 1:5). In that the Holy Spirit is their undergirding strength in the midst of ongoing trial, the last thing they would want to do is reject the one who gave them the Holy Spirit.

The second reason why 1 Thessalonians 4:8 is of significance is because of its placement in the text. Paul's words about the Holy Spirit occupy the very center of this important chapter. Conceptually, the Holy Spirit joins Paul's exhortation to sanctified living and his incisive words about the second coming. So the very arrangement of the chapter visibly demonstrates that eschatology (the second coming) and ethics (sanctification by the Spirit) are inseparable for Paul.

For these reasons, it should come as no surprise that Paul's ethical challenge comes at the very opening of the chapter. As was the case in several churches, especially the church in Corinth, the problem of sexual immorality was also present in Thessalonica. Thus, Paul exhorts that they must avoid sexual immorality of all kinds and live a sanctified, pure, and holy life.[4] Although Paul does not explicitly state that they are to be sanctified in the Holy Spirit, this is Paul's characteristic expression for holiness (Rom 15:16; 2 Cor 6:6; Titus 3:5).

In addition to sexual impurity, their missteps concerning the parousia resulted in another type of problem. Their false notions about the second coming led to the shirking of their social responsibility, especially in the area of work. Though pronounced in 2 Thessalonians, the problem of excessive idleness was present across the board. The phrase "idle and disruptive" occurs no less than three times in 1 and 2 Thessalonians (1 Thess 5:14; 2 Thess 3:6-7, 11).

This was a terrible witness to those who were outside of the church (1 Thess 4:11-12). Paul confronts such error head on. Believers should not associate with those Christians who refuse to work. Also, there is to be no benevolence extended to anyone who doesn't earn a living. If they don't work, they shouldn't eat (2 Thess 3:10).

---

[4]Paul makes a clear antithesis between sexual uncleanness (*akatharta*) and holiness (*agiasmos*) in 1 Thess 4:7. The word for holiness literally means "set apart" in the sense of Christians separating themselves from any illicit sexual conduct or from persons who willingly commit such conduct. Not to live a sexually pure life is to grieve God and by extension the Holy Spirit who has been given to them by God (1 Thess 4:8).

With regard to the second coming, the crux of the matter can be found in 1 Thessalonians 4:13. Some of the Thessalonians had "fallen asleep" and there was still no second coming. It is interesting that Paul uses the euphemism "fallen asleep" in the same manner of Jesus in John 11:11-14. Here Jesus refers to the death of Lazarus as "sleep" until he must pointedly inform his disciples that Lazarus is dead. Nevertheless for Jesus and for Paul the image of sleep conveys a powerful message. For those who are "in Christ" death is a temporary state, analogous to sleep. Just as Lazarus was "awakened" by being raised from the dead, so too will every believer be "awakened" at the general resurrection of the dead. All of this will occur at the parousia.

In clearing up their confusion about the second coming, Paul asserts that belief in the parousia is integrally connected to faith in Jesus' resurrection. If you have faith that Jesus was raised from the dead, then you must have faith that he is coming again.[5] In a counterintuitive way, Paul informs the Thessalonians that the dead in Christ will actually take priority over those who are alive at the time of the second coming. Those who have already died in the faith will be raised from the dead first. After this happens, those who are alive at the time of the second coming will be "caught up" to join them and the Lord.

It is at this point that Paul resorts to the use of Jewish apocalyptic language and imagery. The word *apocalyptic* comes from the Greek word *apokalypsis* and literally means "the unveiling" or "uncovering." It is a genre or type of Jewish literature that describes the sudden and often violent in-breaking of the kingdom of God. Prime examples of this kind of literature are found in the books of Daniel and Ezekiel. Yet Jesus' words concerning the end time contain apocalyptic themes as well, as does the book of Revelation. In fact, the very first word of the book of Revelation is *apokalypsis* because it is the "unveiling" of God's final plan for the world. Paul's words about the Lord coming down from heaven, a mighty shout of an archangel, and a trumpet blast all reflect apocalyptic imagery.

---

[5]The resurrection of Christ was a point of contention and confusion among several of Paul's congregations. Some of the Corinthians flatly denied that Jesus rose from the dead. Paul firmly corrects them and points out the theological consequences of such a denial (1 Cor 15:1-58).

Continuing on, Paul begins to speak in ways that sound similar to Jesus' teaching on the end times. Paul says that the Lord will come as a thief in the night, even when people are calling out peace and safety (1 Thess 5:2; Mt 24:43). He continues that just like the sudden onset of birth pains, so shall the coming of the Lord be (1 Thess 5:3; Mt 24:8; Mk 13:8).

Paul's note about the living being "caught up" is only found here in the New Testament. It is from this verse that belief in the rapture is derived. It should be noted that as was the case with the phrase "second coming," the actual word *rapture* does not appear in the Bible. However, it ultimately finds its basis in Paul's use of the word *harpazō*. This unique word conveys a sudden, violent catching up.[6] All of this is intended to reinstate the blessed hope that every believer, whether alive or dead, will be "caught up" by the Lord at the second coming.

A false report, signs of the second coming, and sanctification in the Holy Spirit (2 Thess 2:3-12). The logistics of ancient letter carrying may have worked against Paul's first counsel to the Thessalonians. Something odd had occurred between the time of his first letter to them and the time he sent his second letter. Someone had sent a false report to the Thessalonians, either by word of mouth, under the guise of prophecy, or in a forged letter, stating that the second coming had already happened. To lend credibility to their ruse, they indicated that this new teaching had come directly from the apostle Paul (2 Thess 2:1-2).

In an effort to clear up this confusion, Paul revisits a theme that he briefly introduced in the opening of his letter. In 2 Thessalonians 1:6-7, he assures the Thessalonians that God will punish their tormentors and grant them solace when the Lord is "revealed" (again, *apokalyptō*). Here he includes the added feature of Jesus coming in blazing fire with powerful angels (1 Thess 1:7; see also Mt 13:30-40). Apocalyptic imagery abounds. Once again, eschatology mandates Christian ethics. In light

---

[6]The Latin form is *rapere* from which the word *rapture* is derived. It is from this same word that we get our modern term for "raptor." So just as a raptor swoops down and snatches up its prey, the Lord will descend from heaven and catch up the living saints (Mk 13:26-27; Lk 21:27).

of Christ's return, Paul prays that God will make them worthy. Every deed and desire must be ordered by the Lord.

In 2 Thessalonians 2:6-11 Paul rehearses a number of end-time events that must happen prior to the second coming. His main point is that wickedness and sin must increase before the end will come. In terms reminiscent of Jesus and parts of the book of Revelation, Paul instructs that a great falling away must first occur before the second coming. Here Paul uses the word *apostasia* from which we derive the word *apostasy*. Those who are weak in faith will fall away prior to the parousia. Paul then speaks of an arch-sinner who not only opposes God but presents himself as God so that he might be worshiped in the temple. Paul calls him the "man of lawlessness," "son of destruction," and "the lawless one." His works are in accordance with Satan and he is able to do lying wonders and miracles (see also Mt 24:4-6; Mk 13:21). Paul then gives the reason why this arch-sinner has not yet gained the ascendency. There is someone who is restraining this evil one and will continue to do so until God's appointed time. There is endless speculation about who "the restrainer" is, but three things are fairly clear. First, the one who holds back is on God's side and opposes the lawless one. Relatedly, the restrainer prevents evil from having its way in the world. Finally, the restrainer must be taken out of the world before the end comes. In that Paul has already spoken of the saints being "snatched up" by the Lord, perhaps Paul is speaking here of the Spirit-filled church. That is, the presence of the Holy Spirit in the church, together with the preservation of morality affected by that presence, will be taken out of the world. Paul does not entertain a dualism between God and the son of destruction. In a manner similar to what we read in Revelation, the defeat of the lawless one is anticlimactic. He will be consumed with a mere breath of the Lord at the time of the second coming (Rev 20:5-15).

True to form, Paul joins eschatological vision with practical Christian living. He is grateful for the sanctifying work of the Holy Spirit in their lives (2 Thess 2:13). Paul exhorts them to stand firm in "the teachings" he has passed on, either by word of mouth or in writing (2 Thess 2:15). The word for "teachings" is *paradosis* and is used of early Christian confessions and ethical instruction (1 Cor 11:2, 23; 15:1-3). No doubt these teachings contained practical guidelines for Christian living.

The charismatic presence of the Spirit (1 Thess 5:19-22). The Holy Spirit serves as bookends for 1 Thessalonians. At the beginning, Paul reminds the Thessalonians that the gospel did not come in word only, but also in the power in the Holy Spirit (1 Thess 1:5). Near the end in the paraenetic section, where Paul includes ethical exhortations, he affirms the gifts of the Spirit (1 Thess 5:19-22). Here Paul commands the Thessalonians not to quench the Spirit. The word-picture used is of pouring water on a fire. They must not dampen the energy and fire of the Holy Spirit! No doubt charismatic utterances are in view because Paul prohibits contempt for prophecy. This prohibition is surprising for a number of reasons. Some, as in Corinth, had misused the gifts of the Spirit. One might think Paul would choose to ignore those who cared little for the gifts. After all, he had enough trouble with those who were overzealous for the *charismata*. Yet, he does not do this. Just as Paul commanded the wayward Corinthians not to prohibit speaking in tongues, he forbids the Thessalonians from looking down on the gift of prophecy. In every instance Paul willingly promotes the manifestation of the gifts in the church. Yet Paul is balanced in his counsel. They are not to be naive with respect to the gifts of the Spirit. Thus Paul exhorts them to test all prophecies. Keep what is good; toss out what is bad.

SUMMARY THOUGHTS

Paul is writing to a church that has been persecuted from the beginning. They are suffering even as he writes. They must imitate Paul in his suffering for the gospel. If God can sustain him, then God can sustain them. The blessed hope of the second coming is a powerful incentive to keep the faith despite present hardships. One day, the Lord will return and make everything right.

Yet for the Thessalonians, hardship and heresies have taken a toll. Some are tempted to give up and return to their old sinful habits. Paul urges them to resist that temptation. They are to receive the sanctification, power, and gifts that can only come from the Holy Spirit. Throughout both epistles, Paul engages their struggle and confusion about the second coming. He does not give up on them. His goal is to reinstate the blessed hope of Christ's return so that they might be strengthened.

WHAT DOES IT MEAN FOR ME?

Paul is writing to a hurting and confused church. But they are good people. They are not using the grace of the gospel as a pretense to sin. They have simply grown weary and Paul is committed to help them in the power of the Lord. Paul's help for them can also be a help for you. Prayerfully consider the following points in your continuing journey of discipleship.

+ Paul did not sugarcoat what lies ahead for the Christian. When he was with them, he told them that persecution would come. At the time of writing, he reminds them that persecution awaits the Christian (1 Thess 3:4). Have you fully accepted that the true way of faith involves suffering and persecution? For sure, the faith is not all gloom and doom. Thank God for that! But things being the way that they are, suffering for Christ is part of the journey.

+ How do you view the second coming of Christ? Has the blessed promise of his return become dim in your faith? If Christ were to come at this very moment, would you be overwhelmed with joy or would you harbor some misgivings? We should all strive in prayer to be like Martin Luther: if we knew that Jesus would return tomorrow, we would plant a tree today!

+ In some way the eschatological zeal of the Thessalonians had morphed into personal idleness and annoying behavior. What a terrible witness for the Lord! None of us would choose to live in such a manner. Yet temptation can be subtle. Belief in the parousia never promotes escapism. Rather, true faith in the second coming will inspire joy in the Lord and a deeper longing to be sanctified in the Holy Spirit.

✦ Pentecostals and charismatics have always had a special interest in eschatology or the "study of the last things." This interest arises out of their commitment to biblical theology. For them, there is no speaking about God apart from the Bible. Since the Scriptures point out "the end" from the beginning, an eschatological lens for interpretation is always close at hand. For all these reasons the subject of eschatology is an exciting one. Yet the Bible always joins eschatology with personal Christian ethics. Pray now that through the power of the Holy Spirit the prospect of Christ's coming might inspire you to holy living.

✦ Paul waited until the very end of his letter to address the charismatic gifts of the Spirit. Perhaps this was part of his literary strategy. Often the very last thing we hear is the very first thing we remember. It's hard to forget, "Quench not the Spirit!" "Despise not prophecy!" Pray about what these final and pointed commands might mean for you and your growth in the Lord.

13

The HOLY SPIRIT
in the PASTORAL EPISTLES

THE SPIRIT OF POWER, LOVE, AND SELF-CONTROL

But when the kindness and love of God our Savior appeared, he saved us, not because of righteous things we had done, but because of his mercy. He saved us through the washing of rebirth and renewal by the Holy Spirit, whom he poured out on us generously through Jesus Christ our Savior, so that, having been justified by his grace, we might become heirs having the hope of eternal life.

TITUS 3:4-7 NIV

FIRST AND SECOND TIMOTHY and Titus are commonly referred to as the Pastorals. This title is intriguing for several reasons. First, in writing his epistles Paul speaks directly to "the saints" without so much as mentioning a single pastor. Only in 1 and 2 Timothy and Titus does Paul explicitly address the acting pastors of churches. Second, oddly enough, the word *pastor* does not appear in the New Testament.[1] Yet, Timothy and Titus are certainly pastors. They preach, teach, and discipline the members of the church (1 Tim 4:11; 2 Tim 4:2; Titus 2:1-5). Also, they are responsible for sound doctrine, church leadership, and discipline in the church at large (1 Tim 3:1-10; 5:20; Titus 1:7-13). In sum, it would not be incorrect to say that Timothy and Titus function as archbishops or regional overseers (Acts 20:28; Phil 1:1).

---

[1]What we do have is the word *poimenas* or "shepherds" (Eph 4:11). There are also many forms of the verb *poimainō,* "to shepherd," (Acts 20:28) but no singular noun form for the word *pastor.*

The Pastorals are being studied together because they share many elements in common. For example, in all three epistles one senses that the apostolic age is coming to an end. Paul says that the time of his departure is at hand and he has given his all for the ministry. Paul realizes that a second generation of leadership is coming on the scene and that Timothy and Titus are an important part of that leadership (2 Tim 4:6-8).

One also senses a degree of anxiety on the part of the apostle. To some extent he feels abandoned in the twilight years of his ministry (2 Tim 4:5-16). He has concerns about his successors. Timothy and Titus must be up to the task, taking full advantage of the gifts and calling of the Spirit (2 Tim 1:7, 14). Hence Paul issues strong commands, exhortations, and words of encouragement. His disciples must be prepared to take over leadership of the church (1 Tim 1:18-20; Titus 2:15).

A major part of their calling was to mentor and discipline other ministers in the church. It is for this reason that qualifications for bishops and deacons are set forth in detail (1 Tim 3:1-12; Titus 1:5-9).[2] It is interesting that the same qualifications are given for their wives as well. This may indicate that Paul has ministering married partners in mind.

Another common theme in the Pastorals is the problem of false teachers and heresy. The transition from Judaism to Christianity was an uneven one. The trouble in the Pastorals seems to have arisen from certain sectors in first-century Judaism, or what Paul calls the "circumcision group" (Titus 1:10-11). An annoying and spiritually vacuous chatter drew in the uninformed and embroiled them in endless "word fights" (2 Tim 2:23). Religious myths, complex genealogies, and purity regulations had clouded the simple yet effective work of Christ (1 Tim 1:4-7, 2 Tim 2:14-23; Titus 1:10-15; 3:9). Mixed in was the misguided notion that marriage detracted from one's spiritual status before God (1 Tim 4:3).

Yet the Pastorals evidence significant differences as well. For example, in 2 Timothy, Paul is in prison (2 Tim 1:8, 16). This is not the case in his

---

[2]The descriptions of some of these qualifications are quite colorful. A bishop must be a "one-woman man," he must not "hover over" wine, he must not be a "fist fighter" and not a "newly planted" convert (1 Tim 3:2-3, 6).

other two letters. In 1 Timothy, Paul instructs his disciple to stay in Ephesus and adds that he hopes to visit him soon (1 Tim 1:3; 3:14). With regard to Titus, the apostle wants him to continue the ministry in Crete. Paul invites Titus to visit him in Nicopolis where he plans to overwinter (Titus 1:5; 3:12).

There is another difference, one more subtle in nature. Just when Paul needs Timothy to take up the reins of leadership, there are signs that Timothy feels overwhelmed by the task (2 Tim 1:7). He does not want to experience the pain Paul is going through.[3] He is ashamed that his mentor is suffering like a common criminal (2 Tim 1:8, 12). To some extent, Timothy has allowed his calling and spiritual giftedness to fade from view (1 Tim 1:18; 2 Tim 1:6). He also lacks focus and discipline (2 Tim 2:3-6). He also is worried about how others view his youth (1 Tim 4:12). All these concerns may have taken a toll on his physical health as well (1 Tim 5:23).

Paul must address an array of problems in the Pastorals. Yet he presents a common solution for them all. The Holy Spirit is the divine person and power who calls the leadership of the church, who sorts out troublesome heresies, and who can embolden ministers to lay hold of their vocation in Christ. Paul reminds his charges that it was the Spirit who vindicated the entire redemptive work of Jesus (1 Tim 3:16). It is the Spirit who not only renews us unto salvation but also helps us guard that salvation unto eternal life (Titus 3:5; 2 Tim 1:14). Paul exhorts that the Holy Spirit is the only true source of godly power, peace, and self-control (2 Tim 1:7). Finally, it is the prophetic word of the Spirit that speaks to the moral decline that will occur in the end times (1 Tim 4:1).

For all these reasons, the Pastorals grant unique insight into the context of ministry in the first-century church. What we find is that life in the church is charismatic through and through. For example, Paul reminds Timothy that his divine calling was confirmed by prophecies (1 Tim 1:18). He also speaks of spiritual gifts that were conveyed by the

---

[3]Paul commands Timothy not to distance himself from the more onerous challenges of ministry. He coins a unique term, *sygkakopatheō*, which literally means to "experience pain together." Timothy is to join with Paul in his sufferings for the gospel.

laying on of hands and prophecy (1 Tim 4:14). At several points in the Pastorals, Paul encourages the lifting up of hands in intercessory prayer. Indeed, an active prayer life characterizes the entire church. Paul exhorts that all should pray, lifting up holy hands with a pure heart. Prayer for civil authorities and for the unsaved are to be continually offered to the Lord for he desires the redemption of all (1 Tim 2:1-8).

PAUSE FOR PRAYER

The first-century world was one of intense religious pluralism. Many of the gods and goddesses of the Greco-Roman pantheon, as well as the ancient mystery religions of Egypt, were fearsome and vindictive. Paul is careful to assure Timothy that none of these harsh qualities characterize the true God. God has not given us a Spirit of fear but of power, love, and self-control.

We must be careful not to transfer our own misguided notions to how we perceive and relate to God. Negative experiences from our childhood, or even adult relationships that have gone wrong, can cloud our understanding of God. We must hold on to this unshakable truth. The Holy Spirit will never seek to intimidate us. Fear is not listed among the fruit of the Spirit. Anxiety and worry have nothing to do with the Spirit of God. The Holy Spirit is given to empower us. The Spirit is given so that we might genuinely experience the love of God. The gift of the Spirit has a healing effect on our spirit that is manifest in emotional and mental wellbeing. Pray now that God will help you reject any false notions about him. Pray that God will enable you to receive the power, love, and self-control that can only come from the Holy Spirit.

THE PRESENCE OF THE HOLY SPIRIT
IN THE PASTORAL EPISTLES

The Holy Spirit and salvation (Titus 3:5). The Pastorals are not known for teaching doctrine. Leading pastors like Timothy and Titus do not need to be taught the basic principles of the faith. Nevertheless, every major aspect of Paul's doctrine of salvation is present in the Pastorals. When referring to the confessional statements of the church, Paul flatly states that Jesus came into the world to save sinners, of whom he is the worst (1 Tim 1:15). The redemption of Christ is destined for the elect and is received by faith alone (2 Tim 2:10; 3:15). All of this comes by the pure grace of God, yet we are each called to live a holy life (2 Tim 1:9; Titus 2:11).

One of the more interesting Pauline statements about salvation is found in Titus 3:5. Here Paul says that God saved us through the washing and renewal of the Holy Spirit.[4] The phrase "washing and renewal" speaks of being regenerated by the Holy Spirit.[5] Here Paul employs concepts that sound more like the Gospel of John than what we find in his epistles. In effect, Paul is basically saying the same thing as John 3:3. One cannot enter the kingdom of God unless one is born again.

The Holy Spirit and ministerial vocation. The theme of ministerial calling is very prominent in the Pastorals. That is why all of Paul's counsel to Timothy and Titus is predicated on their calling in the Holy Spirit.

The "safeguarding" Spirit (2 Tim 1:13-14). Paul had invested a lot in Timothy and Titus. For example, he had entrusted a "pattern of teaching" to Timothy. Also, his entire life in Christ served as a model of faith, love, and a willingness to suffer for the gospel. The apostle describes all this effort and care as a "deposit" that must be guarded. Fortunately, this critical safeguarding is not up to Timothy alone but is secured *through the Holy Spirit.* The word for "through" is *dia* and conveys the idea of "conduit," "channel," or "pathway." So the Holy Spirit is actively preserving the ministerial investment that Paul has made in Timothy's life. No doubt it was a comfort for Timothy to know that God's protecting Spirit actually dwelt in him and was always available to him.

The "vindicating" Spirit (1 Tim 1:18-20; 3:16). First Timothy 3:16 may be part of an early Christian confession. In fact, a critical term in this verse is *homologoumenōs* and means "saying the same thing" or "by

---

[4]The phrase "washing and renewal" reflects the grammatical construction of *hendiadys,* or using two words to express a single idea.

[5]Paul's word *palingenesia* literally means "birthed again." Moreover, the word *anakainōsis* means "made new again." The prefix *ana* can also be interpreted as "from above." Conceivably, the word could mean "made new from above."

common confession." The theological content of this confession is impressive. In just a few lines, the incarnation, the authenticating presence of the Holy Spirit, the divinely appointed role of angels, the international mission of the church, and the ascension of the Lord are all set forth as binding tenets of the faith.

The phrase "vindicated" or "justified" by the Spirit may refer to the resurrection of Jesus. This is precisely what Paul indicates in Romans 1:4 and 1 Corinthians 15:14. On the other hand, since "vindicated by the Spirit" comes right after the incarnation but before the ascension, it may refer to the miracle-working power of the Spirit in the life of Jesus. This rendering coincides perfectly with what we find in the Gospels. Jesus continually referenced the charismatic power of the Spirit as the authenticating sign that he was indeed the Messiah of God. It appears that this miracle-working power of the Spirit was so important for the early church that it became part of an early confessional formula about Christ.

As the book of Acts clearly teaches, the vindicating presence of the Spirit in Jesus' life was also powerfully present in the life of the early church. This transference of the Spirit from Jesus to the disciples is evident in the Pastorals. Paul reminds Timothy of prophecies that were once made concerning him (1 Tim 1:18-20). Ostensibly, some type of charismatic utterance of the Spirit, perhaps on the order of the prophecy given in Acts 13:1-2, was pronounced over Timothy at the beginning of his ministry. Paul's purpose here is that Timothy might recall the content of these prophecies and be strengthened thereby. The implied narrative is that prophetic utterances of the Spirit are sources of spiritual strength and encouragement for those engaged in ministry.

The charismatic Spirit (1 Tim 4:14-15; 2 Tim 1:6-7). In 1 Timothy 4:14-15, Paul presents the reader with a rare yet fascinating insight into early church worship. Here Paul speaks of a *charisma* or "charismatic gift" that was given to Timothy through prophecy. Again, the preposition *dia* or "through" indicates that the "means" or "pathway" through which the gift came to Timothy was by way of prophecy. This prophetic word of the Spirit occurred at the same time that the elders laid their hands on Timothy.

The laying on of hands within the context of worship has a long-standing tradition in Judaism and in the early church. It appears to be of semi-sacramental significance, serving as a point of contact that facilitates the reception of God's grace (Num 8:10-11). For example, Jesus laid his hands on little children to bless them (Mt 19:15; Mk 6:5). Many of his healing miracles were accompanied by the laying on of hands (Mk 10:16; see also Acts 28:8). After they had fasted and prayed, the first believers in Antioch laid their hands on Paul and Barnabas and then sent them on their first missionary journey (Acts 13:1-3). Even the gift of the Holy Spirit was accompanied by the laying on of hands (Acts 8:17; 19:6).[6]

Even so, the church never understood the laying on of hands as some kind of magical ritual. The laying on of hands had no spiritual power in itself. Rather, it represents a kind of acted prayer that earnestly welcomes the presence and power of God. So the charismatic gift granted to Timothy was not automatically transferred by the laying on of hands. Rather, in a manner that is inherent to the mystery of prayer, one could say that the proximity of the Spirit to the environs of this world was narrowed through the laying on of hands. Paul insists that Timothy not neglect this extraordinary experience in the Holy Spirit.

Timothy can pay heed to the work of the Spirit in his life by fanning into flame the gift of God that resides in him through the laying on of Paul's hands. The "gift of God" here probably refers to the gift of the Holy Spirit, for Paul explicitly mentions the Spirit in the very next verse (2 Tim 1:6-7). If all of this is on target, we can learn a lot about Paul, Timothy, and the Holy Spirit from these two verses. First, just as Paul had done for the disciples in Ephesus, he laid his hands on Timothy and prayed that he might receive the Holy Spirit. Second, in some way Timothy had allowed the presence and power of the Holy Spirit to grow dim in his personal life. Worse still, the power, love, and soundness of the Spirit had been displaced by a spirit of fear and anxiety. To correct this, Timothy must fan the glowing ember of the Spirit into a vibrant

---

[6]Simon the Magician was to learn this the hard way (Acts 8:17-24). Similarly, the seven sons of Sceva failed in their attempt to highjack the good things of the Spirit (Acts 19:14-16).

and life-giving fire. In this way, the Holy Spirit will once again be the principle energizing presence in Timothy's life and ministry.

This tremendous experience of public affirmation should teach Timothy another important lesson. Since laying on of hands is a sign of affirmation and endorsement, he must exercise caution in this regard. As he lays his hands on persons and prays, he must not publicly approve of someone who is living in sin (1 Tim 5:22).

The Spirit of prophecy and the end times (1 Tim 4:1-8; 2 Tim 3:1-9). The writers of the New Testament consistently link the Holy Spirit with the end times and the Pastorals are no exception. In these letters Paul contributes some unique material about the end times but also carries forward some common themes as well.

The precise phrase "The Spirit clearly says" only appears here in the New Testament. The word for "clearly" or "expressly" is *rhētōs* and is also unique to this passage. Since *rhētōs* primarily relates to spoken words, as in the sense of "rhetoric," one wonders about the precise meaning of 1 Timothy 4:1. Is Paul referencing some repeated utterance of the Spirit that was spoken aloud during early Christian worship services? This seems to have been the case with words like *Abba* and phrases such as "Jesus is Lord." Could there have been an articulated prophetic utterance that said perilous times would come in the last days? Has this prophetic word become so common that Paul can now refer to it for purposes of instruction? Or does the phrase "The Spirit clearly says" simply serve the same purpose as "Hear what the Spirit says," an oft-repeated phrase in the book of Revelation (see Rev 2:7, 11, 17, 29; 3:6, 13, 22)? Then again, "The Spirit clearly says" may simply refer to the Spirit-inspired Scriptures (see Heb 3:7-11; 10:15-16).[7] In any case, the phrase "The Spirit clearly says" is rare but its content is common. What the Spirit says is that in the last days evil will increase, a common Jewish apocalyptic theme and one shared by Jesus and the early church. What Paul says in 1 Timothy 4:1 sounds very similar to what he has said in 2 Thessalonians 2:3. In both places the apostle speaks of apostasy, or

---

[7]Paul's conventional quotation formula for Scripture is *gegraptai* or "it stands written." He never writes, "The Spirit says" much less "The Spirit clearly says."

falling away from the faith. The general idea of apostasy is repeated in 2 Timothy 3:1 as well. Here Paul states that terrible times lay ahead during the last days.

In the Thessalonian correspondence, Paul presents the big picture of what must come to pass prior to the last days. However, in the Pastorals, Paul zooms in on the kinds of apostasy that will characterize the final days before the coming of Christ. Persons will be more open to deceiving spirits than to the Holy Spirit. They will pay heed to heresies taught by demons rather than submit to sound doctrine. To make matters worse, these false teachers practice religious asceticism, forbidding persons to marry and designating certain foods as unclean (1 Tim 4:1-4).

In a similar way, 2 Timothy details some of the sinful qualities of the apostates. A carnal egocentricity drives these heretics to an arrogant self-indulgence characterized by a brutal disregard for the needs of others. Such persons are impulsive, instinctively follow the ways of the flesh, and do great harm to others (2 Tim 3:1-6).

What makes this scenario even more frightening is that all of this is happening within the church. Demonically inspired false teachers are gathering to themselves persons who are more attracted to the deeds of the flesh than to truly loving God. The whole mess is wrapped in a cloak of religiosity but has no real interest in the true power of God. These misguided souls are always eager to learn about spiritual things, so called, but never submit to the Holy Spirit.

Although the trouble is complex and multifaceted, Paul's answer is straightforward. First, Timothy must look to Jesus as his prime example for fighting evil in the end times. Just as Jesus made a good confession of faith before Pontius Pilate, Timothy must do the same in the face of end-time heretics and adversaries. Relatedly, he must distance himself from evildoers and be spiritually prepared to meet Jesus at his second coming (1 Tim 6:12-16). Again, the principle of personal ethics and the eschaton are brought together in Paul's thought (Titus 2:12-15). The second coming is a time of moral accountability and Paul wants Timothy to be ready. Second, Timothy must give heed to Paul's example and counsel. On the one hand, he must expose the heretics and their false teaching (1 Tim 4:1-6). On the other hand, he must hold on to the teaching he has received from the apostle Paul. Moreover, he is to emulate Paul's pure intentions in ministry and follow his example in every regard. Above all, Timothy must immerse himself in the Scriptures. Only the Word of God can teach him what he should do and say in every situation in ministry (2 Tim 3:10-17).

SUMMARY THOUGHTS

First and Second Timothy and Titus are the only epistles directly addressed to pastors in the New Testament. As such, they give us unique insight into the leadership of the early church. For example, the Pastorals reflect the state of the church at the close of the apostolic period. The astute reader can pick up on an underlying sense of urgency on the part of the apostle Paul. Paul wants to make sure that Timothy and Titus are ready to take up the helm when he passes from the scene. They too must know what makes for good church leadership and how to discipline that leadership when the occasion arises. They must also know how to handle heretics and counter their false teachings. Above all, they must resist being embroiled in worthless arguments that have nothing to do with true faith.

When addressing all these concerns, Paul points to the powerful and varied ministry of the Holy Spirit. When it comes to authentic ministry, regeneration by the Holy Spirit is paramount. Also, the calling of the Spirit must be accompanied by the gifts of the Spirit. All that comes from the Holy Spirit must be safeguarded and cultivated. A minister must be able to hear the voice of the Holy Spirit, especially the Spirit's warning about heresy and apostasy in the last days.

WHAT DOES IT MEAN FOR ME?

Throughout the Pastorals, one senses the caring heart of the apostle Paul. He recognized the special callings of Timothy and Titus. He affirmed the gifts of the Spirit in their lives by laying his hands on them and praying. They became his disciples and he was careful to provide them with a good model for them to copy in ministry. He wants them to be his successors in the church and will counsel and exhort them until the very end.

All of this provides invaluable guidance for us as believers and leaders in the church. Prayerfully consider the following in your effort to grow in grace and to effectively serve the Lord.

+ The central theme of the Pastorals has so much to offer us in ministry. Paul was the mentoring pastor of these two great pastors. Each of us needs a mature spiritual mentor in our lives. We need a sterling example of faith and ministry so that we can render the same level of service to the Lord. There are a number of ways to pray here. First, if you don't have a reliable mentor in the Lord, pray that God would send one your way. Joshua had Moses, Elisha had Elijah, Mark had Peter, and Timothy and Titus had Paul. Second, pray that you might become a mentor to someone in ministry. No doubt persons have contributed to your life and ministry and now it is your turn to invest your gifts and experiences in others.

+ Timothy and Titus were frustrated with trying to sort out the many myths, false teachings, and religious-looking practices that existed among their congregations. Their troubles can certainly serve as a point of prayer for us. How much of our work is spent on things that do not matter to the kingdom of God? Are we easily lured into pious-sounding arguments that add nothing to the church? Pray now that the Holy Spirit will grant you the wisdom to discern the truth from what is false, to perceive what is important from what doesn't matter. There are things that look and sound spiritual, but they are really just frustrating diversions that keep us from being effective ministers for God. Pray that you can know the difference and act accordingly.

+ There is a mystery to God's redemptive work in the world (1 Tim 3:16). We are completely saved by grace, but there must be a faith-filled response to that grace. That is why Paul commands

Timothy to guard the good deposit that dwells within him. Pray that God will continually reveal ways in which you can guard the good deposit that he has placed in you.

✦ Somehow Timothy had become fearful, felt powerless, and lacked stability in his heart and emotions. In response, Paul directs him to the true nature and character of the Holy Spirit. If you are experiencing the same things as Timothy, prayerfully read Scriptures that speak of the Holy Spirit. We must consciously appropriate the power, love, and stability that can only come by way of the enablement of the Spirit (2 Tim 1:7; see also 1 Thess 1:5).

✦ The Pastorals let us know that it is possible to lose sight of the gifts that the Lord has given us. Yet Paul states we can bring these gifts back to life. We can fan into flame the glowing ember of the Holy Spirit that remains in our hearts. Pray that God will enable you to clearly see what gifts he has implanted in your life. Pray also that he might reveal how you can cultivate these gifts to full effectiveness in ministry.

✦ Paul exhorts Timothy to recall points of affirmation in his life. He speaks of prophecies, laying on of hands, and the like. These great experiences can serve as foundation stones that grant us stability and strength in ministry. Pray that the Lord bring to your mind points of affirmation and empowerment in your life. Pray that these affirming experiences empower you to actualize your calling in new and creative ways.

✦ The end-time prophecy of the Spirit is not very encouraging. The Spirit says that things will become increasingly worse in the last days and the church will not be exempt from troubling times. Yet a well-placed warning can save us from grief. The Spirit has given us a "heads up" so that we might not be caught off guard. Pray that you will be the kind of person who will rise above the apostasy of the last days and serve as a strong pillar of faith unto the second coming of Christ.

14

The HOLY SPIRIT
in HEBREWS

THE TESTIMONY OF THE SPIRIT

*God also testified to it by signs, wonders and various miracles, and by gifts
of the Holy Spirit distributed according to his will.*

HEBREWS 2:4 NIV

THE EPISTLE TO THE HEBREWS marks a transition within the New
Testament canon. With the study of Hebrews, the work moves on from
the Pauline corpus and enters the General Epistles. These letters are
called "general" not because of their content but because of their destination. Unlike Paul who clearly addresses his recipients, as in "to the
Romans," "to the Galatians" and the like, the General Epistles speak
more broadly with regard to destination. Hence we have expressions
such as "to the Hebrews," "to the twelve tribes scattered abroad" (Jas 1:1),
and "to the exiles scattered throughout the provinces" (1 Pet 1:1).

Hebrews grapples with a problem that is present in nearly every book
of the New Testament. That problem is the relationship between historic Judaism and the birth and growth of Christianity. The complexity
of the relationship lies in the fact that it is a living relationship, one that
is on the move, progressing along the path of God's perfect will in
Christ. As such, the writers of the New Testament are constantly engaged in a "yes . . . but no . . ." dialogue with the Judaism of their day.
Yes the historic roots of Christianity and Judaism are the same, but no
they are not theologically and experientially identical.

This continuity/discontinuity rubric was inaugurated by the coming of Jesus and the outpouring of the Holy Spirit at Pentecost. These two paradigm-altering events mean that the old must give way to the new, and nothing can be the same again.

Yet some in the church were very slow to accept that God's end-time plan of redemption had finally arrived in Christ. The writers of the New Testament, and especially the apostle Paul, continually confront this kind of spiritual inertia and are at pains to overcome it. For example, Paul clarifies the relationship between Judaism and Christianity in terms of human development. Judaism represents the faith in its childhood, but Christianity is the faith of adulthood. He argues that adolescence is real and important but that one is not meant to stay there (Gal 4:1-11). Continuing, Paul explains that the relationship between Judaism and Christianity is like the growth of a tree. The roots and trunk are real and necessary, but it is the branches that express God's vibrant, forward-reaching redemption in the world (Rom 11:17-21).

This is precisely the challenge confronting the writer of Hebrews. Messianic Jews are being pressured by their Jewish contemporaries to reinstate Judaism as the sole religious paradigm for their lives (Heb 10:1-12). Even though they have certainly received the gospel in all of its fullness (Heb 10:32), they have grown weary of being badgered for their faith in Christ and want to "shrink back" from God's offer of grace (Heb 10:38-39; 12:3). Many want to reenter the synagogue and blend into the Judaism of their day as though the Christ-event never happened (Heb 6:1-6).

The author of Hebrews meets this challenge head on. He presents two major arguments against the notion of returning to a form of Judaism that rejects Christ. The first and foundational argument is that Jesus is better than anything that Judaism has to offer. Jesus is coequal with the Father and is thus the supreme and final revelation of God (Heb 1:1-3). His prophetic status is beyond Moses (Heb 3:2-6); his priestly office is eternal on the order of Melchizedek (Heb 5:6-10; 7:1-28); and his sacrifice is ever present, completely effective, and never ending (Heb 9:26; 10:10-12). For all these things, his covenant surpasses all previous covenants and engenders a better way of faith (Heb 7:22; 8:6-12). Now that the Messiah has come, the salvific significance of the sacrifices, offerings, and rituals of the temple have been surpassed in Christ.

The second major argument emphasizes the essential role of the Holy Spirit in the life of the believer. To trust in a form of Judaism that rejects Jesus as the Messiah is to reject the end-time testimony of the Holy Spirit. This is true because the miracle-working power of the Spirit is God's own testimony for Christ and the church. The charismatic presence of the Spirit points the way to full and complete redemption. To deliberately disassociate with the church is to turn one's back on Jesus and his cross and to treat the strategic plan of the Father with contempt. In sum, to take the giant step backward into the synagogue is to deny the dynamic redemption of the Trinity. It means to lose the fellowship of the Spirit and be closed off to the revelatory voice of God. To neglect so great a salvation is an insult to the Spirit of grace.

PAUSE FOR PRAYER

In Hebrews, the Holy Spirit is the voice of God. When referring to Scripture, Hebrews employs phrases like "the Holy Spirit says" or "the Holy Spirit also testifies." So for Hebrews, there is no message from God apart from the Spirit of God. Correspondingly, there is no hearing from God apart from the Holy Spirit. There is a divine/human cooperation at work here. The Holy Spirit speaks, but we must listen. Pray now that there will be an ongoing sensitivity to the address of the Spirit in your life. Pray that as you read the Scriptures, you will hear the living voice of the Holy Spirit and discern God's perfect will for your life.

THE PRESENCE OF THE HOLY SPIRIT IN HEBREWS

The testimony of the Spirit: signs, wonders, and miracles (Heb 2:1-4).
Hebrews employs a number of methods to prove that the new covenant in Jesus is far superior to the old covenant made with Moses. For example, the author argues *a minore ad maius*, or "from the lesser to the greater." Jewish tradition taught that the law was delivered to Moses by

the hand of angels (see Acts 7:53; Gal 3:19). By contrast, the gospel came directly from God by way of his only Son, Jesus Christ. If the mediated and temporary revelation of the law was spiritually and morally binding, how much more authority is in the eternal gospel of God's Son, Jesus Christ? That is why the recipients of Hebrews dared not let the gospel slip from their grasp.[1]

To add strength to his argument, the author summons the charismatic witness of the Spirit. The word for "witness" in Hebrews 2:4 is a legal term that indicates corroborating testimony in a court of law.[2] The Father has not only spoken the gospel in words but has also acted in the deeds of his Son and through the power of the Holy Spirit. This means that the miracle-working power of the Spirit is God's own testimony to the authenticity of the new covenant in Christ.

This theme of the witness of the Spirit is found throughout the New Testament. When justifying his special calling as Messiah, Jesus referenced the miraculous power of the Holy Spirit (Lk 4:16-20). The same holds true for the ministry of the first apostles in the temple. The validity of their words about Jesus was substantiated by signs and wonders (Acts 5:12). In a similar manner, Paul demonstrates the authenticity of his ministry by pointing to the power of the Spirit (Rom 15:19). Finally, the Corinthians should know that Paul is a true apostle because of the signs, wonders, and miracles that accompanied his ministry (2 Cor 12:12).

The phrase "signs, wonders, and various miracles" as found in Hebrews 2:4 is practically a stock expression in the New Testament. For example, some combination of the words "signs and wonders" appears nine times in the book of Acts alone. Additionally, each of these words conveys a slightly different aspect of the power of the Spirit. The word *sēmeion* or "sign" speaks to the teaching effect of the miracle.

---

[1]The image conveyed here depicts a moment of negligence on the part of a boat tender. The mooring rope has slipped from his grasp and the boat is silently gliding away. He's now a castaway, cut off from his only hope of rescue. In a spiritual sense, this is what will happen to anyone who neglects the salvation of the Lord.

[2]The association of the Holy Spirit with the concept of legal testimony is not unique to Hebrews. The Gospel of John frequently refers to the Spirit as the *paraklētos*, or legal defense attorney, who defends the faith in the hostile courts of this world (John 14:16, 26; 15:26).

The word *dynamis* conveys the sheer power of the miracle. Finally, the word *teras* contains a forward-looking, predictive element.

Clearly there was a widespread and pluriform manifestation of the Spirit in the early church. The Spirit was not only varied in effect but also in meaning. The work of the Spirit meant that Jesus was God's Messiah, the kingdom of God had dawned, and the church was God's Spirit-filled beachhead on earth, portending the complete consummation of all things in Christ.

Hebrews preserves an additional aspect of the Spirit. As a member of the Trinity, the divine Spirit is coequal with the Father and the Son. As God, the Holy Spirit is absolutely sovereign over his will and actions. Hence the Spirit is in control over the granting and distribution of spiritual gifts and over the various ministerial callings in the church (Acts 2:4). It is the Spirit who takes the initiative to express the goodness of God. This means that the Holy Spirit is not subject to any human bidding, but the other way around. As believers, we have the privilege of knowing and doing the Spirit's will for the benefit of the church (Eph 1:17). We can humbly seek the best gifts, but the bestowal of those gifts is subject to the sovereign will of the Holy Spirit (Heb 2:4; 1 Cor 12:11).

The Holy Spirit's testimony to us (Heb 8:1-13; 10:15-17). In Hebrews 2:1-4, the Father testified to the truth of the gospel by way of the miracle-working power of the Holy Spirit. However in Hebrews 10:15, it is the Holy Spirit who testifies to us about the all-sufficiency of Christ. The phrase "First he says . . ." is the standard quotation formula for Hebrews. The author views Scripture as the voice of the Holy Spirit. Clearly Hebrews believes in the verbal inspiration of Scripture and that this inspiration comes from the Holy Spirit.

The testimony of the Spirit spoken of here can be found in Jeremiah 31:33. The prophet Jeremiah, speaking under the inspiration of the Spirit, foresees a new covenant inscribed not on tables of stone but on the minds and hearts of those who truly love God (see also Ezek 36:26-27). Thus in a manner similar to Paul, Hebrews contrasts the superficial quality of the covenant made with Moses with the deeply spiritual covenant effected by Christ (2 Cor 3:6-11). It is on the basis of the new covenant in Christ that God promises to remember our sins no more. For all these reasons, the testimony of the Spirit on the hearts of believers is so much more powerful than dead letters carved in tables of stone.

The message of Hebrews is clear. The gift of the Holy Spirit and all the gifts granted by the Spirit constitute God's testimony to the new covenant in the first century. However, every generation needs God's confirming testimony of the Holy Spirit. That is why, as Peter so clearly taught on the Day of Pentecost, the promise of the Spirit is multigenerational and transcultural. The person and power of the Holy Spirit is God's inestimable gift freely given to all whom the Lord will call (Acts 2:38-39).

The Holy Spirit and the sacrifice of Christ (Heb 9:7-15; 10:15-17). As noted, Hebrews argues *a minore ad maius* in order to prove the superiority of Christ. Hebrews employs another powerful tool of argumentation; that is, he speaks of type and fulfillment.[3] This means that all of the major institutions of first-century Judaism—the law, the tabernacle, the priesthood, the sacrifices, etc.—are merely types that foreshadow the coming of Christ. Stated differently, Jesus is the fulfillment of everything contained in Judaism. Therefore with regard to the problem at hand, the writer of Hebrews asks, "Why would someone want to return to the realm of type when one can enjoy the reality of fulfillment?"

The type and fulfillment pattern is perfectly set forth in Hebrews 9:7-15. Here Hebrews speaks of the temporary and insufficient ministry of the priests in the tabernacle of the Old Testament. The priests and the sacrifices they offer are only a type of the infinitely better sacrifice of Christ. Also, the priests had to offer animal sacrifices for their own sins before they could minister on behalf of the people (Heb 5:3). The point is that the imperfect, external, and repeated sacrifices of the tabernacle could never completely cleanse the human conscience from sin.

---

[3]In so doing, Hebrews echoes elements found in the writings of the Greek philosopher Plato (ca. 428–348 BCE) and later on, the Hellenized Jewish philosopher Philo (20 BCE–50 CE). In this system, present realities are only "types" or "symbols" of more substantial realities in the spirit realm.

Hebrews states that the inherent dysfunction of the priests and the tabernacle constitute a message from the Holy Spirit. This was the Spirit's way of showing that God's complete plan of redemption was yet to come in Christ (Heb 9:8; see also Heb 7:18-19). Through the eternal Spirit, Jesus, who knew no sin, offered up his body in sacrifice for our sins (Heb 4:15). His perfect and all-powerful sacrifice was brought into the very throne room of God in heaven. This deeply spiritual work of God in Christ is able to cleanse our consciences from sin and empower us to serve God and to eventually inherit all the riches of the kingdom. In all these ways, Jesus has been made the mediator of the new covenant, which is far superior to anything offered in the covenant of Moses (Heb 12:24).

The pattern of type and fulfillment and the witness of the Holy Spirit continues throughout chapter 10. The law and the tabernacle are simply a "shadow" or "copy" of the good things to come in Christ (Heb 8:5; 9:23-24). This means the things contained in the law of Moses are not the reality of which they speak. That is why the repeated sacrifices of bulls and goats offered by sinful mortal priests can never fully cleanse the conscience of sin (Heb 10:1-4). All these things simply point to Jesus Christ, the eternal high priest (Heb 5:6-10) who knew no sin and who offered up his own body as a sacrifice for sin (Heb 10:7-14).

So many wonderful truths are set forth in Hebrews. The internal work of the Holy Spirit on the hearts and minds of the faithful is infinitely more effective than legal precepts etched in stone. The eternal and flawless sacrifice of Christ far surpasses the blood of bulls and goats offered by sinful priests (Heb 9:11-14). The power of the cross inaugurates a kind of divine forgetfulness whereby the Father pledges to remember our sins no more. Inspired by the Holy Spirit, the prophets foresaw all of this and their words serve as an infallible testimony to the all-sufficiency of Christ.

Insulting the Spirit of grace (Heb 6:1-6; 10:25-31). Hebrews has been relentless in promoting the absolute supremacy of Christ. Any thought of returning to the synagogue is diametrically opposed to the new covenant in Christ. Consequently, those who deliberately reject the free gift of salvation in Christ are condemned in the harshest of terms. To disassociate with fellow Christians is to regard the cross of Christ with contempt. It is to identify with the enemies of God who, apart from Christ, have no sacrifice for their sins. It is as if they have run roughshod over God's Son. Such persons regard the blood of the new covenant as *koinos*, "common" or "unclean."[4] Furthermore, since Jesus offered up his body through the eternal Holy Spirit, to treat Christ's sacrifice as an unholy thing is to insult the Spirit of grace. The benevolent heart of the Spirit is offended in the most egregious way.

In this way the entire Trinity has been accosted by their incredibly boorish behavior. The Father's final and complete offer of salvation is regarded as nothing. Jesus the Son has been stomped underfoot. The Holy Spirit's offer of grace is treated as some repulsive, unclean thing that must be cast aside. All who express such impiety will not escape judgment.

The warning of the Holy Spirit (Heb 3:7-11). None of this was done in ignorance or for a lack of true experience in God. Hebrews says that those who forsook the new covenant have been enlightened, they have "tasted" the gift of God, they have experienced the fellowship of the Holy Spirit, and they have enjoyed the supernatural powers of the kingdom.[5] At one time, they stood firm in the faith and willingly suffered persecution for Christ (Heb 10:32-34). Yet despite all this, they still cast away their only hope of salvation. For such persons, there is no alternative platform for redemption (Heb 6:1-6).

It is for these reasons that Hebrews includes some ominous warnings from the Holy Spirit (Heb 12:25). No doubt the Spirit is a comfort and advocate for those who believe. Yet in the presence of unbelief and rebellion, the Holy Spirit speaks forth the judgment of God. Hence, "the Holy Spirit says" not to harden our hearts as in the days of the

---

[4]*Koinos* is the same word used by Peter to describe the unclean animals that appeared to him in his vision at Simon the tanner's house (Acts 10:14). Those who trample the Son of God underfoot regard the blood of Jesus the same as the blood of some ritually unclean animal, not fit to be offered on the altar of God.

[5]The word for "partaker" or "fellowship" is *metochos* and means "to have a stake in." At one time, they had "bought into" the person and work of the Holy Spirit in a real way.

exodus. If one does not heed the voice of God, that person will not inherit the promised rest of God. Unless they repent, a day of reckoning is at hand. Barring this, they have fallen into the hands of the only One who can justly exact vengeance. They must return to Christ or they have cast their lot with the enemies of God. Such persons have but one thing to look forward to: divine judgment expressed in unquenchable fire (Heb 10:27).

SUMMARY THOUGHTS

From beginning to end, the author of Hebrews has only one goal in sight. He is determined to present Jesus as the only means of salvation. The religious pluralism of the Greco-Roman world is a hindrance, not a help. All roads may lead to Rome, but not all paths lead to God. Jesus is the only way to the Father. Even Judaism, the majestic religion of the Jews, is devoid of redemptive power so long as it rejects Jesus as the chosen Messiah. Judaism may well be the soil from which Christianity grew, but one cannot stay there. To do so is to remain buried in a faith that has run its course. That course led to Christ. There is no turning back now. Like Lot's wife, to look back is to disparage God's free gift of salvation in his Son. To reject the Father's ultimate and final plan of salvation in Jesus is to regard the cross with contempt and insult the gracious offering of the Holy Spirit. All hope is not lost (Heb 6:9), but the situation is grave. The recipients of Hebrews must return to Jesus, fully identify with the community of faith, and willingly suffer the consequences of confessing Jesus in a fallen world.

WHAT DOES IT MEAN FOR ME?

Hebrews expresses an extraordinary passion for Christ. The author's constant refrain is the exclusivity of Christ. Jesus is our only Savior. Jesus is the locus of God's saving grace in the world. For these reasons, he is absolutely intolerant of any claims to salvation apart from Jesus.

Hebrews also has a passion for souls. The author cares deeply for those who are going astray. He spares no effort in bringing them back into the fold. On the one hand, he knows the matchless love of God. On the other hand, he is aware of the fearful wrath of God. Thus he argues, persuades, and warns.

In some respects the problems in Hebrews are so extreme that they defy contemporary application. Few in the church would think of forsaking Christ for another religion. However, the concerns of Hebrews certainly apply in an analogous way. Cultural and religious pluralism are increasing daily. In many quarters, to stridently claim that redemption can only be found in Christ has fallen out of fashion. Persecution, both subtle and overt, is on the rise. In this sense, the epistle to the Hebrews has a lot to offer. It gives us a lot to pray about.

+ The central theme of Hebrews may be expressed in terms of religion versus relationship. There is something oddly comforting about religion. Its parts and procedures can be identified and practiced. Religion is something that can be done and measured. Yet Hebrews does not trumpet the virtues of religion. Rather, the highest value in Hebrews is entering into a genuine relationship with the living God. This relationship has been secured by the new covenant in Christ and must be received on the basis of faith alone (Hebrews 11:1-40). Once received, this relationship is infused and empowered by the Holy Spirit. Pray now that you forever forsake the path of religion and by faith hold on to that life-giving relationship in Jesus.

+ Hebrews exhorts us to spiritual vigilance (Heb 2:1; 3:1; 10:23). We must not allow the complexities of modern life to distract us from serving Christ. The image of inadvertently allowing our lifeboat to slip away is a haunting one. No one deliberately wants to be abandoned and without hope in the world. Yet our singular focus on Christ can become obscured. We can drift away. Pray now that the Spirit will help you renew your focus on Christ. Pray that you can keep a tight grip on Jesus, our sole lifeline for salvation.

+ Ironically, a major aspect of modern secularism is religious pluralism. All faiths are framed as equally valid. To claim that one's own faith is exclusively true to the detriment of all others is to commit the secular sin of intolerance. Yet this is precisely the message of Hebrews. Pray that God will give you the spiritual clarity and the moral courage to proclaim Christ as the only true Savior of the world, regardless of the cost.

✦ The recipients of Hebrews were being worn down. They were constantly being harassed for their faith in Christ. They were swerving off the narrow path of the gospel. Their knees were about to buckle (Heb 12:12). In response, the author gives the recipients a good dose of "situational awareness." Wake up! Realize what's happening to you! Get back on course! Perhaps you are being worn down in the faith. Hebrews can be a "wake up call" for you. Pray that the Spirit would reveal those areas of your spiritual walk that need to be strengthened. Pray that the Spirit would give you vital course corrections that can get you back on track with the Lord.

✦ For many, life in the Spirit is understood in terms of joyous celebration. Yet the writer of Hebrews preserves another vital tradition about worship. Hebrews promotes a healthy fear of the Lord. If breaking the law of Moses brought judgment, one dare not trifle with Jesus! Pray now that your worship in the Spirit be a well-rounded worship, consisting not only of exuberant joy but also of fearful celebration, all the while remembering that our God is a consuming fire (Heb 12:29).

15

The HOLY SPIRIT *in* JAMES

THE WISDOM OF GOD

*Every good and perfect gift is from above, coming down from the Father of
the heavenly lights, who does not change like shifting shadows.*

JAMES 1:17 NIV

FOR THE PURPOSES OF this study, the epistle of James is prob-
lematic. James may be one of the earliest, if not the earliest, epistles in
the New Testament. As such, this Jewish encyclical is limited in its theological formulation and jargon (Jas 1:1). For example, there is no
mention of the cross of Christ or its atoning benefit for believers. Also,
the word *church* does not appear in James at all. In its place we find the
word *synagōgē* or "synagogue" (Jas 2:2). This may mean that Messianic
Jews of the diaspora may not yet have made a formal break with the
Judaism of their day and are still meeting in the synagogue. Hence,
James's addressees may not have had the benefit of belonging to an
exclusively Christian community of faith.

All of this means that the charismatic activity of the Spirit, so present
among the churches, may not have been as evident among messianic
Jews still attending synagogue. This does not mean that James is un-
aware of the special ministry of the Holy Spirit. The Scriptures state that
he was present in the upper room and spoke in tongues like all the rest
(Acts 1:14). James also knows that Cornelius and his household, even

though they were Gentiles, received the Holy Spirit and spoke in tongues just like on the Day of Pentecost (Acts 10:45-46; 15:7-9).

Nevertheless, James must speak in terms amenable to the special context of his recipients. If they are still meeting in the synagogue and worshiping with non-Messianic Jews, jargon peculiar to the Spirit's work among the churches would not be helpful. In fact, it has been argued that not a single reference to the Holy Spirit can be found in James. There are only two instances of the word *pneuma* or "spirit" in James. The first appears in James 2:26. Here James says that the body is dead apart from the spirit. The word *spirit* in this verse no doubt refers to the human spirit that departs the body at the point of death. The second instance can be found in James 4:5, and the translations are divided on how to interpret the word *spirit*. Should it be "Spirit" (see the NASB) or "spirit" (see the NIV)?

Nevertheless, a case can be made that James contains many elements reflecting the Holy Spirit. A long-standing interpretation is that James's use of wisdom parallels how the Spirit is used throughout the Scriptures (see Ex 31:3; 35:31). Isaiah says that the Spirit of the Lord is the Spirit of wisdom (Is 11:2). This kind of jargon is carried over into the New Testament (Acts 6:3, 10; Eph 1:17). For example, just as Jesus exhorts his disciples to ask the Father for the Holy Spirit (Lk 11:11-13), James exhorts his readers to ask for wisdom (Jas 1:5). Just as the Holy Spirit comes down from heaven (Mt 3:16; Lk 3:22), James represents the wisdom of God as coming down from heaven (Jas 3:17). Moreover, this heavenly wisdom of James consists of qualities that reflect the fruit of the Spirit in Paul (Gal 5:22-23). Even though James does not specifically speak of the gifts of the Spirit, he does say that every good and perfect gift comes down from the Father (Jas 1:17). Finally, some of the worship experiences described in James are linked to the work of the Spirit elsewhere in Scripture. James speaks of anointing with oil, laying on of hands, and healing (Jas 5:14-15). He also welcomes a multitude of strong prayers that have the power to accomplish God's will in a miraculous way.

The sum of the matter is this. Even though James does not mention the church, the cross, the blood of Christ, or the resurrection, he certainly believes these important doctrines of the faith. Similarly, even though he does not explicitly say "Holy Spirit" or "gifts of the Spirit," he certainly believes in these critical components of the faith.

PAUSE FOR PRAYER

If there was ever a need for the wisdom of God, it is now. Traditional values have been turned upside down. A common sense of what is right and wrong has vanished. Somehow, a love for God and his holiness has been construed as hate. On the other hand, an unreflective affirmation of all behaviors, so long as they are consensual, is seen as love. The shining light in this moral morass is James's promise that if we ask God for wisdom, he will certainly grant our request (Jas 1:5). There can be no doubt that God's wisdom is conveyed by the Holy Spirit (Col 1:9). Pray now for the wisdom that only the Spirit can give. Pray that amid the spiritual treachery so indicative of our day, you can be wise as serpents but harmless as doves (Mt 10:16).

THE PRESENCE OF THE HOLY SPIRIT IN JAMES

The Spirit of fidelity (Jas 4:1-5). In all our knowing, we should know this: God is a person. In fact, in a way that can never be fully understood, God is three Persons (Mt 28:19) in one Lord (Deut 6:4). The members of the Trinity have existed from eternity in perfect fidelity to one another. It is God's will that the familial relationship enjoyed by the Trinity be experienced by his people as well. This is why fidelity, or faithfulness in relationships, is so dear to the Lord. In contrast, unfaithfulness is especially grievous to God. That is why Israel's frequent sin of idolatry is described in terms of infidelity or adultery (Jer 3:8-10; Ezek 16:30-35). Such unfaithfulness is an insult to God and invites divine retribution of the strongest kind.

James takes up the motif of spiritual adultery in the Old Testament and applies it to the church. As the prophets of old, James charges his recipients with hedonism, unbridled lust, and adultery. The "friendship" spoken of in James 4:4 surely echoes the inordinate liaisons of Israel's past wherein she committed "adultery" by joining herself to false gods

(Hos 4:10-14). Thus the unconscionable desires of his recipients have compromised their relationship with God. The precious indwelling of the Holy Spirit is being viewed with contempt.

God is not unmoved by their disloyalty. The integrity of the indwelling Spirit is being threatened by an unholy attraction to the world. The person of the Holy Spirit has been insulted and for this reason, the Father has an empathic longing for his Spirit. As was the case with ancient Israel, there is but one hope for restoration: repent.

The Holy Spirit: the wisdom of God (Jas 3:13-17). If the fear of the Lord is the beginning of wisdom for Solomon (Prov 9:10), the indwelling of the Spirit is the reception of wisdom for James. As noted, the link between wisdom and the Spirit in James is strong. For example, James states that the wisdom of God comes down "from above." The imagery of wisdom descending from heaven sounds very similar to the Holy Spirit descending upon Jesus at his baptism (Mt 3:16; Lk 3:22). Similarly, John joins together the ideas of "from above" and the Holy Spirit by affirming that being born from above means that one is born of the Spirit (Jn 3:1-8). And finally, throughout Paul's writings, there is the close association of the Spirit with wisdom (1 Cor 12:8; Col 1:9). All of this supports the view that when James says "wisdom" he is thinking of "Spirit."

Furthermore, when James speaks of "wisdom" he is not talking about retaining complex doctrinal teachings or accumulating facts. Rather, wisdom for James is the outworking of the Spirit in the life of every believer. For him, the wisdom of God is something that can be seen in a good life that is completely consecrated to the Lord. In sum, for James wisdom can be observed in godly service to others done in humility (Jas 3:13). Wisdom is the "good fruit" produced by the Holy Spirit and evidenced in purity, peace, gentle consideration, and mercy (Jas 3:17; see Gal 5:22). Just as the Holy Spirit is a gift that can be asked for, divine wisdom is a gift that can be requested as well.

The Holy Spirit and every good gift (Jas 1:17; 5:13-18). The "coming down from above" jargon is also found in James 1:17. These words, in conjunction with the word *gift*, guide the mind to think of the gift of the Holy Spirit, which comes down from heaven. However, the inclusion of the word *every* tends to broaden the sense of the verse beyond the singular gift of the Holy Spirit. James appears to be speaking of each and every gift among a number of gifts. In an impressionistic way, James conveys that every gift of the Father, the gift of the Spirit, and the gifts of the Spirit, are good through and through.[1] All of this is reliable, stable, and unchangeable. This is true because the God of all good gifts is immutable in his being and character and his glory can never be eclipsed by anything.

From this lofty expression of the benevolence of God, James then addresses good gifts that come from the Lord. He speaks of the gift of wisdom (Jas 1:5), the gift of knowing true worth (Jas 1:9-11), the gift of the crown of life (Jas 1:12), and so forth. Yet perhaps his most explicit references to the supernatural power of God come near the very end of his epistle.

In James 5:14, James affirms the gift of healing.[2] This gift of the Spirit featured prominently in the ministry of Jesus and the early church (Lk 5:17; Acts 4:30; 1 Cor 12:9, 28). He also includes the practice of anointing with oil. Although he doesn't explicitly mention the laying on of hands, the command to anoint with oil and to pray says as much.

The laying on of hands as a point of contact for the effectual grace of God was also practiced by Jesus and the early church (Mk 10:16; Acts 13:1-3). Even the gift of the Holy Spirit was commuted by the laying on of hands (Acts 8:17; 19:6). Taken all together, the anointing with oil, the laying on of hands, and faith-filled prayer create room for the kingdom of God to be realized in power. Not only is the person healed, but James asserts that their sins are forgiven. This might sound arbitrary except James envelopes this whole healing narrative with words of confession, fervency in prayer, and righteousness (Jas 5:16).

James seems to sense that the drama and power of his words, together with the extraordinary example of Elijah, might intimidate the

---

[1] The thoroughgoing goodness of the gifts is conveyed by the word *teleios* meaning "fully developed" or "mature."

[2] James does not use the conventional word for healing (*therapeuō*) but rather the word *sōzō*, "to save." *Sōzō* has a wide range of meanings including "rescue," "deliver," as well as "to save." When used in the context of sickness *sōzō* means "to heal."

more humble members of the church. Thus he is quick to remind his readers that Elijah was a human being just like all of us, yet God still heard his prayers (Jas 5:17). For James, the important thing is not the person who prays but the prayers of the person.

SUMMARY THOUGHTS

As was the case with his half-brother Jesus, James communicates by way of stories, word-pictures, and parables (Jas 1:10-11; 2:1-5; 3:1-12). Often, he speaks on the level of impression, choosing to address the heart and not just the head. For this reason, his words lack the logic and substance so often present in the writings of Paul. Thus, Martin Luther concluded that James was an epistle of straw.

Nothing could be further from the truth. There is more to James than first meets the eye. Even though James does not mention the cross, he boldly states that he is a servant of his glorious Lord, Jesus Christ (Jas 1:1; 2:1). To the dismay of Luther, James extolled the value of good works for salvation. Yet upon closer observance, he was simply calling for an authentic, living faith; a point that Paul would applaud. Some might even conclude that James is devoid of the Holy Spirit. Yet the presence of the Spirit in James occurs at a deeper level than one might expect. For him, the Spirit is the gift of God. The Spirit is the wisdom of God. The Spirit is the miracle-working power of God that answers prayer.

WHAT DOES IT MEAN FOR ME?

James speaks a reality that confronts the delusions of our time. James presents a simplicity that cuts through the stifling complexity of our day. He has no time for a superficial faith whose only goal is to serve the worldly desires of the self. He calls for reality in religion. True faith can be measured by good works that alleviate suffering. James is a New Testament prophet. His voice calls us to prayer.

+ There is no excuse for ingratitude. James says that every good and perfect gift comes down from the Father in heaven. Our lives should be an unending prayer of thanks for all the good gifts that

God showers on us each day. Do you want to have a joy-filled life? Pray that God will give you the gift of unending gratitude.

✦ We are tempted to think of wisdom in terms of intellectual ability or having the right answers. Remember that for James, wisdom does not consist of having good thoughts but in doing good deeds. It is as if the Spirit in James is saying, "Don't overthink this! Just do it!" Simply pray that God would give you the grace to do the right thing at the right time in the right way. When God answers that prayer, as he surely will, you will be a truly wise man or woman.

✦ For James, the wisdom of the Spirit reflects the character of God. When seeking wisdom, do not pray to know more about God; pray to be more like God.

✦ There is no greater joy than sensing that the God of healing and grace is working through you. Yet for James the work of God does not come uninvited. As God grants his Spirit to us, we must move toward him in faith. We must take action in the Spirit. James commands us to anoint the sick with oil. He commands us to earnestly pray for healing. He assures us that God will answer prayer. He comforts us by letting us know that Elijah was just a human being like everyone else and God used him mightily. All of this means that God wants to use you too, just as you are, right now. Pray that as God moves closer to you in his Spirit that you will move closer to him in faith so that you might do his will.

16

The HOLY SPIRIT *in* 1 *and* 2 PETER

GOD'S ANSWER TO SUFFERING FOR CHRIST

If you are insulted because of the name of Christ, you are blessed,
for the Spirit of glory and of God rests on you.

1 PETER 4:14 NIV

FIRST PETER WAS CLEARLY intended to be an encyclical. The letter was meant to circulate among the exiles scattered across a broad region of Asia Minor (1 Pet 1:1). As was the case with the epistle to the Hebrews, Messianic Jews were suffering for their faith in Christ (1 Pet 4:12-19). In fact, some form of the word *suffer* appears eighteen times in this brief letter. Peter often contextualizes their suffering for the gospel by referencing the Holy Spirit. He claims that to suffer for Christ is a sure sign that the "Spirit of glory" rests on them (1 Pet 4:14). Even the suffering and death of Jesus was brought to a definitive end by being raised by the Holy Spirit (1 Pet 3:18).

For Peter, the Spirit puts the concerns of this life in proper perspective. The Holy Spirit expands our horizons to the point of eternity and literally puts time in its place. *Everything* apart from the Trinity is seen to be transitory. Thus our present sufferings are temporary, lasting only "a little while" (1 Pet 1:6; 5:10). Believers are but foreigners in this world (1 Pet 1:17). It is the Spirit who empowers the prophets to escape their time-bound world and gain a glimpse of the gospel. Through the

Spirit, they capture a vision not shared by the angels. It is the selfsame Spirit who inspires Peter and the rest of the apostles to preach the gospel to their own generation (1 Pet 1:10-12). The timelessness of the Spirit was also present in the days of Noah through whom Christ preached to the souls who are now imprisoned (1 Pet 3:19-20).

Second Peter also emphasizes the inspiration of the Holy Spirit. Peter claims that the apostles did not follow cleverly devised myths (from the Greek *mythos*) when preaching the gospel. Rather, they were eyewitness of the Lord's majesty (2 Pet 1:16).[1] Second Peter also picks up on the importance of Noah for a proper understanding of the end times (compare 1 Pet 3:19-20 with 2 Pet 2:5). Both epistles link together Noah, preaching, and the Holy Spirit. However, 2 Peter includes a description of how the Holy Spirit inspired the prophets of old (2 Pet 1:19-21).

Thus for Peter, the Holy Spirit expresses punctuated revelations that consistently address the end of days (1 Pet 1:20; 4:7). The revelation of Christ is at hand (1 Pet 1:5-7), bringing indescribable joy and grace to the redeemed but fearful judgment to the disobedient (1 Pet 4:5, 17).

This present life has meaning insofar as the Spirit has sanctified a distinct and holy people of God. The elect are to be holy, for God, the one who called them, is holy. As such, the saints are to be both temple and priests offering up spiritual sacrifices to the Lord (1 Pet 1:16; 2:5).

Not only have believers been set apart by the Spirit but they have also been gifted by the Spirit. In agreement with Paul's more extensive teaching on the gifts, Peter says that each one is to use his or her spiritual gifts in service to others. Taking care to use one's gifts to the fullest reflects good stewardship toward God. Although Peter does not innumerate the gifts as Paul does, he does describe the gifts as *poikilos*, that is, "diversified" or "manifold." There are many kinds of gifts in the church and their proper use brings glory to God through Jesus Christ (1 Pet 4:10-11).

---

[1]Peter's reference to seeing the majestic splendor of Jesus may be a veiled reference to the Transfiguration. It was here that he, along with James and John, saw Jesus transfigured before his very eyes (Mt 17:1-8; Mk 9:1-8).

First Peter is a word of comfort for the persecuted. Its message will become increasingly important as society becomes more secular and less hospitable to the church. Peter promises that the Holy Spirit is well aware of the plight of God's people. In times like these, Peter's words must not only be heard, they must be received.

PAUSE FOR PRAYER

A major theme of 1 Peter is that believers must take the long view when it comes to suffering. When compared to eternity, our present sufferings are short-lived. Yet this does not mean that suffering for Christ has no meaning. The Holy Spirit can use suffering to forge a unique bond between the believer and Christ. Just as Christ suffered for the kingdom so too must believers suffer for God. Also, suffering can purify our faith, rendering it more precious than gold tried in fire. In fact, suffering for righteousness is a sure sign that the Holy Spirit is present in our lives.

None of this comes naturally for us. Suffering for doing what is right just doesn't seem fair. That is why Peter says we must "arm ourselves" with the same attitude that Christ had toward suffering. His agony on the cross culminated in his death to sin and being raised by the Spirit. Similarly, our willingness to suffer for righteousness' sake means that we have turned our back on the world of sin. We would rather experience the ire of the world than to participate in its folly. Pray now that your suffering for Christ might not be in vain. Pray that the Holy Spirit would grant you the right attitude to receive the full benefits of suffering for God.

THE PRESENCE OF THE HOLY SPIRIT IN PETER

The Holy Spirit and election (1 Peter 1:2). The doctrine of divine election is one of the most comforting and confounding teachings in the Bible. It is comforting to know that from eternity past, God knew his elect and determined to save them in Christ. It's confounding because all persons, regardless of whether they are elect or not, are expected to exercise faith and believe the gospel. It is comforting to know that God is sovereign and is in absolute control of all things. It is confounding in that we are personally responsible for our own moral choices and will be judged accordingly. It is comforting to rest in the eternal security of God's saving grace. It's confounding that some persons are not numbered among the elect and have no hope of salvation.

Although the doctrine of election entails many cardinal teachings of the faith, these truths exist in tension. At the heart of this tension is a sense of arbitrariness. Some are chosen while others are not. The absolute sovereignty of God seems to undermine human free will and moral accountability.

Peter's words about the Holy Spirit tend to dissipate some of this tension. He explains that God's foreknowledge is not the only operative factor with regard to the elect. There is a mutually supportive synergism between divine election and the sanctifying presence of the Holy Spirit (1 Pet 1:2). The word for sanctification is *hagiasmos* and literally means "separateness" or "holiness." So the elect have experienced the active, separating work of the Spirit in their lives. As such, those who have responded to the Spirit constitute God's special people, the church. Although Peter does not describe the mechanics of this sanctification, throughout the Scriptures believers are enjoined to cooperate with the Spirit in holiness (Rom 6:13; 12:1-2). As was the case with Paul, so it is with Peter. The coming of the Lord mandates holiness (2 Peter 3:11). In addition, Peter says that those who have been separated in the Spirit have also been obedient to Jesus Christ. Peter explains the elective process by assuring that the atoning blood of Christ is effectual for those who have faith. Sanctification, obedience, and faith all play a part in God's election. Again, we may never be able to fathom how all these elements come together to constitute the elect. Yet Peter confides that the Spirit is actively involved in the creation of God's elect. Just as God's special person, Jesus, was chosen before the foundation of the world (1 Pet 1:20), God's special people, the church, was chosen from the foundation of the world (1 Pet 2:9).

The Holy Spirit "rests" on the persecuted (1 Pet 4:14). For Peter, if the infinite goodness and holiness of Jesus invited the wrath of those steeped in sin, his disciples can expect no less (see also Jn 15:20). Simply put, to be like Christ is to share in the experiences of Christ and that includes suffering for Christ. Yet taking on the sufferings of Christ constitutes a special kind of fellowship with the Lord. It is a fellowship of those who are mature in faith and enjoy a boundless and complete commitment to Christ.

Relatedly, Peter speaks of being verbally abused or insulted (*oneidizō*) because of "the *name* of Christ" (see also 1 Pet 3:16). One of the ironies of the Bible is that the word *Christian* or *Christians* is quite rare. For example, the first instance of the word *Christians* is found in Acts 11:26. It was in the church at Antioch that believers were first called Christians. Believers did not call themselves Christians, but this was the label affixed to them by unbelievers. The suffix "ian" is a diminutive and so the word literally means "little Christs." Probably the opponents of the church used *Christian* in a negative way to shame the early church. King Agrippa's sarcastic response to Paul seems to be in the same vein. He questioned Paul about whether he really thought that in such a short time he could persuade the king to become a "Christian" (Acts 26:28).

Regardless of their pejorative intent, the term *Christian* stuck, for Peter has no problem addressing believers as those who bear the name of Christ. Moreover, his use of the term also occurs in the context of persecution. There can be little doubt that a willingness to be called a Christian made one subject to insult and persecution in the first century.

With regard to the Holy Spirit, Peter arrives at a fascinating theological conclusion. He claims that if someone is insulted because of the name of Christ, "the Spirit of glory and of God" *rests* (*anapauō*) on them. The precise phrase "the Spirit of glory" is only found here in the Bible. No doubt this is Peter's way of expressing the oft-repeated phrase "the King of glory" (Ps 24:7-10) or "the God of glory" (Ps 29:3; Acts 7:2; see also 1 Cor 2:8). Peter sees the Spirit as being equal with God. The phrases "of glory" and "of God" reflect Hebrew parallelism whereby repeated elements add majesty and force to one's expression. The Spirit is the glorious Spirit of God.

The words "the Spirit of glory . . . rests on" sounds very similar to the grand messianic prophecy of Isaiah 11:1-2. Here, the coming Messiah is described as a shoot springing forth from the stump of Jesse. The hallmark of this promised Messiah is that the Spirit of the Lord will rest on him. The word for "rest" here in the Septuagint is *anapauō* and is the same Greek word used in 1 Peter 4:14. Also, when Jesus spoke in the synagogue in Nazareth, his key point was that the Spirit of the Lord was on him and that it was the Spirit who empowered him to actualize the kingdom of God (Lk 4:18; see also Is 61:1). Peter implies that Christians have the same empowering Spirit resting on them as well.

Peter clearly links the Spirit's presence with suffering, but why? Perhaps it's because those being persecuted are *makarioi*, "blessed" or "happy" (see also 1 Pet 1:6). *Makarioi* is the same word used by Jesus in the Beatitudes (Matt 5:1-12; Luke 6:20-23). Here Jesus says that those who are persecuted for righteousness and slandered on account of him are *makarioi*, or "blessed." The persecuted share the same experience as the prophets in times past. Peter's point is that the Holy Spirit inspired the prophets and they were persecuted (2 Pet 1:21). Also, the Spirit was on Jesus without measure and he was persecuted unto death, even the death of the cross. This can only mean that the Holy Spirit is especially present in the lives of those being persecuted for Christ.

Preaching in the Spirit (1 Pet 1:12; 3:18-20; 2 Pet 2:19-21). The extraordinary presence of the Holy Spirit is described in terms of anointing. For example, King David was anointed with oil and from that moment he was empowered by the Holy Spirit (1 Sam 16:13). Isaiah claimed that the Spirit had anointed him to preach the gospel to the poor. This Spirit-inspired word was ultimately fulfilled by the greatest prophet of all, Jesus Christ (Lk 4:18). When Peter preached to Gentiles for the first time, his first descriptor of Jesus was that he was anointed with the Holy Spirit and power (Acts 10:38).

The joining together of anointing, Holy Spirit, and preaching is continued in 1 Peter. Curiously, Peter says that the prophets foretold of the grace of the gospel, even though they did not understand what they were talking about! Perceiving their own limitations, they diligently sought the full meaning of what the Spirit was saying (1 Pet 1:10-11).

Even though the prophets received a partial revelation, it was not a flawed revelation. Their message did not originate with them nor did they speak out of their own volition. Rather their message came directly from God as they were carried along by the Holy Spirit (2 Pet 1:19-21). The word for "carried along" is *phero* and was used to describe a sailing vessel as it was driven along by the wind. This is an appropriate image for inspiration. Just as the movement of the ship is not generated by the ship, so too the work of the prophet is not due to the effort or will of the prophet. It is God, through his Spirit, who is at work in the prophets. Similarly, just as the wind is invisible to the human eye, so too is the person of the Holy Spirit.

Although their vision was not completely clear, they were not blind to what the Spirit was doing. They knew that the voice of the Spirit *in* them was not actually intended *for* them. Their prophetic word was really for the first generation of the church. Their Spirit-inspired revelation is secure and reliable and merits utmost obedience by the Christian. The voice of the Spirit is as a clear, illuminating beacon of truth that pierces the darkness of this age, shining ever brighter until the dawn of the eschaton (2 Pet 1:19).

Continuing on, Peter asserts that the same Holy Spirit who inspired the prophets of old is still at work in the preachers of the church. Echoing Pentecost, Peter declares that the Spirit who inspires the preaching of the gospel is the Spirit who was sent from heaven (1 Pet 1:12; see also Acts 2:1-4). Like the prophets, even the angels don't fully understand what God is doing in the gospel. All of this accentuates the special privilege enjoyed by the first followers of Jesus. Through the Spirit, believers know what prophets and angels could only hope to know. Yet privilege entails responsibility. The end-time community needs to live up to the revelation of the gospel. They need to be spiritually vigilant and clear-headed as they await the final installment of God's grace to be revealed at the second coming of Christ (1 Pet 1:13).

There is another place that Peter might link the presence of the Holy Spirit and preaching. In 1 Peter 3:18, Peter says that Jesus was put to death by way of the flesh but made alive by way of the Spirit. The word for "Spirit" is *pneuma* and can either refer to the Holy Spirit or the human spirit. That is why some translations have that Jesus was made alive in his human "spirit," rather than made alive in the Holy "Spirit."[2] Also the grammatical form of *pneuma* in 1 Peter 3:18 can communicate the means by which something is accomplished. The sense would be Jesus' experience of death came by way of the flesh yet his being made alive again came by way of the Holy Spirit. If this is the case, 1 Peter 3:18 would be Peter's way of saying that Jesus was raised from the dead by the Holy Spirit (1 Pet 3:21; see also Rom 1:3-4; 8:11).

Continuing on to 1 Peter 3:19, Peter then links the Holy Spirit with one of the most unusual events of preaching ever recorded in the Bible. Immediately after mentioning being raised by the Spirit, Peter includes the words "by whom" or "through whom" Jesus preached.[3] So Peter is referencing Jesus preaching through the Holy Spirit. In sum, for Peter, as the prophets spoke by the Holy Spirit and as the apostles preached through the Spirit, Jesus also preached by way of the Holy Spirit.

Yet questions remain. To whom did Jesus preach, where did he preach, and when did he preach? As to whom, Peter says that by the Spirit, Jesus preached "to imprisoned spirits" (1 Pet 3:19). As to when, Peter makes a reference to the days of Noah, as he does in 2 Peter 2:5 where he states that Noah was a preacher of righteousness. As to where the preaching took place, one's mind is drawn again to the spirits in prison.[4]

---

[2]With regard to the last few words of 1 Peter 3:18, the NAS says, "but made alive in the spirit," but the NIV has "but made alive in the Spirit."

[3]The initial words of 1 Pet 3:19 consist of the preposition *en* and the neuter relative pronoun *hō*. The preposition can communicate means or agency, or in this case "through," and the neuter pronoun must refer to the Spirit. Taken together, the phrase may be translated, "through whom." The main verb of the clause is "preached" and the implied subject of the verb is Jesus, yielding the sense, "through the Spirit, Jesus preached."

[4]From all of this, one might conclude that after his death on the cross, Jesus went and preached to all the souls who did not make it on the ark with Noah and his family. All cobbled together, many in the church arrived at the colorful notion that through the Spirit, after Jesus died on the cross, he descended into hell and preached the gospel to all those persons who perished

Summarizing then, Peter is simply continuing the theme of the Spirit's presence in preaching across the ages. Thus by way of the Holy Spirit, Jesus preached through Noah to his generation. But his hearers were disobedient and so they all died in the flood. Consequently, their spirits are now in prison, just as everyone who rejects the gospel is destined for eternal punishment (1 Pet 4:6).

Regardless of interpretation, one thing is clear. Just as the Spirit preached through the prophets, Noah, and Jesus, the Spirit continues to preach through those who proclaim the gospel.

The Holy Spirit and service gifts (1 Pet 4:10-11). Peter's treatment of the gifts of the Spirit is not nearly as developed as that of the apostle Paul. Nevertheless, he echoes common expressions and themes. For example, Peter speaks of divine virtues that are reminiscent of the fruit of the Spirit (2 Pet 1:5-7; see Gal 5:22-23). Also, Peter speaks of a "gift of grace," twice repeating the Greek root for "grace" in a single line. He emphasizes that the exercise of the gifts should never be self-serving but rather be employed for the benefit of the whole church. His use of the word "speak" is frequently linked to the speech gifts set forth in 1 Corinthians 12-14. His addition of the phrase "as the very words of God" points to the supernatural quality of this gift of speaking. His word for "serves" is related to the word for service gifts found in 1 Corinthians 12:5.

Peter describes God's grace as *poikilos*, meaning "varied," "diverse," or "manifold." In its most ancient use, *poikilos* meant "multicolored." So out of the "diverse" and "multicolored" grace of God, each one has received their special gift to serve.

Although lacking in detail, Peter clearly believes in the exercise of special gifts of grace in the church. Among these are gifts of divine speech and divinely empowered gifts to serve the church. The gifts find their source in diverse grace of God and are intended to benefit the whole body of Christ.

---

in the flood. Indeed, the Athanasian Creed (ca. sixth century) states that after suffering on the cross, Jesus "descended into hell." The idea was that the deceased at least got a chance to hear the gospel, even though they were already in hell.

Summary Thoughts

One could argue that Peter's letters suffer from their placement in the canon. That is, his epistles are overshadowed by more prominent portions of the New Testament such as the Gospels and Paul. This is unfortunate because Peter is a powerhouse for doctrine and spiritual guidance. Peter tells us that the Holy Spirit is equal to God and is actively involved in divine election. The Spirit puts suffering for Christ in proper perspective. Also, the Holy Spirit informs us that our suffering has a purpose. Suffering for Christ births a kind of fellowship that results in our blessing and brings glory to God. All of this is comforting for believers for this deep fellowship engenders holiness and a hopeful longing for the second coming of Christ. In the meantime, the Holy Spirit affords the church with an extraordinary opportunity. The Holy Spirit can anoint our words on the order of the prophets of old so that when we speak forth the gospel, they are as the very words of God.

What Does It Mean for Me?

As the world continues to spiral out of control and the hostility toward the faith increases, the wisdom and comfort of the apostle Peter will become most welcome. Even now Peter is a treasure trove of blessings for those who seek power in prayer. Prayerfully consider the points set forth below. Invite the Holy Spirit to speak to you so that you might hear the voice of God in 1 and 2 Peter.

+ Every true believer enjoys fellowship. Yet there is a special kind of fellowship that no human can provide. This fellowship consists of that deep, mature identification with the sufferings of Jesus. It is not enough to know Christ in the power of his resurrection alone. For the mature, one needs to experience the fellowship of Christ's sufferings as well (Phil 3:10). If you have been chosen to partake in this kind of fellowship, be assured that the Holy Spirit rests on you. You are blessed.

+ We can understand the doctrine of election even if we can never fully comprehend it. Yet you can certainly know this. If the sanctifying presence of the Spirit is in your life, you are among the elect. If you long to be obedient to Christ, you are elect. If the precious blood of Jesus is your only hope for the forgiveness of sins, you are elect. Pray that you can ever rest and rejoice in God's elective grace, living a life of unending thanks to him.

✦ Thank God we are not called to craft clever little "feel good" talks for the church (2 Pet 1:16)! Peter says that we are to speak as if we are speaking the very words of God. This can only happen by way of the pan-generational anointing of the Holy Spirit. Just as the Holy Spirit anointed the prophets, the apostles, and even Jesus, that same Holy Spirit can anoint us to address the unique and living contexts of those we are sent to serve. Pray now that the Spirit of wisdom and revelation would anoint your speech as the very words of God.

✦ We have been recipients of "privileged information." Through the Spirit, we know and experience the gospel in ways unknown by prophets and angels. Yet with privilege comes responsibility. Each of us has a vocational mandate to actualize the gifts that have been given us. Pray now that you will always use your extraordinary privilege in Christ to serve others and to glorify God.

✦ Suffering for Christ is precious because the Holy Spirit is present. Suffering is meaningful because it purifies our faith and brings glory to God. Suffering is bearable because of the soon return of Christ.

✦ With regard to this last point, the second coming is referenced at least six times in 1 Peter alone. In each instance, elements of moral accountability and spiritual vigilance are present. Pray that the initial sanctification by the Spirit becomes an ever-increasing work of holiness intently awaiting the revelation of Christ.

17

The HOLY SPIRIT
in the JOHANNINE EPISTLES

THE SPIRIT OF LIGHT AND LOVE

We are from God, and whoever knows God listens to us; but whoever is not from God does not listen to us. This is how we recognize the Spirit of truth and the spirit of falsehood.

1 JOHN 4:6 NIV

THE JOHANNINE EPISTLES will be studied together because they share common themes and jargon. Since the word *pneuma*, translated "Spirit" or "spirit," only occurs in 1 John, it will receive the lion's share of attention, with 2 and 3 John being used in a supplementary manner.

In 1 John, the apostle is battling dangerous heretics who threaten to destroy the faith. These false teachers rejected Jesus altogether. For them, the man Jesus was of no importance for spiritual life whatsoever. He certainly was not the Christ, the anointed of God (1 Jn 2:22-23). In fact, belief in the incarnation was an abhorrent myth that ruined their upward journey into the realm of pure spirit (1 Jn 4:2; 2 Jn 7). For these false prophets, the blood of Jesus was an unclean thing that possessed no atoning value at all (1 Jn 1:7). They were so "spiritual" that they claimed to have no sin (1 Jn 1:8) and that they had never committed a sin in their entire lifetime (1 Jn 1:10). Moreover, for them, life in the body was inconsequential for faith. Thus they behaved immorally and continually walked in darkness (1 Jn 2:11), all the while believing that they were climbing a stairway to heaven (1 Jn 3:6; 2 Jn 9).

Current scholarship debates the influence of early Gnosticism in the first-century church.[1] However, it is not impossible that some form of early Gnosticism had made inroads into the faith. With a rejection of all things material, Gnostics sought to ascend into the realm of pure spirit by way of "secret knowledge." This knowledge could only be received by the spiritual elite and, of course, that elite group was them. In their own eyes, they became so spiritual that they abandoned the Johannine community, causing all kinds of disruption to the church (1 Jn 2:19).

John is fully aware of the danger at hand. He mercilessly attacks the heretics and their heresy. They are trying to lead true believers astray (1 Jn 2:26). They are deceivers, liars, and false prophets (1 Jn 2:4, 22; 4:1; 2 Jn 7). As far as John is concerned, they are antichrists. Their journey into darkness is so heinous that these rogues have probably committed the blasphemy of the Holy Spirit (1 Jn 5:16).

When refuting their false doctrine, John turns to the person and work of the Spirit. Only the Holy Spirit can discern what is true from what is false. He is the Spirit of Truth, not the spirit that is at work among the false teachers (1 Jn 5:6). God the Father has given the Holy Spirit to every true believer. It is the indwelling of the Spirit that conveys the authentic presence of God in one's life. Because of this cooperative presence of the Spirit and the Father, the believer is enabled to test the spirits to see if they are from God (1 Jn 4:1-3). The true Spirit of God testifies to the genuine humanity of Christ yet equally affirms that the man Jesus was the Son of the living God (1 Jn 5:6-8). The gift of the Spirit empowers believers to recognize true spiritual life from bogus claims that don't match up with the life of Jesus. This means that authentic knowledge from the Spirit does not consist of abstract ideas that

---

[1]For arguments against the influence of early Gnosticism on the Johannine community see Charles Hill's *The Johannine Corpus in the Early Church* (Oxford: Oxford University Press, 2004). See also Urban C. Von Wahlde, *Commentary on the Three Johannine Epistles*, vol. 3 of *The Gospel and the Letters of John* (Grand Rapids, MI: Eerdmans, 2010). For additional thoughts see Olugbenga Olagunju, "Apostolic Witness of Jesus Christ in 1 John 1:1-4 and Its Relevance to Combating Contemporary Heretical Teaching About the Person of Jesus Christ," *JBL* 3, no. 1 (2020): 70-133.

only an "elite" can receive. Rather, knowledge of God is observable. It consists of keeping God's commandments and walking in the light just as Jesus walked in the light (1 Jn 2:3; 3:22; 5:3). For John, knowledge of God is seen in meeting the physical needs of one's neighbor (1 Jn 3:17-18). Simply put, knowledge of God is demonstrated by loving the Father *and* the Son and by loving one's neighbor as oneself. Real spiritual knowledge comes by way of an anointing from the Holy One. This anointing is real and teaches the faithful all things (1 Jn 2:20-27).

PAUSE FOR PRAYER

A constant refrain of John is that God is never honored by anything that is untrue. By extension, since the Holy Spirit is the Spirit of truth, the Spirit will never promote anything that is false. This is why Spirit-filled believers must ardently cling to what is true and candidly point out what is false. This is of preeminent importance with regard to worship in the Spirit. Although we are exhorted not to quench the Spirit (1 Thess 5:19), we are clearly commanded to test the spirits (1 Jn 4:1). As the Spirit's power sweeps throughout the world, pray that truth, obedience, and honor for God be abundantly evident among all who believe.

THE PRESENCE OF THE HOLY SPIRIT
IN THE JOHANNINE EPISTLES

The sanctifying assurance of the Spirit (1 Jn 3:24; 4:13). John is writing to a community in trauma. They have suffered the intense pain of a church split (1 Jn 2:19). This has rattled their confidence. Doubts have arisen. Perhaps those who left the fellowship are right about God and the Spirit and the ones who remained are wrong. Perhaps those who seceded are the children of God and those who remained have been excluded from God's family.

When addressing these doubts and confusion, John looks to the Holy Spirit for answers. He teaches that the indwelling of the Holy Spirit is evidentiary proof that one is a child of God. Twice John emphasizes the wonderful truth that God has given his Holy Spirit to the church

(1 Jn 3:24; 4:13). The gift of the Spirit testifies to a kind of reciprocal indwelling whereby the believer lives in God and God lives in the believer (1 Jn 4:15-16).

The indwelling of the Spirit produces an experiential knowledge that can be seen in obedience (1 Jn 2:3-6; 2 Jn 6). Furthermore, this knowledge is "known" in the context of mutually supportive relationships. An authentic relationship with the Spirit engenders a sincere longing to keep God's commandments (1 Jn 3:2-3). This desire is evidence of a life that is totally immersed in God (1 Jn 1:7; 3 Jn 3-4). It is a life journey that "walks" in the light (1 Jn 1:7) and is theologically parallel to Paul's "walking in the Spirit" (Rom 8:4-5; Gal 5:16).[2] Such a life is evidence of God's intent to dwell in his people. All of this results in a deep-seated assurance that the entirety of their lives has been taken up with God and this assurance is secured by the gift of the Holy Spirit. The message his recipients need to hear is this: they are right and the heretics are wrong. They are the children of God and the heretics are the antichrists.

Discerning the Spirit and testing the "spirits" (1 Jn 2:18-23; 4:1-3; 5:6-8; 2 Jn 7). As was the case throughout the church, John's community experienced considerable charismatic activity in their worship services. Some of these manifestations were from God and some were not. Without a doubt, his recipients were perplexed about how to determine the difference. How can one distinguish the work of the Holy Spirit from those who are simply promoting their own agenda? How can one tell the difference between the true Spirit of God and the various spirits expressed by people, some of whom are ill-motivated?

John presents some very clear criteria in answer to these questions. First, believers are always to aspire to faith, but they are not to be gullible. John prohibits the church from believing every spirit (1 Jn 4:1).[3]

---

[2]The word for "walking" is *peripateō* and literally means "to walk about." The word describes the entire concourse of life. John states that the heretics walk in darkness (1 Jn 1:6; 2:11) but believers are to walk in the light (1 Jn 1:7) even as Jesus walked in the light (1 Jn 2:6).

[3]John uses the Greek negation *mē* plus the present imperative which means to stop something that is already underway. This means that the Johannine community was in fact already believing false spirits.

Some of John's recipients were naive in this regard. False prophets claimed to hear from God and many felt obligated to believe them. John warns that many false prophets have gone out into the world. In a manner that sounds very similar to Paul, the church must "test" the spirits (see 1 Cor 12:10).[4] Believers are not to take every spirit at face value but discern what is true from what is false.

John describes the nature of the test and how it works. The Holy Spirit will always magnify the Lord Jesus Christ. So every spirit that "confesses" that Jesus has come in the flesh is of God (1 Jn 4:2). The church can rest assured that an unreserved affirmation of the incarnation comes from the Holy Spirit. Since the early Gnostics were repelled by anything material, some may have spoken a "prophetic word" claiming that Jesus Christ did not come in the flesh. Basically, these heretics were saying that the man Jesus was not from God. John says that this is not the Holy Spirit but rather the spirit of the antichrist (1 Jn 4:3).

John then includes another important component of the test: the mutual indwelling of the Holy Spirit. Those who are truly indwelt by the Spirit of truth exist in the sphere of God's truth. They only heed the voice of the Spirit. When the Spirit testifies that the Messiah was born in the natural way, the faithful gladly receive it but the heretics do not (1 Jn 5:6). When the Spirit testifies that Jesus was baptized in water, believers affirm this as a matter of faith. The false prophets refuse to accept it (1 Jn 5:8).

In sum, John teaches that there is a communal hearing within the church. This common witness is birthed and maintained by the Holy Spirit. Those who do not know God do not have this witness. Thus the false prophets do not listen to the testimony of believers because the rubric for their lives is the spirit of falsehood and not the Spirit of truth (1 Jn 4:3, 6). These deceivers are cut off from the living voice of the Spirit in the church.

The anointing of the Holy Spirit (1 Jn 2:20, 27). John also conveys the communal witness of the Spirit in terms of anointing. The link

---

[4]The word for "test" is *dokimazō* and was used for testing the value of coins. In the same way, the Johannine community is to apply rigorous tests in order to determine what is of God and what does not come from God.

between anointing and the extraordinary presence of the Holy Spirit is common in Scripture (see 1 Sam 16:13; Lk 4:18; Acts 10:38). Thus when deconstructing the clever arguments of the heretics, John speaks of an anointing from "the Holy One" (1 Jn 2:20). John's joining of words such as *anointing, the Holy One,* and *the truth* naturally brings to mind the revelatory presence of the Holy Spirit. In fact, John's assertion that the anointing "teaches you all things" is practically equivalent to the teaching ministry of the Holy Spirit as set forth in the Gospel of John (Jn 14:16-17; 14:26; 15:26).

The false prophets clearly feel that they possess a superior knowledge of God and that the Johannine community needs their teaching. John counters that the saints enjoy the abiding anointing of the Holy Spirit. They have no need to be taught by any of the troublemakers. The internal abiding of the Spirit of Truth ensures that *all* true believers know.[5] John is rejecting the esoteric knowledge of the false prophets who contend that only a few persons can know the deep things of God. By contrast, John states that the Spirit shares truth with everyone who has genuine faith in Christ.

SUMMARY THOUGHTS

John is faced with a twofold task. He must isolate and rebuke the heretics yet affirm and encourage the true children of God. He turns to the Holy Spirit to accomplish these tasks. Without exception, the Spirit is linked with orthodoxy. The Holy Spirit and the true spirit of faith always agree. They both corroborate or "confess" the truth. The word "confess" is from *homologeō* meaning "to say the same thing" (1 Jn 4:2, 3, 15). The heretics *say* a lot of things (1 Jn 1:10; 2:4, 9), but only the Holy Spirit *confesses* the truth.

John is a practical theologian. Knowledge of the Spirit is seen in obedience to God's commandments and living a pure life (2 Jn 6). The love of God is demonstrated in alleviating the real-life suffering of those in need (1 Jn 3:17-18).

---

[5]Some ancient manuscripts have 1 Jn 2:20 ending with the words "you know all things." However, the more reliable reading is the more awkward, "all you [pl] are knowing."

All of this means that John is both comforting and challenging at the same time. In these brief letters, the apostle of love has gifted to us a vision of the incarnate Word. He has anchored God in flesh. He has grounded the Spirit in obedience and love.

WHAT DOES IT MEAN FOR ME?

The genius of John is that he is able to use very simple vocabulary to communicate the deep things of God. This special gift calls for a very careful reading of his letters. His words direct us to ask questions that reveal the very contours of our soul. Do you want to grow in grace and in the knowledge of the Lord (2 Pet 3:18)? Listen to the voice of the Spirit in 1 John.

+ Can you fully confess that Jesus has come in the flesh? John teaches that this confession is critical for knowing the Spirit of God. Have you thought deeply about what the incarnation means for the faith? Does your spirit agree with the Holy Spirit in this regard? Pray that the Spirit continually reveals to you the deep riches of the incarnation.

+ How exactly do you understand the phrase "the knowledge of God"? Do you think in terms of abstract theological constructs and finely tuned dogmas of the church? For John, "the knowledge of God" is not found in doctrinal formulations but in communion with the Holy Spirit. Knowing God means being spiritually transformed by his presence. Knowing God means entering a reciprocal relationship that is received in love and expressed in obedience. In a world that is inundated with terabytes of information daily, God does not need another know-it-all. What God wants is Spirit-filled believers who long for purity and the power to express God's love in obedience.

+ If John visited our churches today, he might ask, "Are you faithful or gullible?" The Holy Spirit is never honored by a lie. The Son is never glorified by confusion. John commands us to be discriminating in our acts of worship. We are to test the spirits to see if they are from God. Hold on to what is true. Cast off what is false. Pray that God grant you the Spirit of wisdom so that you might know the difference.

✦ So many Christians chase after charismatic superstars so that they might receive one more, fleeting spiritual fix. John claims that we all have an anointing from the Holy One. The source of all spiritual blessings resides in each believer. God can certainly use persons in unique ways and not all believers have the same gifts. But this does not mean that any believer has more of the Holy Spirit than another believer. We all have that special anointing within which the Holy Spirit can lead us into all truth. No Christian should feel that they are dependent on others to know God. The Holy Spirit will teach us everything we need to know about God. When he does, we must obey.

The HOLY SPIRIT *in* JUDE

PRAYING IN THE SPIRIT

*But you, dear friends, by building yourselves up in your most holy faith
and praying in the Holy Spirit, keep yourselves in God's love as you wait
for the mercy of our Lord Jesus Christ to bring you to eternal life.*

JUDE 20-21 NIV

JUDE IS ONE of the most neglected books in the New Testament. This
is true for several reasons. The epistle is very brief, consisting of only
one chapter. Also, Jude reveals that his letter is somewhat an after-
thought. His original intention was to write pastorally, but dire circumstances have caused a change of mind (Jude 3). He now devotes the
lion's share of this short epistle to combat heresy. In so doing, he often
draws on obscure, apocalyptic imagery.[1] Perhaps most disconcerting,
Jude quotes from two apocryphal works, Enoch and the Assumption of
Moses (Jude 9, 14-15). The net result is that Jude comes across as harsh,
negative, and for some, less than inspiring.

Nevertheless, Jude is the brother of James (Jude 1). Arguably, this
would make Jude the half-brother of the Lord Jesus. Since Acts explicitly notes that the brothers of the Lord were present in the upper
room at Pentecost (Acts 1:14), and that they all spoke in tongues

---

[1]The final judgment unto condemnation is a common element in apocalyptic literature and is
mentioned no less than three times in Jude (see Jude 4, 6, 15). Similarly, the final destruction
of the wicked features prominently in Jude as well (Jude 5, 6, 7).

(Acts 2:4), Jude was a Pentecostal of the first order. A careful reading of Jude indicates that supernatural revelation was an accepted part of Christian worship. For example, he refers to dream revelation in Jude 8. The thought that God would reveal himself by way of dreams was a long-standing religious tradition in Judaism (see Gen 28:12; 40:5-23). Dream revelation played an important part in Matthew's Gospel (Mt 1:20; 27:19). Also, when speaking of the last days outpouring of the Spirit, Joel affirms that the saints will dream dreams (Joel 2:28). Unfortunately, the heretics in Jude were misusing the gift of dream revelation to promote their distorted beliefs and practices.

Jude mentions the Holy Spirit near the end of his epistle. He states that the heretics don't have the Holy Spirit (Jude 19). On a more positive note, Jude includes the Holy Spirit in his final exhortation to believers. He speaks of spiritual edification, the sincere expression of God's love, and a judicious offering of mercy (Jude 20-23). All of this is followed by one of the most beautiful doxologies in all of Scripture (Jude 24-25).

For all these reasons, Jude merits our special attention. In the midst of his condemnation of the heretics, Jude holds out special blessings for those who seek them.

PAUSE FOR PRAYER

There is a time to change your approach. For Jude, that time had come. He left off his plans for writing a pleasant pastoral letter and launched into a relentless rebuke of those who would distort the faith.

A trait of true spiritual leadership is knowing when to change your mind and then to take immediate action. Pray that the Spirit grant you the discernment to know when it's time to change your mind. Pray too that the Spirit might grant you the knowledge to take appropriate action to preserve the gospel and protect the church.

THE PRESENCE OF THE HOLY SPIRIT IN JUDE

Devoid of the Spirit (Jude 19). Of all the indictments Jude brings against the heretics (and there are many), the worst of all is that they do not have the Holy Spirit. What could be more pitiful than persons *who think* that they have some stake in the life of the church, yet whose only influence is divisiveness and debauchery? In essence, such persons are devoid of the Holy Spirit. Yet Jude's zeal for the faith and his love of the saints precludes any pastoral care for the troublemakers. He is totally focused on preserving the gospel and protecting the church. There is a justifiable severity to his words. The heretics have secretly infiltrated the church. They have twisted the grace of God into license and denied the lordship of Christ (Jude 4). They blaspheme the things of heaven and lust after things on earth. They feign the gift of dream revelation so that they might sow the seeds of sin and sexual perversion throughout the church. They are obnoxious pests who have nothing good to say except to those from whom they expect a favor. Jude captures the manifold nature of their sin with this one phrase: they do not have the Holy Spirit.

Praying in the Spirit (Jude 20-21). In the Spirit of the prophets, Jude thunders forth judgment. Yet near the end of the epistle, his tone makes a dramatic shift. Jude breaks off his attack against the heretics and begins to speak words of faith to the church. His message literally becomes "constructive" in that he encourages believers "to build themselves up" (Jude 20).[2]

The building motif is common in Scripture. Paul assures his hearers that the Word is able to build them up (Acts 20:32). Believers are exhorted to build others up and to seek those gifts that build up the church (Rom 15:2; 1 Cor 14:12; 1 Thess 5:11). Yet Jude is the only one who expects believers to build *themselves* up in *their* most holy faith. The word *heautou* is clearly reflexive and directs the action of the verb back on the self. The emphatic inclusion of the word "your" lends support here. The plural forms in Jude 20 still have the corporate identity of the church in mind, but the direction of the edification is not outward but inward. Jude is thinking of ministering to oneself within the context of the faith. But how?

---

[2]The Greek word for "edify" is a compound word (*epoikodomeō*) that means "to build upon." The image of raising up an edifice comes to mind. In Jude's case, however, the construction materials do not consist of bricks and mortar but the most holy faith of the church.

Some translations include the word *and* in Jude 20 yielding the expression, "building yourselves up in your most holy faith *and* praying in the Holy Spirit." The inclusion of *and* creates two distinct clauses and separates the ideas of "building up" and "praying." However, the Greek text does not have the conjunction *and*. The original text simply follows with a construction that communicates the idea of "means" or "instrument." In this case, the verse would read, "building yourselves up in your most holy faith *by* praying in the Holy Spirit."

As a point of comparison, 1 Corinthians 14:14-15 is the only other place where praying in the Spirit is mentioned in the context of self-edification. Here Paul clearly says that he is praying in tongues and adds that he does not understand what he is praying. Again, some translations insert the word *my* in 1 Corinthians 14:15, rendering the phrases, "I will pray with *my* spirit" and "I will sing with *my* spirit." However, the Greek text does not have the word *my* but simply has "by spirit." Thus Paul could be referring to praying and singing by means of the Holy Spirit. In a similar manner, Jude may be encouraging his recipients to build themselves up by praying in tongues and that this prayer comes by means of the Holy Spirit.

Summary Thoughts

Chances are you haven't heard a sermon from Jude in a long time, if ever. His relentless barrage of judgment and punishment does not bode well in the church today. Yet Jude is clearly in tune with what was going on in the church. When conditions merit, he does not hesitate to change his approach. He takes on the onerous task of dismantling false doctrine and rebuking those who teach it. Yet in the end, he includes some of the most beautiful words in all of Scripture. He reminds his recipients that they have an obligation to minister to themselves. A primary means to this end is praying by means of the Holy Spirit.

WHAT DOES IT MEAN FOR ME?

The harsh tone of Jude can be off-putting. But if we stop there, we can miss a blessing that only Jude affords. There is much in this short epistle to pray about and to pray for.

+ There is a danger of being too inflexible when it comes to living out our faith. But Jude is spiritually nimble enough to change course in order to keep pace with the Spirit. Pray for an intimate and unbroken communion with the Spirit so that you will know when it's time to change your mind and go in another direction for the Lord.

+ Sometimes we are so busy ministering to others that we forget to minister to ourselves. The history of the church is littered with the unpleasant memory of those who were once in ministry but have succumbed to ministerial "burn out." Only by "building ourselves up" in the faith can we ensure that our work for God will continue over the long haul.

+ When the disciples asked Jesus to teach them to pray, he gave the wonderful example of the Lord's Prayer. Also, some of the most beautiful prayers that have ever been prayed have been preserved for us in the church. Yet there is a kind of prayer that comes only by means of the Holy Spirit. This Spirit-inspired prayer has a ministering effect on us like no other prayer that we can pray.

The HOLY SPIRIT
in REVELATION

THE SPIRIT OF PROPHECY

On the Lord's Day I was in the Spirit, and I heard behind me a loud voice like a trumpet, which said: "Write on a scroll what you see and send it to the seven churches: to Ephesus, Smyrna, Pergamum, Thyatira, Sardis, Philadelphia and Laodicea."

REVELATION 1:10-11 NIV

THE BOOK OF REVELATION IS UNIQUE. All other books of the New Testament address the Spirit as the occasion demands. Revelation is presented as a single prophetic word that has been spoken by the Spirit of prophecy (Rev 19:10). For example, at the very outset John says that he was in the Spirit on the Lord's Day (Rev 1:10). At the end of Revelation he writes, "The Spirit and the bride say, 'Come!'" (Rev 22:17). Also, the phrase "hear what the Spirit says" appears no less than seven times in Revelation. In sum, the voice of the Holy Spirit permeates the book of Revelation from beginning to end.

Its very name, Revelation, reflects the illuminating work of the Spirit. Indeed, the first word of the Greek text is *apokalypsis* meaning the "uncovering" or "unveiling" (Rev 1:1). The hermeneutical challenge is that the *apokalypsis* is conveyed by means of apocalyptic. Apocalyptic is that special literary genre that speaks of the sudden in-breaking of the kingdom of God. The otherworldly power of the kingdom is so contrary to this present age that apocalyptic is full of bizarre images and symbols. The violence and strangeness of the revelation signals the end of days.

This relentless stream of cryptic visions and symbols makes Revelation difficult to understand. Yet there is another reason for the difficulty. At points the intent of the Spirit is not to reveal but to conceal (Rev 10:4)!

John frequently refers to the revelation of the Spirit as "the prophecy." For example, he describes his vision as the words of *the prophecy* or the scroll of *the prophecy* (Rev 22:7, 10, 18-19). In fact, John's prophecy contains prophets who prophesy (Rev 11:3-6). The entirety of Revelation is a divine mystery that, counterintuitively, has already been announced by the prophets of old (Rev 10:7). Yet not every prophet is of God and not every prophecy is true. As is so common throughout the New Testament, Revelation warns against false prophets who perform lying wonders that deceive many (Rev 13:13-14; 16:14; 19:20).

Even though Revelation speaks of things to come, there is a finality to its message (Rev 10:6; 16:17). The book sets forth the last days, but focuses on *the* last day, Judgment Day. The day of reckoning has arrived and there is but one option left: repent. For those who ignore the warnings of the Spirit, the implacable wrath of God awaits them. It is for this reason that the wrath of God is mentioned no less than ten times in Revelation.[1] The Lamb of God has now become the Lion of Judah. For those who refuse to repent, the One whose robe is dipped in blood treads the winepress of God's wrath and fury (Rev 19:11-21).

Yet this shockingly fearful vision of John is also a vision of comfort and hope. Those who have suffered for God will be given rest (Rev 14:13). Those who have been martyred for the faith will be avenged by God (Rev 6:10; 19:2). The curse will be swept away, the righteous dead will be raised, and the kingdom will be realized in all its fullness (Rev 21:1-4; 22:1-3). On the one hand, the vindication of the saints is sweet. On the other hand, the time of grace has come to an end. The ensuing judgment is nothing less than sickening (Rev 10:9-10).

---

[1]See Rev 6:16, 17; 11:18; 14:10, 19; 15:1, 7; 16:1, 19; 19:15.

Throughout all the dread and drama of Revelation, the reader should keep this in mind. What John saw in the Spirit was a revelation from Jesus Christ (Rev 1:1). Moreover, the Spirit of prophecy bears witness to Jesus (Rev 19:10). John states that what the Spirit says to the churches are the words of the Son of God (Rev 2:18). All of this means that the majestic sweep of God's redemption in Christ, both the promise and the peril, are contained in this last great book of the Bible.

PAUSE FOR PRAYER

The phrase "I was in the Spirit" appears twice in Revelation (Rev 1:10; 4:2). The precise meaning of John's words is open to interpretation. One thing seems clear. Being in the Spirit means transcending the confines of this world. It means that the horizons of one's experience have been expanded to encompass the things of God. Believers have not been sentenced to live world-weary, threadbare lives. Those who are "in Christ" have that wonderful prospect of being "in the Spirit." Why not pray for that grander vision of God that can only come by being "in the Spirit"?

THE PRESENCE OF THE HOLY SPIRIT IN REVELATION

Hearing the voice of the Spirit (Rev 2:7, 11, 17, 29; 3:6, 13, 22). The phrase, "Whoever has ears, let them hear what the Spirit says" appears seven times in Revelation.[2] No doubt John is echoing the words of Jesus in this regard.[3] The inclusion of the command "let them hear" calls for obedience to the voice of the Spirit. Even though John addresses the seven churches of Asia Minor (Rev 1:4, 11), the "Whoever has ears" citations address the church across the ages (see Rev 3:22; 13:9).

John speaks directly to "the one who is victorious" or "to the one who overcomes." There can be no doubt that at the time of John's writing, the church was experiencing severe persecution. Many were being martyred because of their testimony for Christ (Rev 2:10, 13). Yet they did not renounce their faith. Rather they triumphed by way

---

[2]See Rev 2:7, 11, 17, 29; 3:6, 13, 22. Rev 13:9 simply has "Whoever has ears, let them hear."
[3]See Mt 11:15; 13:9, 43; Mk 4:9; Lk 8:8; 14:35.

of the cross of Christ and by their forthright testimony for Jesus. Also, those who overcome are promised extraordinary blessings from God (Rev 2:7, 17, 26; 3:21).

The word for "triumph" or "overcome" (*nikaō*) is also used in 1 John. Here John says that everyone who has been born again overcomes the world. "The world" encompasses every flesh-driven system that sets itself over against God and his truth. John is careful to add that the power to overcome the world is our faith in Christ (1 Jn 5:4; see also 1 Jn 2:13-14; 4:4).

In sum, John's repeated exhortation to "hear what the Spirit says" applies to every person who has been born of God. Every believer is to have that sensitivity to the Spirit not only to hear the word of the Spirit but also to obey the word of the Spirit. An effectual "hearing" is evidenced by "overcoming" everything and everyone who opposes God's truth in Christ. This kind of victory does not reside in the self. Rather, its power is the atonement of Christ on the cross and the time-honored testimony of the church.

This is what the Spirit says in Revelation: God's power is present. God's victory is certain. God's blessings are secure.

The Spirit of prophecy (Rev 1:3; 19:10; 22:7, 10, 18-19). The repeated command to "hear what the Spirit says" indicates that the gift of prophecy was active in the Johannine community. Indeed, the words *prophet, prophecy,* or *prophesy* appear twenty times in Revelation. These elements are so commonplace that John senses no need to explain how prophecy works or what a prophet is. He simply labels his revelation as "this scroll of prophecy," indicating that he too is a prophet (Rev 22:19; see also Rev 1:3). All these things are givens for John and his community. They are simply part and parcel with life in the early church.

The relationship between the Holy Spirit and prophecy is so close that John refers to the Holy Spirit as the "Spirit of prophecy" (Rev 19:10). Indeed, all of Revelation is presented as one multifaceted prophecy that originates with the Holy Spirit.

It should be noted that all the words in Revelation that refer to prophets and prophecy are built on the Greek root *prophē.* The core meaning of this root is "to foretell" or "to speak forth." So there is a predictive element to prophecy whereby the prophet reveals the future. There is also an element of exhortation to prophecy whereby the prophet has been empowered to speak forth the will of God.

Both the predictive and the exhortative elements of prophecy are found in Revelation. For example, the Spirit directs John to speak about the second coming of Christ, which is imminent, yet future (Rev 1:4, 8). Most of the rest of the book predicts and describes a period of great tribulation that is to come upon the whole earth (Rev 3:10). John's counterpoint to tribulation is the future restoration of all things, the removal of the curse from the face of the earth, and the establishment of the new Jerusalem (Rev 21:1-7; 22:1-5).

Yet Revelation is not an exercise in spiritual fortunetelling. The Spirit is not revealing the future simply for the sake of the future. The Spirit pronounces judgment on ungodly behavior in the here and now (Rev 1:1–3:22).[4] The Spirit gives strong warnings about the judgment that is to come (Rev 8:13; 11:14). The Spirit gives clear instructions for John to follow (Rev 10:1-4; 14:7). The Spirit speaks words of comfort to the faithful who endure until the end (Rev 14:13; 19:9; 20:6; 22:14).

The multisensory revelation of the Spirit (Rev 1:10; 4:6-8; 5:13; 14:2). When we think of prophets and prophecy, we naturally think in terms of speech gifts (see 1 Cor 12:8-10). The instances of spoken communication in Revelation are too numerous to mention. In addition to speaking, however, the Spirit uses several other ways to address John in Revelation. In fact, Revelation is not so much a spoken word that is heard as it is a vision that is seen (Rev 4:3; 9:17; 15:1). The phrase "I saw" appears more than thirty times in Revelation. Some of the things that John saw in the Spirit were common to apocalyptic literature but are completely strange to us (Rev 4:6-8). We need to remember that John is seeing things "from the other side" so to speak and these things address

---

[4]To overly fixate on the future consummation of the age is to miss a major theme of Revelation. The significance of the end of the world is that it grants meaning and perspective for the present. The present suffering and even death of the saints is not in vain because God is sovereign over all things and everything is going according to his plan.

a world that is running out of time. Even when John explains what he saw, the precise meaning of the vision often eludes us (Rev 12:1-17; 13:17-18).

The Spirit speaks in words, makes known through images, but also communicates by way of sounds (Rev 8:6; 9:9; 14:2). John hears trumpets and the ear-splitting roar of torrents, as bombastic as thunder, which oddly reminded him of harpists. The wingbeats of heavenly creatures sound like a stampede to him.

The Spirit also reveals by way of touch, taste, and smell. John is revived by a single touch from one like the Son of Man (Rev 1:12-17). The beauty of God's revelation tastes sweet (Rev 10:9-11) and the prayers of the saints smell like incense (Rev 5:8).

Transported by the Spirit (Rev 17:1-9; 21:10-27). Perhaps the most unusual experience of John is found in Revelation 17:3. He says that he was carried away in the Spirit.[5] Since John was confined to the island of Patmos, this carrying away must be understood in a spiritual sense. That is, he was transported in his spirit to see another scene in the expanded vision of Revelation. John is not the only New Testament figure who was carried away like this. Jesus was transported while being tempted in the wilderness (Mt 4:5-8). Also, Philip appears to have been physically "raptured" (from the Greek *harpazō*) from Gaza to Azotus (Acts 8:39-40). When Paul was carried away into the third heaven, he was not sure if this occurred in the body or out of the body (2 Cor 12:2). In any case, once John is carried away, he realizes that he too is in the wilderness.[6]

John's transport in the Spirit is both a blessing and nightmare. In the desert, he certainly has an encounter with God. On the other hand, he sees the horrifying vision of sin personified (Rev 17:1-9). Although John is taken to a place of terrifying revelation, he is not left there. The Spirit

---

[5]The phrase "in the Spirit" conveys "means" or "instrumentality." So the means or instrument by which John was "carried away" was by means of the Holy Spirit.

[6]The word for "wilderness" is *erēmos*, which for the Middle East means desert. In the Bible the desert is the place of supernatural encounter. It is the place where God met Moses in the burning bush (Ex 3:2-4). Elijah was sustained by the hand of God in the desert (1 Kings 17:1-6). Yet the wilderness is a place of spiritual peril as well. It can be a place of aimless wandering unto death (Num 14:32-33). It can also be a place of spiritual warfare with the devil (Mt 4:1-11).

also carried him away to an exceedingly high mountain and showed him the new Jerusalem coming down out of heaven (Rev 21:10-27).

The Spirit and false prophecy (Rev 16:13; 19:20; 20:10). Revelation includes a theme that is present in nearly every book of the New Testament. Some "prophets" are really *false* prophets. Not every "spirit" is the Holy Spirit.[7] For example, the Spirit affirms the church at Ephesus because it has tested those who claim to be apostles and discovered that they are lying (Rev 2:2). On the other hand, the church in Thyatira is rebuked for entertaining a false prophetess (Rev 2:20). "Evil beasts" are performing lying wonders. Their chief spokesperson is also a false prophet who performs miraculous signs on their behalf to the deception of many (Rev 13:1-13).

All of this requires vigilance on the part of the church. Longing for the power of God, especially in trying circumstances, can dull one's sensitivity to the Spirit of truth and open the door for error.

The Spirit of comfort, peace, and hope (Rev 20:12-15; 21:1-4). Revelation contains enough judgment, wrath, and hellfire to last an eternity. Yet this extended prophecy also includes some of the most comforting words in all of Scripture. It is comforting to know that all the injustices of this world will finally be accounted for by a truly righteous and good God. It is comforting to know that all evil of every kind will finally be defeated—for good (Rev 20:12-15). There is peace for the saints and for all of God's creation, for God dwells among his people and the curse is ended at last (Rev 21:1-4; 22:3). There is hope, for John assures us that Jesus is coming soon (Rev 22:7, 12, 17, 20).

SUMMARY THOUGHTS

The book of Revelation was the last book to be officially included in the canon. By the end of the fourth century many in the church couldn't make sense of its strange visions, images, and symbols. To make matters worse, heretics were using Revelation for no good. They misconstrued the symbolism of Revelation to spread false doctrine.

---

[7]Paul warns of "false apostles" (2 Cor 11:13). Jesus repeatedly warned of "false prophets" (Mt 7:15; Mk 13:22; see also 2 Pet 2:1). John informs his readers that the spirit of antichrist is already at work in the church (1 Jn 4:3).

Yet every good story requires a good ending. Revelation is a very good ending to the good story of God. It is the end of the end in which the Alpha and the Omega declares, "It is done!" (Rev 21:6; see also Rev 16:17). Also, amid all of the frightening scenes of judgment, the image of God wiping away the tears of the saints is unforgettable.

Finally, Revelation explicitly states that all its content is from the Holy Spirit. As such its message agrees in content and tone with the rest of the inspired Scriptures. The Spirit testifies about Jesus, so much so that the voice of the Spirit and the voice of the Lord are practically indistinguishable (Rev 2:18; 3:3; 19:10). In accordance with the rest of the Bible, Revelation joins eschatology and ethics. The end is near, so it is God's last call to repent (Rev 2:5, 16; 3:3).

This last point brings the message of Revelation home. One cannot read through this powerful book without engaging in some serious soul searching. Prayerfully read through the following points and be open to "what the Spirit says to the churches."

What Does It Mean for Me?

John repeatedly says, "He who has ears to hear, let him hear!" Surely more than the ability to hear sound is being spoken of here. Some degree of spiritual receptivity is implied by the command "let him hear." In order to hear the voice of the Spirit, one must be sensitive to the voice of the Spirit. This kind of spiritual hearing comes by being immersed in the Word of God and by incessant prayer. Pray that you will ever have ears to hear the voice of the Spirit. Pray too that you will have a compliant heart that obeys the voice of the Spirit.

+ John conveys many messages in this last, great book of the Bible. One of these messages is that the meaning of God's revelation is not always clear. That is, the Holy Spirit can communicate in ways that are uncommon to the thought forms of this world. So when you hear the voice of the Spirit, that voice may not lend itself to a point-for-point reckoning with life in the here and now. It might be wise to resist the impulse to render an immediate interpretation of the

Spirit, allowing time for the substance of the revelation to play out in your life.

+ All the ethical exhortations in the Bible seem to converge on the book of Revelation. In Revelation, God's call to repent is pronounced on a cosmic scale. Yet the principle of individual accountability is present as well. Revelation draws a clear line in the sand. Are you on God's side or are you on the side of the world, together with its power structures and values? If you are on God's side, are you willing to suffer for your faith in Christ? If so, pray for that special kind of patient endurance that can remain strong until the second coming of Christ!

+ Sometimes we become world-weary in the faith. The wicked seem to go unopposed while the righteous suffer for their faith in God. We wonder how long sin will prevail on earth. Feelings like this are nothing new. The psalmist felt the same way until he saw things from God's perspective (Ps 73:12-19; see also Jer 12:1). Revelation gives us God's perspective. The wicked will be punished, and the righteous will be rewarded. Through Christ, God has already triumphed over the forces of darkness. Victory is assured. It's just a matter of time.

+ In the midst of divine revelation and while being completely enveloped in the Spirit of prophecy, the apostle John was ever mindful of false apostles, fake prophets, and lying wonders. To confront the spurious is to be in tune with the Holy Spirit. Pray that God will grant you the gift of discernment to tell what is of God and what is not. Pray that he will give you the ability to test the spirits so that the church might be strengthened and every true believer edified.

FINAL THOUGHTS

THE INCARNATE WORD was conceived by the Holy Spirit. The inaugural word of John the Baptist was that Jesus would baptize in the Holy Spirit. The inaugural word of Jesus in Nazareth was that the Spirit had anointed him to preach the gospel. The inauguration of the church was marked by the baptism in the Holy Spirit. From there the Holy Spirit empowered the people of God, the Holy Spirit revealed the will of God, and the Holy Spirit dispensed the gifts of God. The reign of the Spirit continued unabated and his voice spoke forth in the end-time prophecy of John in Revelation. Throughout the epistles the presence and power of the Spirit is assumed and encouraged. The indwelling of the Holy Spirit is the definitive mark that uncircumcised Gentiles have been adopted into the family of God. In fact, the Holy Spirit is the seal of God on every Christian, regardless of whether they are Jews or Gentiles. It is the Spirit who works miracles among them and grants gifts that, at times, were abused but never censored. The Holy Spirit is God's advanced deposit ensuring our complete salvation, which is the redemption of our bodies. This means that the generative Spirit at the dawn of creation is the generative Spirit that effects the new birth in every believer. It is this selfsame generative Spirit who will transform our mortal bodies into the likeness of his glorious body and by extension restore the entire cosmos to that pristine state ordained by God.

Between the alpha and omega of our rebirth and glorification, the Holy Spirit remains so near to the redeemed that he actually lives within them. Of all the temples constructed in this world, the God of all creation chose to indwell the bodies of the saints by his Holy Spirit. His is the animating presence of the redeemed who empowers them to walk in the Spirit, to pray in the Spirit, and even sing praises in the Spirit. The Spirit is their Advocate and Comforter who leads the saints into all truth and even intercedes for them when they don't know how to pray. In all of this, believers are the fertile ground out of which God produces his fruit of the Spirit.

If one could go back in time and suggest to the first believers that all of this goodness would come to an end with their passing, such a suggestion would be met with incredulity. How could the end-time presence and power of the Holy Spirit be limited by their mortality? Indeed, all the benevolent graces of the Holy Spirit are powerfully active in the global church today. In little more than a century, those who self-identified as Pentecostal or charismatic increased 600-fold, from less than a million in 1900 to over 600 million today. All of this has occurred in the absence of a common catechism or a comprehensive plan for church growth. Moreover, this incredible rate of growth shows no signs of slowing down. On the contrary, Pentecostals and charismatics are being added to the church by the tens of thousands every day.

The oft-heard critique that this level of spiritual intensity and numerical growth is unsustainable has fallen flat. On the contrary, practically every facet of the church has been influenced by the movement. Their exercise of spiritual gifts, exuberant worship, zeal for evangelism, and creative leadership structures have transformed, and some say reformed, the church for good. The influence of Pentecostals and charismatics on the church is practically immeasurable and certainly irrevocable. One hesitates to mention the enormous sociological and political effects that the movement continues to produce.

The success of the movement defies description. No wonder words like *explosion, fire, seismic, tsunami,* and *storm* often accompany Pentecostal and charismatic studies. However, all of these descriptors also share a common yet unexpected quality. They all have the potential to wreak havoc and destroy. That is, the extraordinary growth of the Pentecostal and charismatic movements constantly runs the risk of getting ahead of sound doctrine, faithful practice, and authentic discipleship.

Such words of caution have nothing to do with "quenching the Spirit." On the contrary, true biblical teaching, proper worship, and an insistence on genuine spiritual growth are themselves works of the Spirit. The prophets warn against false prophets. The faithful are commanded to test the spirits. Paul, the apostle who taught the most on the gifts of the Spirit, is also the apostle who gives proper guidelines for the exercise of those gifts. He requires that all things be done decently and in order. Do such notables issue these careful instructions because they don't love the church? No! These warnings spring forth from their love for the church. God has entrusted the church to manage its own household. The gates of hell will not prevail against the church. Only the church can do that.

Yet the favor of the Lord rests on those who love him. There can be little doubt that in the main, those who view the Spirit as *the* active hand of God in the world today, truly love the Lord. They also have a love for the poorest of the poor and have no problem with welcoming the disenfranchised. They have proven to be incredibly adaptable, able to make something out of nothing, known for building churches not out of bricks but out of sticks. They are no stranger to persecution and no amount of persecution can stem their zeal for the Lord. For them, it is a comfort to know that the persecuted church in the book of Revelation is the church that stands firm in the faith at the second coming of Christ.

So what is the sum of the matter? The meteoric rise of those who claim the fullness of the Spirit will continue unabated. The Holy Spirit will continue to give gifts to those who seek them and have the faith to receive them. The prophetic voice of the Spirit will not be silenced. On the contrary, in these last days the Holy Spirit will continue to be poured out on all flesh. These Spirit-empowered witnesses will stand steadfast for Jesus, spreading the good news of the gospel unto the uttermost parts of the earth.

SCRIPTURE INDEX